Praise for Mike Sager

"Sager plays Virgil in the modern American Inferno . . . Compelling and stylish magazine journalism, rich in novelistic detail."

—Kirkus Reviews

"Like his journalistic precursors Tom Wolfe and Hunter S. Thompson, Sager writes frenetic, off-kilter pop-sociological profiles of Americans in all their vulgarity and vitality . . . He writes with flair, but only in the service of an omnivorous curiosity and defies expectations in pieces that lesser writers would play for satire or sensationalism . . . A Whitmanesque ode to teeming humanity's mystical unity."

—The New York Times Book Review

"Mike Sager writes about places and events we seldom get a look at—and people from whom we avert our eyes. But with Sager in command of all the telling details, he shows us history, humanity, humor, sometimes even honor. He makes us glad to live with our eyes wide open."

—Richard Ben Cramer, Pulitzer Prize-winning author of *What It Takes: The Way to the White House*

"Mike Sager is the Beat poet of American journalism, that rare reporter who can make literature out of shabby reality. Equal parts reporter, ethnographer, stylist and cultural critic, Sager has for 20 years carried the tradition of Tom Wolfe on his broad shoulders, chronicling the American scene and psyche. Nobody does it sharper, smarter, or with more style."

—Walt Harrington, author of *Intimate Journalism.*

"I can recognize the truth in these stories—tales about the darkest possible side of wretched humanity. Sager has obviously spent too much time in flop houses in Laurel Canyon."

—Hunter S. Thompson, author of *Fear and Loathing in Las Vegas*

Praise for the Stories in
A Boy and His Dog in Hell*

"This collection of pieces from Mike Sager is just brilliant—brave, written with soul and beauty, and unflinching in the depiction of a real America that needs to be revealed. Bravo to Sager for being one of the few writers left willing to do it."

  —*Buzz Bissinger, author of Friday Night Lights and A Prayer for the City*

"Like a silver-tongued Margaret Mead, Sager slips into foreign societies almost unnoticed and lives among the natives, chronicling his observations in riveting long-form narratives that recall a less tragic, less self-involved Hunter S. Thompson and a more relatable Tom Wolfe."

  —*Performances Magazine*

"Sager has made a career of finding the unexpected story and telling it with empathy and narrative skill—a talent that's on display throughout this eclectic and consistently arresting collection."

  —*Publishers Weekly*

"His self-effacing style evokes George Orwell's famous dictum that good writing should be as transparent as a pane of glass...The long opening scene in "Kobe Bryant Doesn't Want Your Love" is a gorgeously observed vision of Bryant taking a shot at the hoop and worth the price of the book. No camera could show as much as Sager does as Bryant sinks a single foul shot. I'd submit the scene as Exhibit A for why, in an age of video, writing still matters."

  —*San Diego CityBeat*

*Many of the stories in *A Boy and His Dog in Hell* were originally included in *Wounded Warriors*, which is no longer in print.

Also by Mike Sager

MIKE SAGER

A BOY AND HIS DOG IN HELL

& Other Stories

Cover and Interior design by Siori Kitajima, SF AppWorks LLC
SFAppWorks.com
Photo by Jeff Share on assignment for *Rolling Stone*

Cataloging-in-Publication data for this book
is available from the Library of Congress.

ISBN-13:
Hardback: 978-1-950154-37-1
Paperback: 978-1-950154-27-2
eBook: 978-1-950154-36-4

Published by The Sager Group LLC
www.TheSagerGroup.net

A BOY AND HIS DOG IN HELL

& Other Stories

MIKE SAGER

THE SAGER GROUP

Artifex Te Adiuva

Hard Work
Well Enjoyed
Builds a Man
Makes a Life
Day by Day

The business I am in is a strange one. I intrude into people's lives for an hour or a day or a week, and I scrape their lives for what I can, and then I display the scrapings to strangers. I get paid for this; whether it is a moral calling or not, I do not know, but I have no other craft.

—Bob Greene, "American Beat," Esquire, September, 1981

Contents

Over the past two decades, Trevor Brazile has won more professional rodeo championships, 23, than any other cowboy in history. Going into this year's Wrangler National Finals Rodeo in Las Vegas, Nevada, he's once again leading the all-around standings—though not by much. Putting it mildly, it's been a challengin' couple of years.

The boy in the alley calls himself Zeke. He's thirteen years old; he has a part-time job selling cocaine on a corner. He swears he didn't fight no pit bull dogs to the death. He didn't hang no dogs from no roof with telephone wire, neither. That's what he told the judge, anyway. Life and death on the mean streets of North Philadelphia's Little Puerto Rico.

Charlie Van Dyke is six-foot-three, 650 pounds, give or take a few dozen. He is required by law to buy two seats on an airplane. He uses long brushes to wash himself, a specially designed portable personal bidet. His wife, Kathie, is five feet, 120 pounds. "She's a committed cellulite surfer," Charlie says with a wink. A fat man in a low-fat world.

By some account, Christopher Michael Langan is the smartest man in America, with an IQ of 195. He is certainly the smartest nightclub bouncer in America. As he likes to say, quoting Kermit the Frog, "It ain't easy being green." Welcome to the HiQ Nation, where smartest, it turns out, isn't necessarily best.

Against all odds, Bill Hicks was a comic's comic. A critic's comic. In a class, really, all his own: Three albums, two HBO specials, a BBC special, eleven appearances on Letterman, the subject of a lengthy *New Yorker* profile. The best-known unknown in the business, he was destined for stardom, until tragedy struck.

After fighting in Vietnam, unwilling to return to America, these vets put down stakes in a place they thought would be better than home. From the sex bars of Bangkok, to the blood-red sunsets over the Mekong River, to VFW Post 10249 in Udon Thani—what happens when you follow that wild hair to the end of the earth.

He's got Martin Luther King's dream, James Brown's hairdo, and a date with political destiny. Black folks love him. The rest aren't so sure. "I just haven't learned how to talk to white folks yet," he says. At home and on the road with the Reverend Al Sharpton during his early years, before he ran for U.S. president and became a mainstream chat show host.

Back in the day, when gangs fought for turf and respect, V-13 ruled the streets of Venice, California—proud *vatos* in their Pendleton shirts and hair nets. They drove shiny low-riders and sold heroin to the *miatas*, the poor blacks across the street. Then crack arrived in the neighborhood and the tables turned. Life inside an L.A. gang.

Manute Bol measures seven feet seven inches tall and weighs 208 pounds. The first time he tried to dunk, on a makeshift basket in his village in Sudan, he broke a few teeth on the rim. Now he's the NBA's newest star. He ejected Kareem Abdul-Jabbar's dunk, Larry Bird's lay-up, Kevin McHale's fadeaway jumper. But he still forgets to duck into doorways now and then.

The Forgotten at Forest Haven 261
Forest Haven was a live-in facility for children and adults with Intellectual Disability located in Laurel, Maryland, and operated by the District of Columbia. The site was opened in 1925 and closed on October 14, 1991, by order of a federal judge after years of alleged abuse, medical incompetence, and several deaths. *The commonly used vocabulary of the era is retained.*

The Hausslings: All in the Family 271
Ruthann and Henry Haussling of Northern Virginia have seven adopted sons, all under 13 years old. To the social service agencies of Virginia and the District of Columbia, they were burdensome special-needs children whose natural parents could not raise them. But up the gravel road past the cornfield, in a big brick house on a hill, the boys are just Hausslings.

Farmers Harvest Fruit of Bountiful Summer 279
Ninety miles west of Washington, D.C., at the foot of the Blue Ridge Mountains, fall has come to Greg Smith's farm in Culpeper, VA. The sun is round and low; the verdant countryside is fading, and the smell of mature Yellow Delicious apples hangs sweet in the crystal air. Winter is coming; there is much to do. There are signs the coming cold will be long and deep.

The Hunt: Special Bond for Father, Son 283
A hunt is a ritual: the guns and the gear, the primitive mile-stone of the first kill, the lore of manhood passed from generation to generation. For father and son Jim and Troy Norine, the hunt is not about killing. It's about holding yourself real still, the smell of damp earth and distant woodsmoke. It's about love and kinship and being together in the great outdoors.

Eagle at Sea: The Rigorous Life Before the Wind 291

The USCGC Eagle is a 295-foot sailing barque used as a training ship for future officers of the United States Coast Guard. Each summer, Eagle deploys with more than 300 Coast Guard Academy cadets on various missions around the globe. A story of a reporter's three weeks at sea, with nary a sight of land, on a ship that looks a lot like a pirate's.

The first to be buried here, in 1946, was John Doe. Two John Does and two Jane Does followed, followed by a Christine Marie Doe, Infant Unknown. Though the others there have names duly recorded on small granite headstones, the histories of nearly all have been lost in the shuffle of paperwork and time. But not all were forgotten. An investigation back in time.

Foreword

You could say Mike Sager stumbled into journalism as a way to save his ass.

Three weeks into classes at Georgetown University law school in Washington D.C., he'd realized how much he wanted to be . . . a writer. Having lied to his parents—assuring them a deferred admission to the following year's class had been easily secured—he pulled up the only writing contact he had: the mother of a fraternity brother happened to be an editor at the *Washington Post*.

When Sager got the call from the *Post*, he put on his three-piece interview suit, packed his new graduation-gift briefcase full of college-era writing clips, and drove to the august newspaper, situated only a few blocks from the White House. Promptly he failed the spelling and typing tests administered by the paper's human relations department.

Several dozen desperate phone calls followed over the next month before he landed a full-time spot as a copy boy on the graveyard shift. His assigned post—which required no spelling or typing—was a closet-sized space housing some fourteen news service teletype machines (AP, UPI, Reuters, and others). Before mobile phones and the Internet changed newspaper reporting forever, the wire room was how news-gathering organizations kept up with worldwide events. The cacophony of sound emanating from the printing machines—the hammering, sawing, buzzing, and dinging—was deafening. There was a metal bar-type stool and a large window at the front of the room, which gave Sager a front seat to the daily drama at one of the best newspapers in the world.

Unbeknownst to Sager, he'd arrived at the *Post* at a moment in cultural history when journalism was at its zenith. A few years earlier, relentless investigative reporting by the team of Bob Woodward and Carl Bernstein for *The Washington Post* helped usher a crooked president, Richard M. Nixon, out of office. Journalism was considered the highest of callings; it was equated with the best intentions of the political idealism fostered by the social protest movements of the 1960s.

At the same time, a longer form of non-fiction writing was in vogue. The well-known author, cultural critic, and magazine writer Tom Wolfe—with his talent for coinage and self-promotion—called it "The New Journalism." The idea was to meld investigative reporting and cultural anthropology with the creative elements of a novel. Reporting the story was only the first part of the job. Next came the grace of the telling. Wolfe and others believed that by using the techniques of fiction—scene, setting, action, dialogue, and point of view, with a particular emphasis on character and setting—a deeper, more entertaining, more thoughtful, and ultimately more informative story could emerge.

Along with Woodward and Bernstein, reporter/writers like Robert Caro (*The Power Broker*) and David Halberstam (*The Best and the Brightest*), created massive character-driven narratives, while New Journalism stylists such as Wolfe, Joan Didion, Gay Talese, and Hunter S. Thompson had a more distinct flair. All shared the ability to immerse themselves in reporting. While some writers have used the banner of New Journalism to stretch the truth—or even make stuff up—the true practitioners know that careful reporting cannot be faked or written around.

Of course, Sager wasn't familiar with any of this when he started work as a copy boy at the *Post* in 1978. A history major in college, Sager didn't come from a bookish family. He wasn't versed in the classics; he didn't read magazines or newspapers. He just knew that he loved to write and would find a way to do it.

A former jock—he played varsity soccer at Emory University—Sager threw himself into his new job as if he was playing a sport, with the intensity of a 5-foot 5-inch guy with something to prove. Like many young reporters at the *Post*, Sager burned with ambition to succeed. Unlike most, he had no Ivy League credentials, no flair for office politics, no family connections, and no facility for French or other foreign languages.

He made up for his lack of experience by working long hours, soaking up everything he could learn. The late 1970s was a time when the Drug War raged and the murder rate in the nation's capital hovered among the highest in the nation. Sager's familiarity with the worlds of his other early seventies teenage preoccupations—music and drugs—had lent him some street knowledge that made up for his lack of social polish. Within the year, Sager's freelance work for the Metro and the Virginia Weekly sections, carried on outside of his 40-hour weeks as a copy boy, earned him a promotion to staff writer. At the time, Bob Woodward was the lead editor of the *Post's* Metro staff. It was he who delivered the news to Sager, inside his glass cubical in the heart of the newsroom, in the late afternoon, right in the middle of deadline. The day was Sept. 12, 1979, also the day of his first front page story in the *Post*.

From there, starting with a stint at night police, Sager was given an old-school newspaper education, rotating through all the traditional stations of reporting—night rewrite, courts, general assignment, and politics—learning the standards and practices of the Fourth Estate from the very best in the business.

When he wasn't covering his beat or doing spot stories assigned by the editors, Sager used his own time to work up enterprise features, longer stories told with more literary flair. In college, he'd minored in creative writing, but his work was not memorable. "I could write a decent sentence, but I had nothing say," he has said. But with journalism, he'd found the motherlode. He didn't need to *say* anything, just put in the work. "You hunted up the details, the interviews, the background. Then all you had to do was get out of the way," Sager said.

Three years into his stint at the *Post*, Sager was assigned to a new editor named Walt Harrington, who would go on to write *Intimate Journalism*, one of the seminal textbooks on literary non-fiction. It was Harrington who opened Sager's eyes to Wolfe's anthology, *The New Journalism*, which Sager found "mind-blowing. Here I was, a typical kid, trying to re-invent the wheel. I sat up all night reading the book. From the moment I started reading it, I knew it was exactly what I wanted to do." For the next three years, Sager read every bit of New Journalism he could find. Under Harrington's tutelage, he began to put the pieces together that would become his own voice and style.

Seeking, in his own words, "more room to stretch my fingers," Sager quit the *Post* after six years to become a freelance magazine writer. As much as he loved the people he worked with, he knew he wasn't quite one of them. He started locally in DC, at *Washingtonian* and *Regardie's*, and then eventually moved on to stints as a contract writer for *Rolling Stone*, *GQ*, and *Esquire*. Combining his rigorous *Post* training in newsgathering with the techniques of his anthropological hero, Margaret Meade, Sager would, over the next four decades, make a career "finding the quotidian within the extreme, the tender amid the grotesque," according to the author and popular Columbia Journalism School professor Sam Freedman.

Sager takes us inside different worlds in a way that is immediate, vivid, and dramatic. He doesn't hover 20,000 feet above his subject and just give you an overview—instead, you are right there on the ground level. He has a rare ability to get people to tell him things that they wouldn't tell other people, maybe not even themselves. He earns their trust by hanging around, by not pushing or manipulating. By being genuinely interested.

Because Sager doesn't put any barriers between us and his characters, and because he renders them so thoughtfully and with such compassion, readers are allowed to focus on the drama of the stories. Above all, Sager doesn't get in the way of the story. He is not a commentator or a pundit. He doesn't analyze, his pieces don't have an obvious aim or thesis. His prose is so direct and unfussy, it's almost invisible, like a camera. And yet there is a propulsion to it because in almost every sentence you'll find a fact—that blessed newspaper training again. The sentences flow with a definite rhythm, but Sager's style is unadorned with falsity, unburdened by over-interpretation. He's a natural storyteller. You never get the feeling he's there just to show off, only to entertain you.

***

It was at *Rolling Stone* that Sager's career took a leap, owing mostly to the mentorship of editor Robert Love, who assigned Sager his first true crime story, a genre in which he could amalgamate his reporting skills and his literary aspirations. Along with the New Journalists, Sager's bible for the form became Truman Capote's masterpiece of reportage, *In Cold Blood*. Thanks to Love's generous assignments, Sager had great stories to tell.

Sager's 1989 *Rolling Stone* article, "The Devil and John Holmes," published ten years after his promotion from copy boy to reporter, became the inspiration for P.T. Anderson's classic porn saga, *Boogie Nights*, and also for *Wonderland*, starring Val Kilmer and Lisa Kudrow. It remains one of the greatest true crime magazine stories ever published. Twenty-one years later, Sager's portrait of failed NFL quarterback Todd Marinovich would win the National Magazine Award for profile writing. It was later the basis for *The Marinovich Project*, an Emmy-nominated ESPN documentary. Along the way, more than a dozen of his articles would be optioned for or inspire Hollywood feature films, including *Veronica Guerin*, starring Cate Blanchett, and *Betrayed by Love*, starring Patricia Arquette.

With the help of editor Peter Griffin, Sager pioneered *Esquire*'s hugely popular *What I've Learned* series of celebrity interviews, and did scores of celebrity profiles large and small, as well as dozens of personal essays. With the coming of the internet came several short-lived regular columns, both local and national, the most notable for *Playboy*, called "Go Ask Sager."

Though he is perhaps most widely known for his crime stories, Sager has, over the past 40-plus years, written dozens of deeply reported narrative stories of a genre some have called "literary anthropology."

Taken together, the stories in *A Boy and His Dog in Hell* present an omnibus of American life, and, in turn, of Sager's life. The legal world's loss has been our gain.

—Alex Belth

Author's Note

These stories are particularly dear to me.

Looking back, I consider them milestones, pieces that have defined and distinguished my work over forty some years of journalism—adventures, high jinks, near-death moments, and wrenching intimate encounters that have helped to shape me as a writer and as a man.

Included in *A Boy and His Dog in Hell* are 19 stories about people from a wide variety of circumstances and cultures—all of them distinctly American. In this time of deep division, I hope these profiles stand as a testament to an over-arching humanness that spans our great differences. Over the course of my career, I have learned nothing if not this: Even as we are each of us wonderfully odd, curious, entertaining, and peculiar, we are all of us very much cut from the same stuff.

While I am fond of the many crime stories and celebrity profiles that have occupied and enriched my life both personally and professionally, *A Boy and His Dog* highlights my work as an anthropologist without portfolio. In a more modern context, each of these stories is very much like a TV reality series, time spent with a person or community of people you would not ordinarily get to meet.

If it was my 11th grade journalism teacher, Dora Simons, who first introduced me to the idea of writing articles, it was the anthropologist Margaret Meade, and her groundbreaking *Coming of Age in Samoa*—assigned for my class in Anthropology 101 during the first term of my freshman year in college—who put me on my present course. Getting from there to here required ample help, particularly from Walt Harrington at *The Washington Post*, my mentor for all things New Journalism; Bob Love at *Rolling Stone*, who taught me extended structure and challenged me with the gift of incredible stories; and David Granger and Peter Griffin, my dynamic duo at *Esquire*. Truly told, Granger was the first to double down on my Harrington-inspired passion for "intimate journalism." Before Granger came along, getting the green light to do my form of anthropology (how dull does that sound in a pitch meeting?) necessarily involved a Dante-esque list of ingredients, including death, drugs, exotic locations and/or mayhem. It was Granger who embraced the form as a way of allowing me to explore the universality of the human condition. First there was Big, about a 650-man, which he championed into print at *GQ*. Later, at *Esquire*, there were dozens more. "Old." "Ugly." "The Secret Life of a Beautiful Woman." "The Man of Tomorrow Goes to the Prom." At some point, someone used the term *Literary Anthropology* to describe my work. I have tried my best to live up.

Warming my hands by the cultural fires of so many diverse characters, groups, and settings over the years, I've observed how strongly our world depends upon cultural stereotypes and clannish dictates, misconceptions, hate and fear, political correctness, and mythology—our notions of what is supposed to be true, what is considered to be true, what other people say you should think and do, what is gospel.

No matter where I've gone, no matter whom I've met, no matter how low or how high, I've practiced a technique of keeping my mind open—I've come to call it *suspending disbelief*. I spend a lot of time. A lot of time. I keep my my mouth shut, my eyes and ears open, and my audio recorder running. I pay attention. I act respectfully. I listen deeply. I earn trust by example. I learn to read the subtext. I keep an open mind and an open heart. Never have I failed to find a human connection—except in those few cases where I was unavoidably beaten, threatened with a gun, or roughed up by soldiers of a desperate regime. In those cases, I was dealing with strangers, people I hadn't planned to be around, who knew nothing about me and didn't care to learn. In such conditions, the only recourse was to survive and retreat. There is evil in the world, yes. But principally what I've learned is that *different* doesn't have to be evil, or scary, or threatening. Knowledge is power. And people are generally just people. Chances are if someone is fucking with you, it's someone who's either desperate or afraid. After every assignment, I have unfailingly returned home with new understanding, new insight, new truths I'd have never imagined unless I'd walked the proverbial mile in the shoes of another.

The stories in this book represent a lot of miles in a lot of different shoes, from cowboy boots to signature Kobe Bryants—a tour of an America few people ever see, safe as they are within the borders of their own colorful square in the nation's patchwork quilt of diverse cultures, communities, and circumstances.

We meet: A pair of young Puerto Rican brothers, living marginally in the slums of North Philadelphia, working the corner selling cocaine and fighting stolen pit bull dogs to the death. The members of a once-proud Latinx street gang, the V-13 from Venice, CA, have lost their fortunes in a cloud of crack smoke. A seven-foot six-inch, Sudanese-born NBA basketball player—the first time he attempted a dunk, he broke his front teeth on the ten-foot rim. He went on to become one of the greatest shot-blockers in the history of the National Basketball Association,

We spend time with blue collar tweakers in Hawaii; Aryan Nation troopers in Idaho; and near-fatally hip heroin addicts on the Lower East Side of Manhattan. We meet the Reverend Al Sharpton at a time, early in his career, when this important civil rights figure and mainstream chat show host was vilified and feared by many Americans of all races. A road trip across country brings me eyeball to eyeball with a number of America's smartest men (and one woman) and demonstrates that having a super high IQ can be as much of a handicap as an advantage. Life, it seems, can be just as challenging on either end of the bell curve. A trip across Thailand brings me together with dozens of American military veterans who'd decided, after the Vietnam war, that they'd rather set down roots in the Land of Smiles than return home. Life as an ex pat: *You're home and yet you ain't.*

We attend the "Superbowl of Rodeo" with the world's winningest professional cowboy, a deep dive into red-state values and the condition of the American Western Ideal. We meet Charlie Van Dyke, 650-pounds, a fat man in a low-fat world. Bill Hicks, a comedian destined for mainstream stardom until tragedy struck. And NBA lightning rod Kobe Bryant, who lifted the craft of basketball into a compelling art . . . and so beautifully made the tricky transition to next chapter . . . before leaving the earth suddenly and way too soon. It was my giddy personal privilege to spend more than a week with Kobe and his wife to report the piece. Included also is a personal appreciation I wrote for *The Atlantic* on the night of his death.

I have also been privileged to add into this collection, with the paid permission of the *Washington Post*, six of the feature stories I wrote during my six years at that great paper, where my career began in 1978. (As of this writing, I have completed paid journalism assignments in each of the past six decades.) Unlike the other stories in this book, all of which have been expanded and refurbished since first publication, I leave these stories untouched. (According to the terms of my agreement with the *Post*, I'm not allowed to change anything. Nor would I want to.) Over the years, teaching young writers, I have often assigned these pieces to grad students. It's good for them to get the perspective: This was my work when I was *your* age.

***

In this world of rapidly changing media—remember, the first televisions were introduced in 1927, less than a century ago—it is has been my good fortune to have plied my trade during the golden age of magazines, when ads were plentiful, books were thick, issues came 12 times a year, and editors thought nothing of letting you spend three weeks living with a 650-pound man, six weeks with a crack gang, or three months circling the globe in search of a Hollywood actor. And they didn't mind paying you a decent enough wage that you could put copious amounts of time into the rest of the process: transcribing, additional research, writing, editing, fact-checking, lawyering, and more. For that I am truly grateful.

For the people who shared their lives with me so I could write these stories . . . for the editors who gave me these assignments and the magazines that gave me the resources and a platform . . . for the readers who spent their time and money . . . for the loved ones who nurtured and encouraged me as I pursued my passion . . . for my son, who taught me as much as all the stories I've written . . . and for so much more, I give thanks.

Please enjoy.

Mike Sager
La Jolla, CA

THE KING OF THE COWBOYS

Over the past two decades, Trevor Brazile has won more professional rodeo championships, 23, than any other cowboy in history. Going into this year's Wrangler National Finals Rodeo in Las Vegas, Nevada, he's once again leading the all-around standings—though not by much. Putting it mildly, it's been a challengin' couple of years.

An hour northwest of Dallas, Texas, the King of the Cowboys is practicing for the richest rodeo of the year—ten days of high-stakes competition that will make or break his season.

His name is Trevor Brazile. He is a modest man of 41, a prodigy in autumn, with boyish dimples and budding jowls, the compact physique of a hockey player—5-foot-10 in his Trevor Brazile signature cowboy boots.

Raised on a feedlot in the dusty north Texas Panhandle, he roped his first calf from horseback at age 3. At age 5 he refused to return to the second day of kindergarten unless his parents installed his roping dummy on the school playground. Over the past two decades, Brazile has won more professional rodeo championships, 23, than any other cowboy in history. Going into this year's Wrangler National Finals Rodeo in Las Vegas, Nevada, known as the NFR, he's once again leading the all-around standings—though not by much. Putting it mildly, as people tend to do in these parts, it's been a challengin' couple of years.

Brazile's 100-acre ranch is nestled into rolling, winter-brown hills a few miles outside the town of Decatur. Bare trees rise like sculptures toward a wan blue sky. Brazile and his crew are busy inside an immense, roofed-in practice pen, down the slope from his big stone house. The dirt is red and fine, a sandy loam. He's been working out all afternoon. The evening chill is beginning to settle. The overhead lights are on. Frank Sinatra is crooning "Fly Me to the Moon" from built-in speakers.

The playlist belongs to Brazile's practice partner, 28-year-old Tuf Cooper, who will also compete at the NFR this year. Tuf is his given name—one of many creative or honorific spellings that distinguish his family line. As it happens, Tuf's dad, Roy Cooper, is in the Cowboy Hall of Fame. When Brazile was coming up as a young rodeo cowboy, the Super Looper was his idol and mentor. Now Tuf is in the game. He's second in the all-around, behind Brazile—the young buck nipping at his heels, just like it was back then with Brazile and Roy.

Compounding our story further is the fact that Brazile is married to Tuf's half-sister, Shada, 38. A stunning sometimes-model and semi-retired professional barrel racer, she herself is a past-NFR qualifier who dabbled at competing as recently as last summer, when she was barely one-year postpartum with the most recent of their three kids. She homeschools the spirited trio in a makeshift classroom—complete with miniature desks and lockers—in a loft on the second floor of their house. Until recently Shada was the force behind a children's clothing brand. She has a social media presence as an influencer on the Western wear fashion scene. When Tuf was 12 and his parents divorced, he lived with Shada and Brazile. Later, in 9th grade, when Tuf turned pro, Shada supervised his home-schooling.

"Basically, if you just look at me, nearly everything I do is a direct influence from Trevor," Tuf says. "Shada was like my second mom."

At the moment, Brazile is in the starting box in his practice pen, seated on a custom saddle cinched to his calf horse, Deputy. Brazile uses a different horse for each of the three events in which he competes; the others are stabled in a state-of-the-art barn next door. Versatility is one of the main reasons Brazile has been all-around champ 13 times. He's also won titles in ten individual events.

Championships are based on year-end aggregated earnings. Few cowboys are good enough to compete at this level in more than one event. And few have the will to hit the exhausting quota of 75 to 100 nation-wide events in each category that are counted toward earnings totals. The rodeo season lasts nearly year-round: The old season ends on September 30 and a new one begins October 1. This past summer, over one six-day period, Brazile and a helper drove 7,500 miles and hit five different rodeos.

To prep himself for the NFR, Brazile has altered the starting box in his practice pen with sheets of plywood to mimic the facilities at the Thomas and Mack Center in Las Vegas, which is smaller than most rodeo venues. Likewise, temporary fencing has been brought in to downsize the ring. To Brazile, no detail is too small: Before he bought the ranch, he says, he took a shovel to the earth at every property he shopped—he didn't want to have to haul in the kind of soft loam that is easy on livestock. "I may not be 6-4 or 225 like some of the competitors, but I don't cheat the process," he will later tell a Vegas crowd at a meet-and-greet.

Deputy is a 15-year-old sorrel gelding with a fancy braided tail and mane—you don't want to rely on a young horse at a critical time. Deputy is probably the fastest calf horse Brazile has ever owned. Coming out of the starting box, Brazile doesn't even have to think about kicking Deputy with his cutter style, double-mounted spurs, which were hand crafted by a well-known artisan from the drive shaft of a Model T Ford automobile. Usually, as soon as the chute opens and the calf bolts, and Deputy feels the tension come off the reins, he is off and running full speed. The secret to Brazile's dominance in rodeo, he says, is "my level of horsemanship is hopefully above my talent level. My horses are where I attribute most of my success; it takes a lot of training."

Because of his dominance in his sport, Brazile is known by some as the "Michael Jordan of Rodeo." Like the basketball great, Brazile makes more money on endorsements and licensing than he does on rodeo purses. Here on an average day in the practice pen, both horse and rider are dressed crown-to-hoof in Brazile's signature clothing and tack, brand named "Relentless"—a handle suggested by one of his business partners but pretty much on the nose. (Brazile is an old-fashioned kind of guy, way too modest to have suggested such a name. But not so modest as to fail to embrace it.) Deputy sports a Relentless breast collar, bridle, saddle pad, and fetlock and hoof wraps. A full line of roping supplies, including practice dummies, is also available.

Brazile's hat is a black, Trevor Brazile signature 100X, made by Resistol, the Texas-based company that sells a million hats a year. The rest of Brazile's outfit is Relentless brand, licensed by cowboy performance-wear giant Ariat to Brazile's specifications: The shirts have extra room in the arms and chest for roping and wrangling. The jeans material, unlike traditional denim, is stretchy for comfort and movement, but can still stand dry-cleaning chemicals and hold a crease, the look pro cowboys prefer. The boot soles feature rubber tread inserts for better traction, which help considerably in events like tie-down roping—Brazile's signature event—where the cowboy, after chasing a calf on horseback and roping it around the neck, jumps off his horse and sprints to the young animal, then picks it up and throws it down onto its side, legs away (called "flanking"); time stops when three hooves are neatly tied together with a hooey knot—a western-style slip-knot—and the cowboy raises his hands.

Ready for his next practice run, Brazile fiddles with his rope— nobody *ever* calls it a lariat. Thirty-one feet long, it is woven of a special poly-grass fiber that doesn't stretch. The material is known to become finicky in different weather conditions. For this reason, pro cowboys carry doughnut-shaped, waterproof rope cans, with a strap for shoulder or saddle horn, bringing to mind a lady's large purse—and watchdogged at events just as carefully. Besides his horse, nothing is more important to a cowboy than his ropes. Like an undergarment, it is one piece of equipment rarely lent to others.

Brazile holds his right arm out from his body at a right angle, elbow bent, hand at shoulder height, palm-forward, the loop of his rope supported by a single finger, the index, giving the impression he's gesturing thoughtfully, *Wait a second* or *I've got an idea.*

Coiled between his teeth is the piggin' string—it's written with the apostrophe. About six feet long, custom-made of little-boy-blue, three-ply polyester rope, the piggin' string is used to make the tie on the calf's hooves. To lubricate the slipknot, Brazile uses baby powder. It must be Johnson & Johnson original formula, nothing else. The smell evokes thoughts of his three young children, ages 11, 9 and 2, and marks a strong sensory contrast to the rest of the immediate atmosphere—earth and manure, wood smoke and hay, sweaty men and animals. When he bites down on the piggin' string, Brazile's dimples show, making him look intense yet also elfin—he is the kind of guy who loves hanging out with his fellas and goofing, even as his eyes are darting toward the next task on his ever-growing list. To keep things tidy, the loose end of the piggin' string is threaded through Brazile's rear-most belt loop. Another long rope, connected to Deputy's bridle, is tucked beneath his belt.

Deputy's ears crane forward. His nostrils flare. Brazile nods his head slowly, gravely, almost imperceptibly, causing the brim of his Trevor Brazile signature cowboy hat to bob. One of his crew jerks a lever, releasing the first in a line of 3-month-old calves, standing rump to face in the confines of a long chute, constructed of round, schedule-40-size steel pipe and stretching from one side of the practice pen to the other—the one end for gathering the calves, the other for releasing. Each calf weighs about 250 pounds. Owing to Brazile's strict protein and vegetable diet, he goes about 185.

The first calf in line is a black baldy: black body with a white face. She's the daughter of a calf Brazile roped at the 2015 NFR, two years ago now, the last time he competed at the NFR and also the last time he won the all-around. To commemorate the victory, he bought the winning calf. Once known by her ear tag, #76, she is now a permanent resident of Brazile's pasture, along with a bunch of other winners and their progeny. His kids named her Sally.

Sally's daughter has no name, but like her mom, she's fast out of the gate.

Brazile and Deputy give chase.

***

From the door of Brazile's practice pen, you can look over yonder on the hill, behind the lake, and see a smaller, 20-acre spread, with its own barn and practice pen. A prominent ranch gate constructed of wood posts and artesian metalwork presides over top the driveway: Roy Cooper: 8 Times World Champion.

Rodeo came to the New World with the conquistadors, along with horses and cattle. The word comes from *rodear*, Spanish for "to surround" or "encircle." Long before professional cowboys were competing for brand sponsorships and five-figure purses, wherever in the world cattle were being raised, ranch hands were competing against each other for pride and amusement. By the second half of the 19th century, public rodeo spectacles were popping up across America in nowhere towns like Deer Trail, Colorado; Pecos, Texas, and Prescott, Arizona. In the absence of movies, theater, or sports teams, rodeo was the ascendant form of public entertainment across much of the agrarian nation.

Like all great American pastimes, rodeo eventually became a big business. Cowboy associations sprung up; promoters and competitors got together to more or less standardize rules, regulations, and titles. The first National Finals Rodeo was held in Dallas in 1959. For many years it was held in Oklahoma City; in 1985 it was moved to Vegas. The sport's governing body, the Professional Rodeo Cowboys Association, PRCA, holds the largest chunk of the game in its hands, sanctioning over 600 rodeos a year in North America, and more around the world. Every rodeo event has an entry fee, paid by the cowboys. There is no guaranteed money.

Typically, a rodeo features seven events, most of which are derived from necessary jobs performed on a cattle ranch. Bareback riding and saddle-bronc riding come from the practice of breaking wild horses for everyday use. Steer roping—also known as steer trippin'—in which the steer is roped by the horns and jerked off its feet, was used to doctor or attend to livestock, as was calf roping, Brazile's only event at this upcoming NFR. For steer wrestling, the cowboy jumps off his horse, grabs the animal's head and horns, and takes it down to the ground. (In days long past, cowboys on the range would also bite the animal's nose or lower lip to help gain control.

That is no longer practiced.) Team roping features two cowboys—one ropes the head and one the hind legs. In areas where families have the space and wherewithal, team roping is practiced as a recreational sport, kind of like doubles tennis. There are tournaments, mixed and single sex teams, age groups, handicaps and purses. Barrel racing is the only women's event regularly featured at PRCA tournaments; the contestants are still called cowgirls, a reflection of the somewhat retrograde values still clinging to the rodeo world.

There is no possible reason one might need to ride a bull, rodeo's most popular event. (In the riding events, the broncs and the bulls are also scored and rewarded championships and money.) Bull riding draws mostly young competitors, who tend to have short careers due to injury—they alone wear protective vests and neck collars and sometimes helmets instead of cowboy hats. Some say the genesis of bull riding involved lots of boredom and alcohol.

From the mid-1970s to the late 1980s, Roy Cooper—a national high school and college champion and PRCA rookie of the year—was the most recognized figure in professional rodeo. "At his prime, he had no competition," says Joe Beaver, an eight-time NFR champion roper, and one of Roy's many traveling partners back in the day. He is now a prominent TV commentator. "Roy was so consistent. He was so fast and so darn good. He rarely made any mistakes. What he could do in the arena was unreal. He's probably the greatest roper there has ever been."

Born to a famous rodeo family, Roy Cooper was one of the first of the great modern rodeo champions. The Super Looper was so good that sometimes, to make things more interesting in a competition, he would rope with his left hand—and still win. In a sport known for the close collaboration between man and animal, Roy would sometimes fly to competitions on a private jet and borrow an unfamiliar horse. "No matter how much he messed around, Roy had this amazing ability to make no mistakes and beat everybody," says Beaver.

Roy Cooper was also known for his appetite for partying, especially during the eighties and nineties, when he turned up everywhere with his best friend, country musician George Strait. Over the course of his career, Cooper qualified for the NFR 20 times. He won eight world championships, six in tie-down roping.

"Roy literally never pulled up at a rodeo that he didn't know in his head, in his mind, in the way he walked around, that he was fixin' to win it," says Roy's former wife, Shari Smith Cooper, the mother of Shada Brazile and Tuf Cooper, and also Tuf's older brother, Clif.

"Roy was like Mohammed Ali. He had his competitors intimidated before he ever walked in the arena, you know?" Shari Cooper says. "But the thing was, at the same time, he was encouraging to his competitors too. He once said he thought the best friend he could ever have in his life would be a guy who could beat him.

"There were times when he was winning the rodeo and he had the best horse, and the second-best roper might need to borrow a horse, and Roy would ride over and say, 'Here, get on him,'" she continues, shaking her head in disbelief, even after all these years and another husband. "It was like *Go ahead, try to beat me*. He had a sense of fairness about beating people only someone truly great at something could have."

There are a million stories about the Super Looper's exploits. Hang out with Roy for an afternoon; he loves to tell them. This one might well summarize: the pilot of a private jet puts the plane on autopilot for two hours so he can participate in a rousing game of strip poker at 30,000 feet with Roy and some lady friends and a huge pile of party favors.

"I had a great life," Roy says, looking out his window at the lake. "I got me a new truck every year and had the best horses I could find. I had new clothes. I had the first bus in rodeo. I bought George Strait's bus, the one he used in (the movie) *Pure Country*. I stayed in suites man, you could buy a suite for $150 back then, you know what I mean?

"I was spoiled. And maybe in a way I didn't appreciate what it meant to be at the top. Some men stand and face their gifts and others prefer to look away," he says, taking a slug of a Fireball mini. "It's a picnic but it ain't no picnic, know what I'm sayin'?"

***

Another of Roy's many and loyal rodeo buddies was a part-time competitor named Jimmy Brazile.

Jimmy was born in Amarillo, Texas, to a produce company foreman and his wife, who had migrated from Arkansas in the early fifties in search of work. One of ten children, Jimmy didn't rope at all until he was 16, when his family moved from a place in town out to a subdivision with five-acre tracts. "Around the corner a ways" lived a girl named Glenda Light. Her dad was a self-taught metal fabricator who made trailers and owned a ranch. "She and her family roped, and she ran barrels and rodeoed and everything," Jimmy remembers. "The first time I visited I said, 'Shucks, I think I can do that.'"

To Jimmy's father, who quit school after third grade, educating his kids was a priority. Jimmy graduated high school and enrolled at West Texas State as an agriculture major. In the meanwhile, he'd become captivated with rodeo and ranching—Glenda Light was no small influence. During college, Jimmy also apprenticed himself to an experienced cowboy in exchange for tutelage and calf roping time. After five semesters, Jimmy left school. He made his living ranching, working at a poultry plant, and giving private roping lessons to kids, in a region where rodeo is as much of a legitimate youth competitive sport as baseball or even football. In his spare time, Jimmy competed in amateur and then pro rodeos. He became one of the few successful left-handed ropers on the circuit—given the setup at most rodeo arenas, it was a handicap and a lifelong disappointment. Had he been right-handed, Jimmy Brazile says, his life may have been very different: he may have been a champion himself.

A few years later, Glenda Light graduated from West Texas with a teaching degree; the pair married and moved to Gruver, a dusty town of 1,100 souls in the Texas Panhandle, about a dozen miles south of Oklahoma. The couple was employed by a family that owned a ranch and feed lot. Glenda and Jimmy lived in a little house on the property. They worked side by side on horseback doing chores; part of their responsibilities included coaching the family's kids in roping and riding.

Trevor came along in 1976. With a partner, Jimmy and Glenda soon opened a feed lot of their own. It was flat country with hardly a shade tree in sight. The little family lived on the premises, which held about 10,000 head of cattle, brought to the lot to be fattened on corn and milo about 90 days before slaughter.

"Even blindfolded, you couldn't mistake the smell of a couple thousand steers," Brazile remembers. "Their constant bawling sounded like a swarm of bees."

"If somebody ever said something about the smell," Jimmy says, "I told 'em: 'It smells like money to me.'"

In time, the family left the feedlot business and moved south to Krum, north of Dallas. Jimmy went to work for Peterbilt. Glenda found work as a schoolteacher and coach. From the beginning Trevor never wanted to do anything but rope and ride. (His father made sure he was right-hand dominant.) By age 11, Brazile was competing in local and regional rodeos. He clearly had a rare talent.

"He'd win all the year-end saddles," Jimmy says. "Most of the time he'd win his age group a year or two before he hit the top age limit. He won '12 & Under' at age 10, '15 & Under' at 13, and same with the 16-19 age group. He'd just dominate each age group as he went along and win the title every year."

Brazile played some baseball in middle school; Jimmy remembers rushing back from a rodeo so Trevor could pitch. In high school, Brazile was a guard on a perennially good basketball team at Krum High School (Bobcats), the only freshman to make varsity. When the coach told Brazile he needed to devote more time to basketball or choose between the sports, the boy was torn. "He said, 'Dad, I don't know what to do,'" Jimmy remembers. "When I'm playing basketball, I feel like should be roping, and when I'm roping, I feel like I should be playing basketball.'" Before long he made his choice. Basketball never had a chance.

As a teenager, to help finance his competition and travel, Trevor broke riding horses and trained barrel racers for pay. He took out bank loans (co-signed by his maternal granddad) to buy calves for roping practice, which he then raised for sale for a profit. He also sold the saddles he won in competitions. "I probably won 70 or 80 over time," Brazile says. "I hated to let them go, but I couldn't afford to be sentimental." Today he has a large collection of prize saddles in a display in his family living room.

When Brazile was 12, his parents split. Glenda remembers: "One time, he came to me and said, 'Mom don't ever make me choose between the two of you.' I told him, 'Trevor you know you can go to your Dad's any time you want.'" Through the ensuing years, parental time was divided evenly; like any youth sports family, his parents took turns driving him to rodeos, depending upon their work schedules. Meanwhile Brazile roped with his dad every day after school; he remained close with both parents.

When Brazile was 15, the great Roy Cooper, known as the Super Looper, told his pal Jimmy to send his boy to one of his roping clinics, held at his ranch in the panhandle town of Childress, Texas. Brazile's talent was immediately obvious. From day one, a relationship blossomed between Brazile and the old pro. Later, when Trevor was a freshman on a rodeo scholarship at Vernon Regional Junior College, about an hour east of Roy's place, he spent all of his free time at the ranch.

"I remember Trevor being like 19, and he'd come down to my arena and he'd be like, 'What are you going to work on today?'" Roy says. "He was so interested and asked so many questions. I knew back then he had what it took. He practiced all day, every day."

***

While Brazile was training with Roy Cooper, he was also developing a relationship with Roy's stepdaughter, Shada, and Roy and Shari Smith Cooper's two sons, Tuf and Clif.

Shari Smith Cooper was born to a banker and his wife—a crafty businesswoman who owned restaurants, a bridal shop, and other businesses. The family also lived in the Panhandle, on a ranch outside Childress, the reason Roy had bought there, of course.

Shari's dad, Clifton Dale Smith, was also a part-time rodeo roper. Clifton had twice been to the NFR. "He never won a world championship, but he was good," Shari says. Together with her parents and her siblings—Suzy, Sealy, Smitty, and Stran—the family would pile into the car and drive to rodeos, pulling a horse trailer behind. (Brother Stran would become an NFR world champion tie-down roper in 2008.) Shari remembers loving the travel, the excitement, the new faces and places.

"I always wanted to be on the road, I always wanted to be traveling," says Shari, an accomplished businesswoman who acts as Tuf's manager—and travels frequently to rodeos and vacation spots with all of her kids and grandkids. "I never wanted to go home. I would watch out the window and know we were getting closer and closer to home, and I would just remember thinking, 'Slow down, don't get there, I don't wanna get there yet.'"

Shada is the daughter of Shari's first husband, Steve Norris; Shari married Norris when the two ran away to Vegas on a lark. Norris was the grandson of a woman who'd inherited an oil concern called the Texas Company, later to become petroleum giant Texaco. She had inherited the company from her uncle, John Warner "Bet-a-Million" Gates, a fascinating Gilded Age industrialist who was an early pioneer of the use of barbed wire and a president of Republic Steel.

After the breakup with Norris, Sheri and Shada moved back to the Smith ranch in Childress. "We grew up racing horses bareback like wild Indians. Just crazy stuff," Shada says. "I was a daredevil, which is what you have to be to barrel race. I look back now and I'm like: *I would not let my kids do that!* I remember once I fell off my horse and rolled over a cactus. My mom had to use tweezers to get out all those little prickly pear thorns. That hurt!"

Later, after a brief second marriage and sojourn in Los Angeles, the vivacious Shari met Roy Cooper at her mom's restaurant in Childress. A romance bloomed. The couple was married in 1987. Shada was 6 at the time. Clif came along the following year, Tuf two years later in 1990.

"Shada has always been an overachiever on everything she's ever done," Shari says. "Monday, she went to tap class. Tuesday, she went to piano lessons, Wednesday she went to gymnastics. Thursday, she went to ice skating lessons. Friday, she went to ballet and modern dance—that's what she liked to do. She was always busy." Later she played basketball and cheered for Childress High School—also named the Bobcats, like Brazil's high school.

"She graduated from high school in three years because she didn't want to waste any time," Shari says. "She never wastes time, even today, she's a whirlwind. She graduated from college (Texas Tech University) in three and a half years, too."

When Clif and then Tuf were born to Shari and Roy, "Shada acted like the boys were her own babies," Shari says. "She fed them and gave them baths. She never thinks of them as her half-brothers. To her there's no doubt they are her full-fledged brothers she helped raise."

"Growing up, I was so happy," Shada says. "But really, there were some problems between my Mom and Roy. Even though they hid it from me really well, I knew. I just kept busy, you know? I wasn't there to see any strife. I was either doing my homework or playing with my brothers or playing outside. Later, when I was 16 and I decided I wanted to rodeo, Roy bought me my first barrel horse. It was a nice horse, a really good horse, and probably expensive. He was always very good to me. And kind. Roy took me to my first little junior rodeo and I won on that horse, and then I had a good college career on him, too."

Shada and Trevor had their first real date when Trevor was a freshman on a rodeo scholarship at Vernon, about an hour east of Childress. A high school junior, Shada might have been a tad young for a college boy. They took it slow but never wavered. As time went on, Brazile found himself becoming close to the whole Cooper clan.

"My first memory of Trevor is when he brought me and my brother a bow and arrow," Tuf Cooper says. "I was probably 6 or 7. I guess he was trying to get in with the little brothers right off the bat."

Brazile went on to West Texas A&M University, but left in 1996, before graduating, to turn pro and join the PRCA. He moved into an apartment on Roy's ranch. During weekdays, when Shada was off at college on a barrel racing scholarship, Brazile would live in the house with Roy, Shari, and their two boys. Other times, Brazile and Roy traveled together to rodeos.

"Trevor was so sweet to the boys," Shari says. "They played Lego like crazy, oh my gosh, they built stuff all over the house. They'd play guns, cowboys and Indians, baseball and basketball or football—they'd play and tackle or they'd wrestle, everything boys do. Then they would tie and rope and ride horses. Trevor became part of the family."

Clif and Tuf were 12 and 14 when their parents broke up, mostly due to Roy's hard-partying ways. That same year, 2001, Shada and Brazile were married.

"A divorce is a rough time in a family's life," Tuf says. "The care Trevor and my sister had for me and my brother made a huge impact. Trevor really guided me to do the right things. He didn't allow me to go and screw up and do something extreme. I don't remember a life without Trevor. I don't remember him not being there for me."

The following year, Brazile won his first all-around championship, followed in the next two years by his second and third. After narrowly missing in 2005, he won the next ten in a row.

***

For two weeks every December, when the rodeo is in town, Las Vegas becomes a celebration of all things Western—even the huge golden lion in the lobby of the MGM Grand is wearing a Texas-size cowboy hat.

Dubbed the "Super Bowl of Rodeo" by the local newspaper, the Wrangler NFR is really more like Mardi Gras—instead of one game, the competition spans ten performances over ten nights. The NFR brings together, in each of its events, the top 15 money winners from the regular season. All of the men and women are fan favorites, the all-stars of their sport. Only six of the usual seven events are featured here—there's not enough room at Thomas and Mack for steer trippin'.

Up and down the Strip are bucking bronc and bull sales, barrel riding competitions, cowboy concerts and cowboy comic shows, demonstrations, exhibits and hospitality activities—even a big tent in a parking lot where a rodeo clown competition is happening, with colorfully dressed and made-up clowns vs. bulls in a small ring. (Like the crowd at an auto race waiting for a crash, the expectation in the stands is a few nasty gorings per show.)

Like the Superbowl or NBA All Star Game, sponsors rule the day—Wrangler, Polaris, Justin, Dodge, and Coors. An affiliation with rodeo is an affiliation with the spirit of the American Western ideal—a largely white, rural and Christian vision of a world where people are homogenous, neighborly, and don't overshare. They're tied to the land. Treat animals as a valuable commodity that require care but not equality. Plan to meet again in the afterlife. Use liberally the affirmatives *Yes, ma'am* and *Yes, sir*, having grown up under threat of a stiff switch. At the Cowboy Christmas show at the Las Vegas Convention Center, a random rack of bumper stickers, displayed innocuously beside a booth selling knickknacks, provides a decent read on community values: *I STAND WITH TRUMP. NO WELFARE FOR ILLEGALS. PETA: PEOPLE EATING TASTY ANIMALS.*

(Interestingly, the largest minority represented appears to be Native Americans, huge fans of pro rodeo, though sparsely represented in rodeo ranks. Most of the men are dressed exactly like every other man in attendance: boots, tight jeans, plaid dress shirt, big silver belt buckle, and a cowboy or trucker hat. So many Indians dressed like cowboys. Nobody pays it any mind.)

One afternoon, after a meet-and-greet with fans at a hotel off the Strip, Brazile is riding in a hotel limo that has been placed at his disposal. The leather seats in the Bentley motorcar are soft, the color of butter, as is the plush pile carpeting, atop of which are resting his black ostrich boots, complete with working spurs that *jingle, jingle, jingle* wherever he walks.

The autograph line at the last event had snaked around a corner. There was a giddy, expectant air among the pilgrims. More than two decades ago, when Brazile first broke in, many of them were children. Now they were bringing their own children to meet him.

Each fan lingered beyond the time it took for Brazile to scribble his signature, to spend a few moments chatting, to bask in the presence of the King of the Cowboys. It is as if, because they've followed him for so long, they feel as though he knows them intimately, too. They speak of a problem training a stubborn horse, a son or daughter's promising career in junior rodeo, a local connection to a distant family member. Some ask intricate questions about roping or riding or training technique—many are in town to participate in a team-roping competition held jointly at a huge hotel just off the Strip. After each audience came the inevitable selfie. Whole families arranged themselves around him; without prompting, Brazile picked up a sick and snotty toddler and placed him on his knee.

As required for official events, Brazile is wearing his signature uniform—a black hat and blue jeans and a black shirt embroidered with sponsors' logos. Traditionally, winners' purses include swag: finely crafted gold belt buckles, fancy hand-tooled saddles, watches, gun cases, spurs and sculptures. Brazile has won so much stuff during his career he's given it to a local merchant in Decatur to catalog and enshrine. The belt buckle he's carefully chosen to wear this week says *2015 World Champion All-Around Cowboy*. That was the year he roped Sally, tying an NFR arena record at 6.5 seconds. It was the last championship he won before his decade-long streak came to end.

After the 2015 NFR Finals, many cowboys' long-simmering issues with the PRCA—about the brutal travel schedule, threats to eliminate events, and inadequate, non-guaranteed payouts (only winners get the purse, but the PRCA takes a cut)—came to a head when Brazile and a group of 80 top competitors formed a parallel body called Elite Rodeo Athletes, ERA. Shortly thereafter, the PRCA passed bylaws barring ERA cowboys from entering their events, including the NFR. The ERA, in turn, filed an anti-trust suit in federal court.

When the dust cleared, the ERA cowboys and cowgirls dropped their lawsuit. Brazile, Tuf Cooper, and many others sat out the 2016 season, opting to participate only in the nine, ERA-sanctioned rodeos and a smattering of other independents—none of which qualified them for the NFR Finals, which is by far the most lucrative rodeo in the world. Brazile's exit from the PCRA also cost him his endorsement deal with Wrangler, the PRCA's premier sponsor. A successful line of children's clothing, conceived and run by Shada, became a victim of the fallout as well.

During his enforced layoff, Brazile says, he found himself with leisure time—something with which he was previously unacquainted.

He's been going hard at rodeo since he was a small child. "It was weird. But also kind of enjoyable. I spent a lot of time going to the batting cage with the kids and working on my 3-point shot," he says, nodding to the regulation height hoop in the driveway.

"It was *different*," Shada says. "We kind of had a normal schedule like normal people. We went to weddings and birthday parties and stuff we'd always missed. I kinda liked being home. I got used to it. People always used to say to me about our life: 'I don't know how you do it.' I never really understood what they were talking about until the layoff. It was the only life we'd ever known."

Returning to competition at the beginning of this 2017 season, Brazile says, "I felt rejuvenated. As much as I've invested and loved this sport, a year off gives you that extra *oomph*. You just crave it that much more."

Even so. . . his performance this past year, throughout this 2017 regular season, has been admittedly. . . *underwhelming*.

"The rust was pretty thick," he says as the limo works slowly through the traffic. Every car around us seems to have at least one cowboy hat visible inside the passenger space. "It was the first sub-$500,000 year I've had in a long time," he says candidly. Of the 20 most lucrative years by professional rodeo cowboys, 10 of them belong to Brazile. And all of those are over the half million mark.

More troubling: Brazile's earnings from sponsorships far exceed his rodeo earnings. Maintaining his sponsorships means maintaining his performance and visibility. Seemingly nothing he uses on his ranch isn't supplied for free by some sponsor. Currently, he endorses or licenses hay, feed, saddles and tack, ropes and roping gear, trucks, trailers, customized living quarters in trailers, off-road vehicles, a performance supplement company, the clothes, and more. Winning is necessary to keep the juggernaut afloat. Born poor and lifted by his own bootstraps, Brazile is acutely aware of the value of his name and brand: It's what enables him to compete more often and, in more events, than other cowboys, and to afford to travel farther to do it.

"There's a lot of winning that didn't get done this year, that normally did," he says. The way his hat weighs down the tops of his ears, folding them forward a bit, adds a suggestion of youth and earnestness.

As the limo works its way slowly through the traffic, Brazile looks out the window. In side view, the softening of his jawline is apparent, the workings of time. He doesn't talk about the nagging injuries. He is not a man to make excuses. Win or go home. That's how it's always been.

***

After the rough regular season, Brazile had gone home and trained hard for Vegas. A steady stream of pro cowboys, relatives and competitors alike, came to the ranch to train with him and get in reps.

Owing to whale sperm injections in his sore right elbow, physical therapy on his sore quad and hamstring—not to mention a steady, well-monitored, low-carb diet and the balm of being home with his family—Brazile had come into the ten days of the NFR feeling as healthy and well-oiled as he had all year. "I was finally feeling like myself again," he says.

The first night in Vegas, he looked like his old self, tying for second place (7.9 seconds).

In round two, he was first (7.4).

In round three, he was third (7.3).

At that point, the King of the Cowboys was leading the all-around earnings in his event with $313,837. And he was leading for lowest average time in the event, which pays another $67,000 at the end of the meet and counts toward the all-around totals. It appeared he was finally back on his game.

Then things began to unravel.

The NFR is a marathon. Along with the strain of ten, back-to-back nights of competition, there are daily appearances and autograph signings, post-rodeo dinners with sponsors, and late-night partying with family, friends, and fans.

In round four, Brazile tied for eighth (9.4).

In round five, eleventh (10.4).

In round six, when Brazile desperately needed to get things back on track, he was disqualified for a "jerk down," meaning Deputy pulled back too hard on the rope after Brazile dismounted to chase the roped calf, a rule installed to accommodate animal rights advocates. Family and friends were aghast, citing the call as evidence of the PRCA's sour attitude toward their fallen poster boy—obvious revenge for his ERA rebellion. *A jerk down call on night six?* Like fouling Michael Jordan out of a finals game. The jerk-down call also disqualified him from contention for lowest average time—you need all ten runs to qualify.

Then last night, round seven, the bottom fell out—he misses the calf completely.

"After I got flagged out for the jerk down, I knew I was out of the average competition, so I came back knowing I had to press for day money," to raise his totals, Brazile says, sitting in the back seat of the Bentley, his tone neither grim nor heroic.

The crowd of 16,000 went silent.

Unfettered, the calf gamboled across the dirt ring, heading for the opening (and a snack of hay and water) at the opposite end of the arena.

"It was *ugly*," Brazile said.

***

Brazile directs the limo driver along a series of obscure alleys and ramps on the back side of the Strip. He has been competing here for more than half his life; he seems to know every shortcut, stage door, and loading dock in town.

We disembark behind the Convention Center, near a stack of hay bales, and filter past a couple of temporary livestock pens— kids aged nine to 19 and their parents fussing over horses and tack. Several adults in the crowd spot Brazile; their eyes track him eagerly, a legend in their midst. Nobody makes any move to approach.

A loading door leads to an indoor rodeo arena. Tons of sandy loam have been trucked in to convert the space. There are bleachers on two sides. Already seated is a large contingent of family—Coopers,

Smiths and Braziles, some call them the First Family of Rodeo. They are here to cheer Brazile's son, eleven-year-old Treston Brazile, as he competes in the annual Roy Cooper Junior Tie-Down Roping Invitational, another of the many attractions in Vegas this time of year.

Treston is a bright and rubbery 85-pounder in a miniature uniform shirt, with sponsor names like his dad's. By the time Brazile arrives, Treston is up on his horse, ready to go.

The boy shares Brazile's brown eyes; he looks a lot in the face like his Uncle Tuf. The event is called 10 & Under Girls & Boys Breakaway, which means the calf is roped, but not thrown and tied. After the loop settles in place around the neck, the roper lets go, and the calf runs out of the arena trailing the rope. The contestant has to follow the calf out of the arena to retrieve his rope.

Brazile tightens the saddle cinches on Treston's horse, checks the other Relentless tack. There's a lot of affectionate patting—of both boy and horse—and a lot of adjusting of equipment, but not many words: The Cowboy Way.

Just then, Roy Cooper appears beside his kinfolk. He's been running clinics and tournaments and giving high-end lessons for years, the natural sideline of a legend. The 62-year-old walks a little gingerly. He's wearing Day-Glo orange sneakers instead of cowboy boots; he's had a long list of surgeries.

Roy Cooper grew up on a ranch in Hobbs, New Mexico. His father, Delbert "Tuffy" Cooper was inducted into the National Cowboy Hall of Fame in 1998. His sister, Betty Cooper Ratliff, is in the National Cowgirl Hall of Fame.

As he was growing up, Roy's dad seemed determined to make his boy into a superstar. "I took the best traits of every roper who ever lived and incorporated them into him," Tuffy Cooper told a biographer, who writes that Roy Cooper, though small and asthmatic in grade school, was entering as many as fifty rodeos a year by the time he was 12. According to an interview with Tuffy, Roy's tie and his hooey knot—the finishing slip-knot on the piggin' string at the end of the hoof tie—were crafted from distinct parts of three different rodeo superstars' techniques.

In 1973, Roy won the national high school championship and accepted a rodeo scholarship to Cisco Junior College in Texas. During his sophomore year, he won the calf roping event at the National Intercollegiate Finals, then transferred to Southeastern University, where he became a journalism major. In 1977, while still a senior, Roy turned pro. In his rookie PRCA season, at age 20, Roy won the tie-down roping championship, and broke the record for the most prize money won by a rookie cowboy. Perhaps one of his proudest moments occurred in 2010, when all three of his sons, Clif, Tuf, and Clint—the eldest by his first wife (who lives in a small house next door to his property)—all competed in tie-down roping at the NFR, a first for the record books.

Roy was in the crowd last night at the Thomas and Mack when Brazile missed his calf. Now, in the ring at his own tournament, he wants to say something to his former protege. . . but then again, he doesn't. The Cowboy Way.

He knows what he did, Roy thinks. *I know what he did. We all know what we did. It's over and done. What else can you say?*

Instead he turns to his grandson, "Ready to get 'er done?" he asks. Playfully, he jostles Treston's shoulder; the kid's tan Resistol hat is knocked askew.

Brazile re-sets it for him.

All three share a laugh.

***

Late afternoon at the MGM Grand, the First Family of Rodeo is having a pre-performance lunch at their favorite spot, just off the casino floor—The Grand Wok and Sushi Bar.

When he's with his family eating meals, or walking through the hallways at the hotel, or nursing a soda water at the raucous, late night after-rodeo evening activities along the Strip, you'd never know the mild-mannered Brazile was in the middle of competing for the biggest prizes of the year, at the biggest rodeo of the year, a rodeo he missed last year for the first time in his long professional life, sponsored by people who rejected his shot at a cowboy liberation movement and rescinded his (and his wife's) sponsorship deals.

And you'd never know things aren't going very well, or that tonight is the tenth and final round—do or die.

Instead, he seems like just another guy in a cowboy hat in a sea of cowboy hats, eating Chinese food with his extended family.

The hotel is one of the major sponsors of the NFR. Most of the finalists are staying here; Brazile, Shada, and the kids are bivouacked in a chic duplex in the Signature Towers, which has its own secret lobby off the main lobby, behind an unassuming pair of double doors. Tuf Cooper is staying in another exclusive part of the hotel called The Mansion. A stand-alone structure hidden deep inside the bowels of the property, it drew its inspiration from an 18th-century villa in the countryside near Florence, Italy. Few people know it exists.

In all there are more than 50 members of the Smith/Cooper/Brazile clan in town.

This group occupies two large tables. In attendance are Brazile and Shada, baby Swayzi, 2, daughter Stile, 8, and son Treston. Glenda Light Brazile Horney is in from her ranch in New Mexico, where she moved several years ago with her second husband, an old high school chum. Blessed with a strong sense of humor, she has obviously passed along to her son, she likes to tell about the first time, in high school, she heard her future husband's name called in homeroom during the morning roll, last name first: Horney, Guy.

Also present are Shari's two sisters. Suzy Smith Yarborough, the eldest, has grown children named Yancy (a former Miss Texas/America who has become an evangelist), Yandy (a working cowboy and former bulldogger), and Yacy (a nurse). Her other sister is Sealy Smith Vest. Her kids are Vandon (an entrepreneur), Stetson (a pro cowboy), and Sawyer (former Texas Tech defensive back and a working cowboy).

As usual, Tuf Cooper is with his girlfriend of seven years, Tiffany McGhan, more on which, later. Across the table and down one chair from Tuf is his older brother, Clif, 29, and his wife Terryn. Owing to the family's tendency to have fun with spelling and names, their daughter is named Ceattle—she is sitting at the moment with her

Brazile cousins at the other end of the table with their two grandmas, Shari and Glenda. Like Trevor and Shada, Clif and Terryn met at a rodeo when they were children. Later, they were team roping partners on their college rodeo squad—they were both on scholarship and pursuing business majors; she was the header and he was the heeler.

Though some say the 29-year-old Clif—a star basketball player in high school—is a superior athlete and better roper than any other Cooper, Clif chose to leave the full-time game in 2015, a year before the whole business with the ERA. Since then he has rodeoed part-time for fun, meanwhile starting a business building and leasing homes. He also works as a personal trainer. Last year, Terryn and Clif won one hundred thousand dollars appearing on a short-lived game show called *Candy Crush*, based on the cell phone game, hosted by Mario Lopez. Their connection to the TV world was her brother, Hayden Moss, a former winner of *Big Brother*, who also appeared on *Survivor*. Their adventures in Hollywood could easily fill another chapter of this story. They sometimes entertain notions of trying again on another show.

Until the banquet of dishes is delivered by the deferential Grand Wok waiters, there is much getting up and switching seats and visiting, as people do, and a lot of light chit chat and discussion of sightings and doings of family members and neighbors and friends drifting through town. Though Brazile and Tuf are running neck and neck in the all-around standings—Brazile is still leading, but only by about thirty thousand—nobody mentions the standings. Or about anything rodeo. Once the food comes, the two men retire to their different tables, each beside his significant other. Serious eating ensues.

By the time the servers begin clearing the table, most of the adults are slouched back and sated, discussing their next move—the clock is ticking. The young cousins have run off with Glenda Horny, an energetic dynamo who has no trouble keeping up. Having had the misfortune of being seated across from a reporter, Clif and Terryn are reflecting deeply about Clif's decision to take a break from rodeo—making him the only one in the inner family who has done so.

Everyone acknowledges Clif is the tallest and most handsome of all the cousins of his generation. Roy Cooper thinks he's the best natural roper, too. Like all of the other beautiful and well-composed women of various ages at the table, Terryn puts one in mind of a contestant for Miss America/Texas. They are nearly always seen together, attached at the hip: Country Barbie and Cowboy Ken.

"I remember when I told her I was finally done, and she cried," Clif is saying about his decision to leave the circuit. "But I just told her, 'I'm tired of all the running around. I'm tired of not being with my family. All I want is a set schedule, just like a normal person. I wanna wake up and have coffee with you in the morning.'"

"We have that now," Terryn says, her head tilts itself lovingly in the direction of her husband's.

"And we can go to the gym and work out together," he says. "That's what I wanted. I wanted a little bit of normalcy."

"And maybe a little less pressure," Terryn adds.

Clif nods in agreement. "If you want to be successful, you have to be conscious of always working, always getting better, every single day," he says. "I come from a family with a huge work ethic. But you have to realize: there's always someone out there thinking, *I better get out and practice today because somewhere, someone else is practicing, someone is working at it, trying to be great.*"

"So you have to put that first," Terryn says.

"After a while you just wonder. *What am I trying to achieve?*"

"Especially if you think there are other things besides rodeo."

"In my case," Clif says, "I was being pulled toward having a better life for my family, taking care of my family, making a long-term plan for myself."

"Because there's no retirement plan in rodeo," Terryn says.

Clif sighs and takes off his baseball style cap, revealing his long golden hair, which is tied up in a definitely non-cowboy-issue man-bun.

"There's no retirement plan in rodeo," he repeats. "There's no benefits package. There's no long-term. It's all short-term success."

"And then you're forty," Terryn says, "and you can't beat the young kids who are coming up behind you."

I look at Terryn. Her eyes are large and deep brown, set off by her dark eyebrows. She is smiling pleasantly; her lips are painted red, a quick re-application after the meal was done. I don't think she's just registered what she said. There is no way she's talking about Brazile and Tuf, about their pitched battle to the finish.

But there you have it.

The inevitability of age and injury.

"I grew up my whole life with these guys my dad knew," Clif says. "There was this one guy, I won't say his name. But he was a several-time world champion. We went to visit him, and I was all excited, and we pulled up at his place. And he was living in a really beat-up old mobile home. It was just a wreck, you know? And that made such an impression on me. I was like, 'Man, that's not gonna be me, *ever*.' I want to have my own plane someday. I want to have a beach house. In 20 years, I want to be able to fly the whole family to my place for vacation. . ."

Somewhere during Clif's soliloquy, Tuf has craned one of his adorable stick-out ears toward our conversation and has begun to listen in.

Finally, with a crooked smile on his face, the most antic of the Cooper kids interrupts his older brother: "You know you'd give your left nut to be competing right now!" Tuf says adamantly.

Clif purses his lips.

He knows his little brother is right.

Absently, he raises his large and strong hands to tighten the flaxen hair of his topknot.

***

The final night of the Wrangler NFR is the money shot, nighttime Vegas in full Western reveal: cowboy boots and lace, turquoise and rhinestones, plaid and denim with a sharp center crease, the air flavored with anticipation and barbecued beef, country-western hits booming from the PA system outside the Thomas and Mack Center. Traffic is snarled. Search lights sweep the sky. Tickets officially run $67 to $300, but many have paid thousands for their seats. Over ten sold-out days, 171,000 people will attend the rodeo.

It takes 2,000 tons of dirt to convert the basketball arena at the University of Nevada at Las Vegas into a rodeo venue. Anyone meaningful to ProRodeo is here for the final night. The members of the extended Smith-Cooper-Brazile clan are scattered throughout the building. Shari Cooper has a seat right next to the starting box. Shada also has a plum location. Her daughters Stile and Swayzi are beside her, dressed in matching gold sparkle dresses with white faux-fur capes. Treston looks like a miniature man in his Western-cut sport coat and tan Resistol hat.

Going into tonight—the tenth and final night of the NFR—Brazile and Tuf are running neck and neck—#1 and #2 in the all-around. Brazile has earnings of $319,337, compared to $286,983 for Tuf, a difference of about $32,000.

But after a strong comeback over the last few days, Tuf is currently first in tie-down roping. And he's second in the average, which carries an additional purse, from which Brazile has been disqualified, having failed to post a score in the last round due to the jerk down ruling.

Though Tuf hasn't performed spectacularly, he's been consistent. Over ten nights, that's maybe the most important.

Tonight, Brazile is the tenth contestant to take his turn. Tuf will go last, 15th.

As Brazile trots Deputy into the arena, the houselights lights dim. The spotlight follows him. The PA announcer is a ProRodeo Hall of Famer too. His name is Randy Corley. He puts one in mind of famous boxing announcers on telecasts from Vegas and elsewhere, only with a southern twang and a gift for working the Lord God into all the introductions—make no mistake, the NFR Finals are a Vegas show, but the sizzle includes a strong helping of tent-revival-style ministry and conservative red-state boosterism.

"Two decades ago," Corley intones dramatically, "this man was winning college championships. Twenty years later, he's the winningest cowboy in professional rodeo!"

The crowd roars.

"That's right, people, THE Trevor Brazile! Six million dollars of winnings! Twenty-three world championships!"

In the stands, Shada's brow furrows. *Man,* she thinks, *no matter who wins tonight, I'm a winner and I'm a loser.*

Brazile sets up Deputy in the starting box, worries his rope into shape, holds his right arm out from his body—the same crooked elbow, the same single index finger pointed up. To win his 24th championship, he needs a first-place finish. Nothing else will do. The time to beat is 8.1 seconds.

Uncharacteristically, Brazile looks nervous and unsettled in the box. He swings Deputy around and backs him up and repositions. He fidgets in the saddle. He fixes his hat. He fiddles with the piggin' string, trying to get it set properly in his mouth.

At last, the dimples show. He nods his head slowly, gravely, almost imperceptibly, causing the brim of his Trevor Brazile signature Resistol hat to bob.

Deputy is the fastest calf horse Brazile has ever owned. And maybe the most game. Brazile never even has to kick him. Usually, as soon as the chute opens and the calf bolts, and Deputy feels the tension come off the reins, he takes off immediately at full speed.

This time, however, when the chute opens and the calf bolts, and the crowd roars, and the showy heavy metal music plays over the PA . . . Deputy doesn't take off immediately at full speed. Instead, he rears up, both front legs in the air, like a sprinter out of form. Brazile urges him forward. A few microseconds of eternity pass. Finally, he digs in his front hooves and gives chase.

Brazile swings his loop over his head—once, twice, three times—and throws overhand, a unique motion said to share kinship with a baseball pitcher's follow-through.

As the loop settles around the calf's neck, Brazile jumps out of the saddle and runs full speed toward the stunned but still-standing bovine.

Deputy stops in his tracks, and begins walking backward, as he's been trained to do (horses don't naturally back up). The other end of the rope is attached to the saddle horn. When the calf runs out of slack, it is jerked backward somewhat violently—hence the jerk-back rule, which was partially inspired by the protests of animal rights proponents, who claim the calves get hurt in the event; cowboys say they are professionals and wouldn't ever want to injure the animals on which their livelihoods depend. All of these events are evolved from the tricks a lone cowboy can use to hobble one of his animals long enough to see to its well-being, to doctor and administer meds and dress wounds.

Brazile grabs the rope's "hondo" (the slipknot of the hooey) with his left hand. With his right, he grabs hold of the calf's flank (the fleshy portion between the rear leg and the belly). In one strong motion, he picks up the animal—older and larger than his practice calves, 100 pounds heavier than himself—and flanks it, taking it down to the dirt.

Straddling the calf, using one knee to hold it in place, Brazile places the slipknot of the piggin' string over the near front hoof, then gathers the two back legs—sinuous, strong, uncooperative. Many a fast run has been ruined by a stubborn leg.

Two wraps pull the loop through: the hooey knot. A bouquet of cloven hooves.

Brazile throws his hands in the air like a gymnast finishing a landing—the signal to stop the clock.

The official time shows on the scoreboard: 9.9 seconds.

***

When the competition is done, the house lights in the Thomas and Mack arena are dimmed. It's time for the Gold Buckle Ceremony.

Spotlights are trained on a small platform that has appeared in the center of the ring, filled now with a thick cloud of theatrical smoke. The platform is crowded with rodeo brass and legends. Around the circumference are nine elaborate, hand-tooled trophy saddles, one for each event (team roping has two winners), plus the all-around.

One by one, the victors are called. They come out holding their gold buckles aloft, accompanied by flashing lights and a heavy metal soundtrack. It's reminiscent of an entrance you might see in pro wrestling, only foreshortened for lack of space.

Last up is the winner of the all-around . . . Tuf Cooper. It is his first all-around buckle.

Like his father before him, Tuf was groomed to be a champion. He won his first roping contest at age six, turned pro at 18. At 23 he became the youngest cowboy ever to reach $1 million in earnings.

With his baby face and cherubic smile, the name of his Lord and savior embroidered along with his sponsor's across his uniform shirts, Tuf has been called the "Justin Bieber of Rodeo." He has a large social media presence. His autograph lines are often dominated by middle-school-age girls. "Grandparents want girls to marry him, and daddies want their sons to be like him," says Shari Cooper, who co-manages him along with his cousin, Vandon Vance.

Unbeknownst to many of his fans, Tuf's heart is reserved for his girlfriend, Tiffany McGhan, a fashion blogger and stylist. Tiffany is a few years Tuf's senior. Tuf was 19 on their first date. He dressed in a sports coat and picked her up in a red convertible Mercedes. Together, the couple completed a rare Dallas sports bifecta: attending both a Cowboys football game and a Rangers baseball game on the same day.

According to Shari, Tiffany has quietly and maturely endured the onslaught of teeny boppers for seven years. Everybody is always asking when the couple will tie the knot.

Now Tuf strides toward the Gold Buckle platform to make official his first all-around title. He's wearing a steel-colored American Brand hat. His blue gingham check shirt and his blue jeans are both "Tuf Cooper Performance" by Panhandle. His boots are light blue ostrich, custom made by Rios of Mercedes.

As they come to the stand, each winner is interviewed by the popular country music radio host Suzanne Alexander, who has anchored the TV coverage on CBS Sports for the past ten nights. Now Alexander sticks a microphone under Tuf's strong jaw. He smiles and reaches across his body with his right hand, taking hold of the mic jointly with Alexander. He tugs lightly, trying to take the mic and hold it himself, but she doesn't want to let it go. They settle uneasily on joint ownership. The cameras capture the moment up close in HD; it plays both at home and in the arena.

Tuf first thanks Trevor Brazile, and also "my family, my dad, my brothers," and all of his fans. Then he says, "Susan, I have something special I want to do now." He makes another attempt to wrest free the mic.

She's not yielding. A mini tug-of-war ensues.

"I got this," he says—this time pointedly, flashing one of those big Texas smiles that lets you know someone is not playin' around.

She relents.

Tuf is all blue eyes and bone structure, his ears bent forward with little-boy earnestness beneath the brim of his hat. For one brief moment, professional rodeo's newest All-Around Champion looks as if he's about to cry.

"Pretty nervous right now," he says into the mic.

Then he takes off his hat, gets down on one knee and proposes marriage to Tiffany.

The crowd goes wild.

***

A few weeks later, back at home, Roy Cooper is hanging out in the den at his ranch, watching football and sipping on a miniature bottle of Fireball Cinnamon Whisky. From the built-in couch where he's lounging, beside a large window, we can see the lake he shares with Brazile. It has a fountain in the middle that wouldn't be out of place in Las Vegas, throwing up a water spout 30 feet high.

A few years ago Roy and Brazile had a truck come over from Arkansas, full of little catfish and bass, five to ten cents apiece.

"Shit, them sons of bitches are like this right now," Roy says, holding his hands a couple of feet apart. He cackles and then reaches over to free another mini bottle of Fireball from a newly opened ten pack that has been delivered from the liquor store by his cook/maid, along with a sandwich she made herself and has urged him to eat, a familiar kind of concerned nagging that comes with long association.

The way Roy figures it, there's a beautiful symmetry to Tuf's relationship with Brazile. "I know Trevor helps Tuf, but it goes the other way, too," he says. "Just like Trevor probably helped me, because I seen how hard he worked at it, and it made me work a little harder, too."

Out the window, we can see Tuf, the youngest of his three sons, and the newly crowned all-around champ, working out with his horse in Roy's practice pen. Tuf has just returned from a celebratory trip with his new fiancée. There's a rodeo in Odessa, Texas, this weekend and he needs to iron out the kinks.

Ordinarily, Tuf would practice with Brazile over at his place, but Brazile has already left for Odessa, wanting to get a head start on the 300+ mile drive.

Before he drove off, Brazile leaned against the front of his heavy-duty, deluxe, six-wheel pickup—courtesy of a local dealership, as are his two large family SUVs. He raised his hat and wiped his brow with his sleeve, the way cowboys do on TV shows. Then he looked thoughtfully into the middle distance.

"I had multiple chances in Vegas to get the job done, and I just didn't, and Tuf executed, and nobody worked harder," he told me. "Listen, it's been fun to watch him blossom and grow. He's like a son to me. And he's also someone I respect. Over the years, he's pushed me some. He probably prolonged my career. The thing is, at the end of the day, I want somebody wearing that gold buckle who my kids can look up to, and that's definitely the case right now."

The sun was setting. His cheeks and his hands were rosy. He'd been practicing since morning in the cold.

"I know I'm near the end," he said. "Sometimes, I feel like I need to find some inspiration to make it work, to keep pushing the way I always have. I don't have anything else to prove."

Epilogue

One year later, just before the 2018 NFR Finals were due to begin, the PRCA announced Brazile would be greatly reducing his rodeo schedule starting in 2019, a kind of graceful semi-retirement, enough to maintain a public profile in the PRCA, with the fans, and with his sponsors.

But without the full-time grind, the 23-time world NFR world champion would no longer be competing in enough rodeos to qualify for any more NFR world championships.

Barring some kind of extreme turnaround, in other words, the 2018 NFR would be his last.

"My priorities have officially changed," the 42-year-old Brazile was quoted as saying. "The way I divide my time has been trending toward where we are today for a while now. Though we rodeoed together as a family, rodeo was taking a lot of my time and attention. Home-schooling our kids is the only thing that made it work as long as it did. Now that they're in public school, the days of being gone on the first day of school, and missing ball games are over. I've always been an all-in kind of guy, and if there's one thing I cannot live with doing halfway, it's being a husband and dad.

"The good news," he continued, "is that this is *my* decision, and I'm not being forced out because I'm hurt or too old."

Over the course of his career, since his rookie season in 1996, Brazile had rewritten rodeo's record books. His 13 world all-around crowns nearly doubled Ty Murray's seven, which is second all-time.

In addition to the all-arounds, Brazile had been one of only three cowboys to win world titles in four events—six world steer roping championships, three world tie-down roping crowns and the world team roping title, as both a header and a heeler. The single-year NFR earnings record of $298,159 set by Brazile in 2015 also still stands. . .

And so it was, on Sunday night, Dec. 9, 2018, in front of 16,917 fans at the Thomas & Mack Center, on his very last chance at winning the gold buckle for the All Around, Brazile went into the tenth round running neck and neck with Tuf.

Tuf, the reigning champion, was in first place, ahead of him by only about $12,000.

Brazile had had an up-and-down season in 2018. Only a big win at the end of the year had elevated him in the standings enough to guarantee his inclusion in the NFR.

When Brazile ripped off a blazing 6.8 in the fourth round to give him a first place, people were thinking, *The King of the Cowboys is back.*

But as the week dragged on, both men performed unevenly. No doubt both had much on their minds; both had huge milestones looming. For Brazile, this was his last chance. After this, there would be no more buckles.

For Tuf, well, win or not, he was getting married directly after the conclusion of the NFR.

Unlike 2017, in this do or die situation, Brazile and Deputy seemed at peace in the starting box. There was no fiddling, no apparent nervousness. After last year's loss, Brazile told me: "The problem was, I'd backed myself into a corner. I was pushing. I had a predetermined shot: I had to do it or fail. Anybody I'm teaching how to rope, I always tell them: you can't rush, you can't press. There's a lot of elements to bring together for a good run. The calf, your horse, yourself. You just have to settle down and let it happen. Unfortunately, I didn't listen to my own advice."

Now the dimples appeared. The head nodded slowly, gravely, almost imperceptibly, causing the brim of his Trevor Brazile signature cowboy hat to bob. The chute opened and the calf took off running.

Without hesitation, horse and rider gave chase, as they had so many thousands of times before.

Brazile swung the loop in a circle over his head. Once . . . twice . . . and then he threw.

And ran and flanked and tied his hooey. Hands in the air.

7.2 seconds.

Good enough for first place.

The crowd went wild.

Then Tuf's turn came. The run looked fast. But then he was disqualified for a jerk down.

The prize money put Brazile well on top, giving him the lead in the all-around with $335,679.98—a margin of $25,322.97.

The King had secured championship number 24.

Breaking into tears in a TV interview before his appearance at the Gold Buckle ceremony, Brazile said, "It's been an up and down week . . . I learned a lot about myself. I could never thank the sport or my fans enough. Everything I've got is because of rodeo."

2019

A BOY AND HIS DOG IN HELL

The boy in the alley calls himself Zeke. He's thirteen years old; he has a part-time job selling cocaine on a corner. He swears he didn't fight no pit bull dogs to the death. He didn't hang no dogs from no roof with telephone wire, neither. That's what he told the judge, anyway. Life and death on the mean streets of North Philadelphia's Little Puerto Rico.

The kid in the alley calls himself Zeke. He's waiting for Beo, his older brother. It's early yet, 8:00 in the evening in spring. Dogs bark behind a backyard fence, rain drums the hood of a car, rap rumbles from a boom box in an open window.

Zeke cups his hand beside his mouth and lifts his chin toward the roof line. "Yoooooooooo!" he howls—a lone, shrill note that pierces the rot smell and the amber light and echoes across the ruins of North Philadelphia. Once upon a time, this area was populated by Irish and Italian immigrants; they worked in the factories along American Street, turning out ball bearings and steel rollers and conveyor belts, little parts of bigger parts that made the machine age run. Today the neighborhood is called Little Puerto Rico. The factories have moved to the suburbs, the Sunbelt, offshore. American Street is wide and empty.

"Yoooooooooooo!" Zeke howls again. He tilts his ear and listens.

From a distance comes a faint response. "Yoooooooooo!"

Beo is coming. He's got the dog.

Zeke crosses a vacant lot, crunching over the tin cans and car parts and bedsprings and pieces of foam and Pampers covering the ground like mulch. He jumps atop an old washing machine and lights a joint. The rain is harder now. He tugs the collar of his jacket closer to his neck. It is a 76ers jacket, red and shiny and much too large for a seventy-five-pound kid. The waistband hits him mid-thigh. The sleeves keep falling over his hands. He took it from somewhere, he can't remember; it was a while ago, before his last stretch at St. Michael's School for Boys. A name is stitched on the left chest in white letters: SAUL.

Zeke has been home from St. Michael's for two weeks. He likes being home, being free, doing anything he wants—like all day today, like tonight, a night sharp with the promise of dogs and drugs, blood and adventure. St. Michael's was far away from the neighborhood, in Tunkhannock, Pennsylvania, in the woods near the mountains. They locked him in there, and he went to school, took baths, watched TV. They tried to make him eat, but the food was nasty, nothing tasted like nothing. Zeke didn't know nobody but one boy. One night the boy tried to pinch Zeke's ass. Zeke punched his lights out. Or so he says.

To hear him tell it, Zeke should never have gone to jail in the first place. It was his lawyer's fault—his lawyer wouldn't let him talk to the judge. Had he been able to talk, Zeke says, he would have got himself off. Like he told that lawyer, he didn't fight no pit bull dogs to the death. He didn't hang no dogs from no roof with no telephone wire after they lost a fight. And he didn't know nothing about no ten dog bodies. He didn't do *nothing*.

The lawyer told him to shut up. Zeke was appearing before the same judge who'd sent him away the last time. This time, his sixth at St. Michael's, Zeke got five months. By his own rough count, that makes a total of three years he has spent locked up in one place or another. He is thirteen years old. When he totals his time, he smiles and shows his dimples. He is a pretty boy, with high cheekbones and dark hair cropped close to his head. His eyes sparkle like the broken glass in the gutter.

Beo rounds the corner, issues a quiet "Yo." He's got the dog by a choke chain. It pulls him through the alley, weaving here and there to sniff and piss, wheezing a bit from the pressure of the chain around its neck. A young male pit bull, about one year old, it is fourteen inches tall at the shoulder, maybe twenty-five pounds. Its brown and tan coloring is called *brindle* by breeders and aficionados; on the street it's *tiger stripe*.

He's a good-looking animal, handsome in the same way a man can be—chiseled jaw and high cheekbones. His body looks like something by Nautilus, with a muscular chest and slightly bowed front legs, as if he's done a lot of pushups and bicep curls. The waist is tapered, the ass small, the gait wide-legged and sturdy.

Zeke neither waves nor says hello. His expression says he doesn't give a shit whether Beo showed up or not. He doesn't even look at the dog. In Zeke's world, he says, "If you want something, you don't get it." Zeke don't want nothing from nobody. If he did, he'd take it himself.

Beo is fourteen, the oldest boy of his mother's seven children by three fathers. Beo is four-foot-eleven, one inch taller than Zeke, five pounds heavier. He's wearing a leather jacket with the hood pulled up over his head. As he comes closer, his soft face and big brown eyes put you in mind of the time Tom Sawyer wore a bonnet to fool the old lady. Like Tom, Beo is a legend, at least around here.

"We tried to catch this kid for two years," says Sam McClain, a Philadelphia police officer. One morning at 6:00, McClain came to Beo's house with warrants for theft, receiving stolen property, dog fighting, cruelty to animals, and killing or maiming a domestic animal. The fire department set up ladders on either end of the block-to-block possible escape routes. Fifteen police officers covered the rooftops and the street.

"Somehow the kid got away," McClain says, only half-grudgingly.

Around the neighborhood, the stories about Beo have reached mythic proportions. One time, it is said, he was running through an alley, trying to elude the cops, and a pit bull flew out of nowhere and locked onto Beo's back. He flipped the dog over his shoulder and crushed its skull with a brick, never even breaking stride. In the next block, a stray German shepherd clamped onto Beo's leg. He beat it to death with a board. In the end, the cops found the two dead dogs but could not catch Beo.

Or so it is said.

According to McClain, Beo is now wanted in connection with a murder. In March a kid answering Beo's description rode his BMX bike past an old woman at high speed and snatched her purse, knocking her down in the process. She died later from her injuries.

Beo says he owns four pit bulls at the moment, scattered at three different houses in the neighborhood to protect them from confiscation by the SPCA. They are named Voltron, Hitler, Murder, and Atlas. By his own account, over the past three years, Beo has had, for varying lengths of time, literally hundreds of pits. He has fought them all, many to the death. They are never around for very long. In one recent five-day period, Beo and Zeke had eight different pits in their possession.

Most of the dogs are stolen; sometimes the boys will trade, either dog for dog or dog for dog plus considerations, for instance, a small amount of cocaine or marijuana. Both of the boys earn money selling powder cocaine on a street corner—they both work regular shifts. Like dedicated fight managers, Beo and Zeke put their dogs in training. They fatten them on twenty-five-cent-a-can dog food and leftover beans and rice, run them around the block behind their bicycles, feed them chicken blood to make them game, take them on safaris around the neighborhood hunting for cats and strays, shoot them up with black-market penicillin and vitamin B12 to help heal their wounds, rub them with motor oil to make their fur grow back over scarred areas.

Unlike his big-shot brother, Zeke has no dogs at the moment, though he had one last night—a white bitch he'd stolen to celebrate his return from St. Michael's. He named her Canna, short for Canna Be Stopped. She was a good fighter. But she wasn't as good as Beo's dog, Murder. The fight lasted only five minutes.

After the fight, Beo and Zeke threw Canna's carcass on a trash heap, then went hunting for a new dog. A couple of miles away, in a back yard, they found a black pit. They stole it and named it Blade. They knew the guy who sold Blade to the man in the house, so they passed the word through the streets: If Blade's original owner wanted him back, he could come see Beo and Zeke. He did. A trade was arranged. That's where Beo has been this evening. Now he's back with the goods.

Beo lets go of the choke chain and the tiger-stripe pit makes a bee line for his little brother. Zeke jumps off the washer and kneels on the ground. The dog is all over him in an instant—licking and wagging and strutting.

Zeke swats the dog on its side, pulls its ears, ruffles its fur and makes him growl. He kisses him on the snout. "What his name?" he asks his older brother.

"Shit, I don't know, man." Beo's voice is husky, his dialect a mixture of Puerto Rican Spanglish and Black Ebonics. "He crazy, though. He went after two cats on the way here."

"He *fat*," Zeke says. "He look *good!*"

"I gonna train him up. He gonna be a champ!"

"What his name?" Zee asks again.

Beo bites on a hangnail, studies his brother for a moment. "What? You want him or somethin'?"

Zeke scuffs his toe on the ground. *If you want something, you don't get it.*

"You want him or not?"

"No, man," Zeke says. "*You* keep him."

Beo grabs the dog by the scruff of its neck, lifts him to eye level and growls. Then he looks over at his younger brother. They share a room together. Since they were little, they have always been together, side by side, best friends and worst enemies. The only thing that has ever kept them apart is St. Michael's. "If I give him to you," Beo asks, "you gonna take good care of him?"

No answer.

"You won't let him get skinny?"

No answer. With Beo, it's hard to know the right answer. Usually, it's best to say nothing.

Without warning, Beo throws the dog at Zeke. It knocks him over; the two tumble as one across the wet cobblestones.

Zeke sits up, delighted. The dog licks his face.

"We'll call you Diablito," he tells his new pit, Little Devil.

"We'll make him a champ!" Beo proclaims, and then he kicks Diablito in the hindquarters, sends him sprawling.

And then he laughs, "*Ah ha HA!*", the way he always does when he's around the pits: head back, eyes wide, left hand squeezing his package.

***

According to the *New York Times*, North Philadelphia is "the 'dog fight' capital of the East Coast." But this story could just as easily be set in New York or Miami or Detroit or Los Angeles. Wherever there are men and boys who need something to be proud of and known for, there are people fighting pit bulls.

On the hard streets of the city (and in the mall parking lots of the suburbs), you are what you own: your sneakers, your bling, your pit. Having a pit is not like having any other kind of dog. Pits do more than eat and shit and walk on a leash. They fight. They are perfect for places like Little Puerto Rico—small enough to keep, tough enough to survive.

"The attraction is basic. Kids need an outlet," Officer McClain says. "You go home every day, you live somewhere shitty, your mother and father are fighting, you got your ass kicked last night. You need a pit to impress your peers, to make you feel good about yourself. With your pit on the street, you're somebody. You've got an enforcer at your side."

Pit bull fighting has traditionally been the domain of skilled professionals—a mostly rural cult of outlaw aficionados who fight the dogs in regulation pits according to rules. They train and care for the animals as they would prizefighters. (More recently, the illegal sport has made headlines in stories involving rappers and athletes, most notably former Atlanta Falcons quarterback Michael Vick.) "Pit bulls have become the macho dog of choice in the urban centers of the country," according to Randall Lockwood, the director of higher education for the Humane Society of the United States. More and more pits are being seen on the streets and in the neighborhood of the nation's cities and towns. As their numbers grow, so does the litany of horror tales.

Law-enforcement officials have reported the increasing use of pit bulls as weapons in crimes ranging from street robbery to rape. "And I know of some cases," McClain says, "where police will hesitate to raid drug-selling sites because they are guarded by an army of pit bulls."

"Nowadays," McClain says, "you walk your pit down the street and people clear the way. It's about power. It's a fad. Every era has its fads. This era has pit bulls. This era is pretty twisted."

***

Pit bulls trace their ancestry to the English bulldog, to a sport called bullbaiting. During the early nineteenth century, peasants would gather for an afternoon, tether a bull to a long lead, cover its horns with pitch, and poke it with sticks. Then they would let two or three bulldogs attack it.

With the passage of the English Humane Act of 1835, which outlawed bullbaiting, dog versus dog became a popular sport, especially in the coal-mining areas of Staffordshire. When the bulldog was brought to America, it was bred, successively, with the terrier, the bullmastiff, the Rottweiler, and the Rhodesian ridgeback. The result of all this selective breeding is known, variously, as the American pit bull terrier or as the American Staffordshire terrier. It is a dog that has been genetically engineered for fighting.

Most wild and domestic dogs, according to research by the Humane Society of the United States, fight to drive away rivals for food, mates, status, or territory. First, the dogs will square off and bluff—growling, barking, baring teeth. Fighting is usually a last resort; the engagements are brief. A fight ends when one of the dogs withdraws or surrenders by exposing its neck and belly.

Pit bulls, however, rarely bark or growl. They will attack without provocation. The gamest of them will fight for hours, until complete exhaustion or death. They wrestle with muscular front legs, lock on an opponent with sharp teeth and powerful jaws. They crush bones, puncture flesh, tear it free from the skeleton. If a dog shows his belly to a game pit, the pit will disembowel it.

A 55-pound pit bites with a force of 1,800 pounds per square inch. The average German shepherd or Doberman bites with half of the force. And the pits' jaws have become specialized over the generations, so it can lock on an object with its front incisors and chew with its back molars at the same time.

According to researchers, pits have been genetically equipped with a higher tolerance for pain than most animals. Pit bulls can climb trees or hang from a tire by their teeth for hours. In Holland, a forty-pound pit recently pulled a two-ton trailer 100 meters along a straightaway.

Defenders of the breed speak of a highly misunderstood dog. Like gun enthusiasts, they fault the human element—the pit-bull owners who misuse their dogs. They extol the virtues of the pit bull—innate intelligence, loyalty, and fine character. In an eloquent paean to the pit bull that appeared in *Harper's Magazine*, Vickie Hearne, a writing instructor at Yale University, rhapsodized over "the seriousness of mind of this breed," its purity of heart, its "awareness of all the shifting gestalts of the spiritual and emotional life around" it. The article—entitled, "Lo, Hear the Gentle Pit Bull!"—portrays the pit as a complex, highly refined dog that is capable of acting with "moral clarity," the result of "qualities that have to do with real love, love with teeth."

Only in the latter part of the twentieth century did the pit bull become maligned. In the early 1900s, the pit was portrayed as the canine embodiment of American virtues—a dog of independence, ingenuity, tenacity, cooperation, and good humor. Petey from *The Little Rascals* was a pit bull. A famous 1914 painting by Wallace Robinson depicts an English bulldog, a Russian wolfhound, a German dachshund, and an American pit bull terrier. Each dog wears the military uniform of its country. The American pit bull is at the center of the lineup, the hero of the piece, which is entitled *I'm Neutral but Not Afraid of Any of Them.*

***

Nine in the evening, Beo and Zeke are in the living room of their family's row house. Beo is pounding a screwdriver repetitively into a piece of cardboard. *Bang, bang, bang.* Zeke is smoking a Newport cigarette. Diablito is asleep at his feet.

"Hey, Zeke."

"What?"

"Who ax you?" Beo laughs his maniacal laugh, "*Ah ha HA!*"

"Fuck you!" says Zeke.

"Shut *up.*"

"*You* shut up!"

"I'm gonna bust yo ass," Beo says, and then he smiles, huge and toothy. They both crack up.

"Hey, pussy," Zeke challenges, "who put the soda in their Cheerios with milk?"

"*Ah ha HA!* I only did that so you wouldn't want none."

And so it goes, another night of going nowhere fast. Beo and Zeke don't attend school. They've never been to a movie. They don't know what a magazine is; they've never heard of *Rolling Stone*—or the Rolling Stones, either. When they have money, they go to the "Indian store," the only business in a several block radius, a liquor store and general market owned by a Pakistani. They have never seen an answering machine, have never used a computer. Their television gets only three channels. The only time they've ever been out of this part of the city was when they had to go to court or to jail or to St. Michael's. Most of what they know comes from rap songs, TV, and life on the streets. Neither one of the boys reads very well, but between them they know every hiding place, every abandoned house, every path through every alley in the neighborhood. When they are engaged in illegal activities, they set up lookouts like a team of well-trained guerrillas, covering all lines of approach. If someone says scatter, they're gone like smoke in the wind.

The origins of the Puerto Rican community in Philadelphia go back to 1943, when a number of workers—who had come to the mainland on labor contracts with the Campbell Soup Company in Camden, New Jersey—took up residence in Philadelphia. By the late 1940s, as economic conditions on their home island worsened, many others followed, hoping to find high-paying jobs in the area's factories. By the early 1950s, there were direct air flights from San

Juan to Philadelphia, making it an attractive alternative to New York City, which already had a thriving Puerto Rican community of its own.

Unfortunately, the influx of the Puerto Ricans coincided with the end of the great days of manufacturing in Philadelphia. As was the case in the rest of the industrialized Northwest, factories were shutting down or moving out. During the 1970s, the number of manufacturing jobs in Philadelphia declined by 40 percent. The population of the city declined by 13 percent. The number of Puerto Ricans increased by 76 percent.

During the 1980s and early 1990s, Puerto Ricans had the lowest levels of education and income and the highest rates of teen pregnancy, infant mortality, and criminal arrests in the city. According to a report by Temple University's Institute for Public Policy Studies, there was little hope for relief. "Puerto Ricans have a hard time in Philadelphia.... As serious as [their] needs may be, they are only one group among many poor people living in a city with limited means to help them."

Despite their disadvantages, when you spend time with Beo and Zeke, it doesn't seem they mind being semiliterate and truly needy. They wear name brands like Adidas and Lees. They have fancy BMX bikes. They have regular employment in the shadow economy—their shifts on the corner selling cocaine. And now they have a new pit bull, Diablito. It doesn't seem to matter they have no future. This is life as they know it. It's the only one they have.

The living room is dark and warm. Heating is included in the rent, which is good, considering their last house burned down after one of the little cousins got too close to a space heater and caught her dress on fire. There is a water-stained hole in the ceiling, beneath some bathtub pipes, and you can hear the leak—*drip, drip, drip*—mixing with sounds of laughter and shouting and the heavy bass of rap songs filtering through the shaded front windows. As the evening wears on, the rest of the Garcia brood lands in the living room with Beo and Zeke. Mami and Popi remain upstairs. You hear them occasionally, like Charlie Brown's parents in *Peanuts*, but they rarely make an appearance.

Sister Angelina is sixteen. Her baby is thirteen months old, named Nikki after a character on a daytime soap. Nikki's eyes are bandaged because Angelina accidentally used the lice shampoo instead of the baby shampoo.

Renata is fifteen. She's just come back from the store with a bottle of soda called Malta. She says that if you're pregnant, you can drink a Malta and take two of these pills called Cortal and you won't be pregnant anymore. Her boyfriend is named Angel. Beo and Zeke refer to him as their brother-in-law. He brings presents all the time; he is allowed to sleep in Renata's room. He deals coke for the Blue Tape Gang up the street. In Little Puerto Rico, gangs are identified by the color of the tape used to seal the little glassine envelopes of cocaine—blue, red, black. The gangs control their own corners. White people drive into the neighborhood, catch a runner on a corner to score. The coke is mostly powder, with a few small rocks, a bad burn. Both Beo and Zeke work for Angel. On the corner where they stand, there are a few scraggly trees with white crosses spray-painted on the trunks, places where kids Beo's age and older have been shot to death in the gang wars.

Ten-year-old Maria is busying herself at the coffee table in the living room, using a butcher knife to cut apart an imitation pearl necklace she found somewhere in the neighborhood. Seven-year-old Elena is playing roughly with a little kitten, throwing it up and down like a ball. Elena says the kitten has already used up three of its lives. One time, Popi threw the kitten out of the third-floor window. It didn't land on its feet, it didn't move. But then, after a while, it got itself back up and climbed the front steps into the house. Another time, the baby sat on it. It seemed dead, so Angel soccer-kicked it into a wall. But two hours later it came back to life and walked shakily to its bowl and took a drink of water. Elena can't remember the third time but she knows it happened. The kitten is cross-eyed. It has no name.

Beo watches idly as Elena plays with the kitten. All of a sudden, he snatches the kitten by the scruff of its neck and starts teasing Diablito with it. He bounces the terrified, cross-eyed kitten on the dog's nose, throws it at him, picks it up before the dog can pounce.

The kitten shrieks, Elena shrieks at Beo. Zeke shrieks at Elena. Maria shrieks at Beo. Angelina shrieks at Maria.

Then Renata hollers she's gonna punch somebody out if they don't shut up. She sounds serious. A scuffle ensues, the volume maxed, everyone shrieking and screaming and laughing and scowling and swatting, literally bouncing off the walls...

And then a bellow from above—Popi!

The stairs shake with heavy footsteps. *Boom, boom, BOOM!*

Juan Garcia is the father of the four youngest children, including Beo and Zeke. He came here from Puerto Rico in the late 1950s. He says he works for a Jew, landscaping rich people's houses on the Main Line—when there is work. Popi hates the dogs. Last week he called the SPCA. They came and took away three pits.

By the time his feet hit the living room floor, Beo and Zeke have vanished.

***

"Tell 'em, Zeke, tell about Tough Boy," prompts Beo.

"Tough Boy—he *tough*," Zeke says proudly.

"Tell about that time with the *bike*."

It's nearly midnight. Beo and Zeke and Diablito have fled to their basement hangout down the street. There are seven boys in attendance, ranging in age from thirteen to sixteen: Sam, Emilio, Macho, Louie, and Li'l Man. All of them have pit bulls. The basement is downstairs from where Louie lives. The kids crash here all the time. It's decorated with old mattresses and sofas, posters of professional wrestlers, a boom box Zeke stole out a car the other night. As the hours pass, boys come and go from the basement. Each time there's a knock at the door, everyone freezes. Every boy in the room has done something illegal today—stolen something, received stolen property, bought or sold drugs, fought their stolen pit bulls, gotten into a fight, snatched a purse. As Beo likes to say, "You ain't broke no laws 'til you get caught."

"Check it out," Zeke says, happy to have been given center stage. "I was riding my bike in the alley, and Beo had Tough Boy. And Beo say, 'Sic him!' you know, so Tough Boy runs me down and grabs my back tire, flips me right off the bike. Then he just held the bike straight up in the air, you know, by the rim of the tire."

"*Ah ha HA!*" Beo laughs. "He *strong*. Zeke was teasing me, you know. He was tellin' me how Tough Boy was a mutt and shit. But really he was *jealous* of him."

"I was not jealous of him!"

"Yes, you *was*. You used to talk a lot of shit."

"I hated that motherfucker!" Zeke says. "I *hated* him."

"Only 'cause he kilt that pit of yours. Tell 'em how Tough Boy kilt that pit of yours."

"Terminator?"

"*That* motherfucker."

"Check it out," says Zeke, "I had this pit, right? He a champ. Name Terminator. He eat up one of Beo's dogs, a tiger-stripe named Buzzsaw. After the fight, Beo had to carry his shit home. His ears was hanging off and shit."

"Das right," says Beo, taking up the story himself. "So after that, I went and I traded this boy dog I had—he was all white, name Cocaine. I went to this guy I know and say, gimme a real killer. So I gave him Cocaine—plus I gave him a gram of Blue Tape—Cocaine plus *cocaine!* And that's how I got Tough Boy. I come back with him and tell Zeke that Tough Boy gonna kill *his* dog. And Zeke say, 'No, man. No *way.*'

"We went to the third floor of this old house and they rumbled. Tough Boy and Terminator. Tough Boy shook him all up. He bit him on the neck. Crunched him on the leg. Bit his fuckin' ear off. Terminator be hollering and screaming, bleeding and pissing and shitting, trying to run away. *Ah ha HA!*" Beo laughed. "That lousy ass motherfuckin' mutt almost jumped out the window!"

"He *did* jump out the window!"

"'Cause he a little pussy like you, *motherfucker!*" Beo says.

"I got a champ now," Zeke says. He raises his chin. "Diablito gonna tear your ass up! He gonna tear your shit right up."

"Yeah?"

"Yeah, mothafucka."

"Let's bang 'em!" calls Macho.

"Let's rumble!" says Sam.

"Let's shake 'em up!" yells Louie.

"*Ah ha HA!*" laughs Beo—head back, eyes wide, left hand squeezing his package.

***

The boys walk through the alley in a hard rain, across a vacant lot toward a fenced-in schoolyard. Beo has Diablito, Li'l Man has Voltron, Louie has Death Man, and Macho has Darth Vader. The dogs pull the boys through the alley, wheezing from the pressure of the choke chains around their necks. Zeke tries to take Diablito's leash out of Beo's hand. "Give him *here*," he implores. "He's *my* dog."

"Who give him to you?" Beo sneers.

By the time they reach the schoolyard, the rain has begun to let up. They find a dark spot near a fence. The boys form a ring. In the center, it's Diablito versus Death Man, Beo versus Louie.

The boys stand five feet part, face to face. They keep the dogs between their knees, squeezing to hold them in place, meanwhile riling the dogs, pinching and scratching at the fur behind their ribs, hissing into their ears, "*Sssssssssic, sssssssssic.*" Shortly, the dogs catch on and nature takes its course. They growl and bare teeth, strain forward. The boys let go. The dogs charge.

Bang! They collide. You feel the ground shake.

Death Man gets a deep neck lock.

Diablito cries and disengages. He turns tail and runs.

Beo laughs and squeezes his package, "*Ah ha Ha!*"

Zeke's face falls. He doesn't say a word.

Beo corrals Diablito, sets him up again between his knees, facing Death Man.

Again, a neck lock. Diablito utters a squeal so horrible and wrenching it turns your stomach. He shakes free and retreats again.

"Pussy!" everyone taunts.

Zeke looks like he's about to cry.

Darth Vader is next, a black pit with distended teats, a new litter. She's fast. She locks Diablito just behind the head. There is much growling and squealing. There is blood.

Next is Voltron. He is Beo's dog, midnight black.

"*Ah ha HA!*"

It is over quickly.

Diablito is lying on his side on the fissured concrete of the basketball court. His breathing is shallow. His blood mixes with a puddle of rain water. His brown eyes, fearful and confused, search the faces of the boys and dogs surrounding him.

Beo calls Zeke a pussy.

Louie calls Zeke a pussy.

Macho calls Zeke a pussy.

Li'l Man calls Zeke a pussy.

Zeke kicks Diablito. He calls the dog a pussy.

Then the boys head back to the basement.

***

Late afternoon the next day, Zeke's living room.

It's raining again. It's quiet. There is no one around. Beo is working his usual shift on the corner, selling cocaine. Zeke has taken the cushions off the sofa and placed them on the floor against a heating vent.

"When your dog lose," he says, "you probably get a little mad, 'cause everybody sayin' your dog lost and your dog a pussy and you a pussy. You get a little mad, but you don't get embarrassed. *No way.* 'Cause everybody be laughin', right? But *you* know you're gonna come back with revenge. Big-time revenge. You gonna tear their shit up. You gonna shake up their dog. You gonna kill their shit. And that's when *you* start bragging, too. That's when *you* be havin' a big smile on your face.

"Diablito was a mutt. Motherfucker wouldn't fight. Kept turnin' his back. Shit. He was a pussy. He don't deserve to live noways."

Zeke closes his eyes and takes a hit off a joint. Diablito is certainly dead by now. Someone has probably called the SPCA; they will come and collect the body from the school yard. Zeke had Diablito for less than one day. Like he says: *You can't care too much about shit, 'cause sooner or later, it be gone.*

Spending time with him out in the streets, you almost forget Zeke's age. He seems as street smart and savvy as any grown man, drinking and snorting and smoking, fighting dogs in a schoolyard, selling drugs for money to buy dog food, committing all kinds of crimes, petty and otherwise. But here, in the warm darkness of his family's tenement living room, it is easy to see Zeke as he really is— thirteen years old, seventy-five pounds, curled up in the corner in a stolen 76ers jacket that is way too big for him.

"When I get older," Zeke says, his voice soft and dreamy, "I ain't gonna hustle or nothin'. I'm gonna buy me a car, a little Mazda with one of those racing engines. I'm gonna buy me a house, some furniture. I'm gonna put the house in the city, but far, far away from my family. I don't want those motherfuckers coming to my house.

"I'm gonna have slaves in my house. I'll sleep late, and I'll have lady slaves fanning me, rubbing my back. I'll wake up, they'll wash me up, wash my hair, hook me up. Then I'll be ready for them to carry me to the kitchen so I can eat my breakfast. And I'll be fuckin' all the lady slaves, too. Some badass bitches. All of them Puerto Rican. And some black ones. And some white ones. Different ones all the time.

"I ain't gonna have no company. Nobody can visit. It the king's house. Nobody visits the king. Like, if you come over, they open the door, my slaves do, and they say, 'What you want?' And you'll say, 'This is Mike, King Zeke know me, I'm baldheaded. I brought some drugs to give to Zeke.' And they'll say, 'All right, but you gonna have to wait.'

"If I decide to let you in, I'll tell 'em all right. Then my slave will come back down. He'll open the iron door, *bang.* He'll open the wood door, *bang.* He'll open the screen door. Come right on in. See the king. Me. I'm over here. You kneel."

Zeke giggles, then he closes his eyes. The pot is low quality; it makes your lids heavy. Cradled in the lullaby of the dripping rain, he nods for a while, a beautiful, mocha-skinned boy with long, thick eyelashes.

Outside the window, someone walks past with a boom box. The boy stirs from his nap, stretches, and yawns.

Zeke picks up the beat from the passing song, makes it into his own. He taps on the wall with his knuckles, blows a bass beat through his lips, beatboxing. Then he begins to recite. This is Zeke's Rap.

My name is Zeke
I'm at the mike
I'll tell you 'bout
My whole damn life
I fight the pits
I'm number one
Look at me havin'
So much fun
To the beat y'all
To the beat y'all
To the beat y'all

BIG

Charlie Van Dyke is six-foot-three, 650 pounds, give or take a few dozen. He is required by law to buy two seats on an airplane. He uses long brushes to wash himself, a specially designed portable personal bidet. His wife, Kathie, is five feet, 120 pounds. "She's a committed cellulite surfer," Charlie says with a wink. A fat man in a low-fat world.

At twilight a full moon has just risen over the terminal in El Monte, bringing in the tide of commuters. The buses squeal and hiss and disgorge their loads, and the platforms fill, and the people spill down the concrete steps toward the kiss-and-ride, looking for their connections, the final leg home.

Out on the avenue, a left-turn arrow clicks green. A small white Toyota crosses the intersection, listing ponderously to port as it goes. It enters the terminal parking lot, heads toward the area designated for compact cars. The sky is a darkening azure, unusually clear for the San Gabriel Valley this time of year, the autumnal haze of particulates and fumes having been cleansed temporarily by a rare easterly wind, the storied Santa Ana.

The Toyota plies the rows, seeking a space. It is a Corolla three-door hatchback, eighties vintage, bumper hanging, a hand-me-down from the mother-in-law. With the motor home out of commission, hunkered in the driveway beside the dead Lincoln and the semi-squashed VW Bug, the Van Dykes have been forced to tag-team the Toyota. She's going to be late; he's having dinner with a journalist, following at the moment a little distance behind in his own vehicle. He must park the Toyota somewhere in this vast lot where she can find it.

A speed bump is sighted; the Toyota's brakes squeak, the car comes to a complete stop. Then, ever so slowly, the front tires creep over the little asphalt berm. At bottom, the chassis sags, the springs complain—a deep, mushy bounce that scrapes the belly of the car, setting up a series of jiggling aftershocks.

Back wheels clear, another bounce; the car turns left, then right. Charlie Van Dyke has a particular space in mind. After twelve years of marriage, you designate such things, you come to agreements on routines and conventions. It may be a vast city parking lot, the terminal where thousands of people from this particular patch of Southern California sprawl come each day to ride buses between lives and livelihoods, but that one parking space, over time, has become theirs—the property of their marriage, something known and understood. She will be looking to that spot. She will be frazzled, no doubt, after a long day, a long commute. Commuting. *Sheesh.* Charlie doesn't understand how people do it. He doesn't know how *she* can do it. He feels for her, but at least it's steady income and health insurance for them both. It occurs to him that for untold centuries, the fields have been located too far away from the village. If people really put their minds to it, couldn't they figure out a way to abolish the need for commuting? They could come up with a better way to live and work, something more spiritually and spatially conjoined, and people would be a lot happier, and the world—particularly California—would be a better place, the urge to hate a little less strong in everyone. Such is the nature of Charlie's running inner monologue. He is a thinker, a dreamer, a scholar, a believer, a lover, a high-tech renaissance man, able to figure out and teach himself—and usually improve upon—each new wrinkle of technology that comes available on the market.

Now, however, he must focus on smaller things, something he doesn't always do as well, things in the here and now that need attending to, like finding the Van Dyke parking space, willing it open, thinking perfectly open thoughts.

It's important for Charlie to come through for Kathie. He has always been her rock, her mountain. She relies on him, takes her cues from him, even talks like he does, very slowly, forming each word precisely, explaining everything completely. Her voice-mail message at the office is a three-act play.

They met over drama, in fact, in eleventh grade, when they were both seventeen, the subjects of an English teacher's matchmaking—seating chart manipulation on a field trip to see the movie *Camelot*. It was an inspired pairing of misfits.

Charlie was on the AV squad, the leader of the nerd clique. Some types of people have always looked up to him, have always come to him for guidance and information. Others have always reviled him—scornful or mean or rude for no reason other than his appearance.

Kathie was tiny—five feet tall and ninety pounds. In first grade, she'd contracted rheumatic fever; she didn't return to school until she was twelve. The youngest child of two overprotective school-teachers, she tended to see herself the way her parents saw her, as fragile and impaired, with scar tissue around the heart. When she finally returned to the classroom, the other kids considered her stuck-up and brainy; in reality, she was incredibly withdrawn, completely befuddled by people's reactions to her. What she learned from her experience is this: When you're insecure or different, when you don't participate, people will assume you're stuck up. They will think you are ignoring *them*. They will interpret this as hostility on your part, and anything bad they are thinking about themselves they will project upon you. It's all about insecurity, she says, how it's so pervasive in our society. It took her years to come to this conclusion. Charlie was the one who helped explain.

In Kathie, Charlie found someone of intelligence and sensitivity, someone who understood what he was talking about, who liked puzzles with thousands of pieces, who could read almost as fast as he. She laughed at his humor, which was always on the warped side. She liked the things he liked: sendups and puns; the TV show *Deep Space Nine*; the Dr. Demento songs "Junk Food Junkie" and "Happy Happy Joy Joy." In truth, she was his greatest fan—her giggly, snorting Horshack laugh always at the ready, her eyes sparkling behind her glasses, which are squarish and thick with oversized frames, just like his.

Late though it is, 7:30 or so, the parking lot is active. Wives, husbands, whole families await their loved ones on the asphalt shores of the home front. They sit inside cars, perch on trunks or on hoods, lean down to talk through open windows, to fit a pacifier into a bubbly little mouth. The sounds from car radios of salsa, classic rock, and rap mix with hypnotic Arabic strings and drums, reflecting the vast diversity of the region, all of it merging and swirling beneath the amber mercury vapor lamps.

The Toyota turns left again, down a row of parked cars, then right, down another.

And what do you know: There it is.

The Van Dyke space.

And it is *open*.

Hail the Goddess.

***

The Toyota pulls in and stops.

There is the ratcheting sound of the parking brake. The car goes dark and silent; the engine ticks off heat. After a moment, the driver's side door squeaks open, the tinny cry of a tired hinge.

A sneaker appears, bright white, size 15 quadruple-E—thirteen and three-quarter inches long, six and five-eighths inches wide.

It is followed by a pink expanse of skin reminiscent of a small Christmas ham. Charlie's ankle—hairless, mottled, flaky, eighteen inches around.

The sneaker plants itself on the asphalt, followed soon thereafter by its twin, and then a knee appears, pulling behind it a lumpy, forty-two-inch thigh. The denim material strains at its double stitching—the Classic 5-Pocket Jean, model No. 2115 from a mail-order company called King Size. He wears size 72, the largest in the catalogue.

Charlie pushes down on the door frame with his large right hand, meanwhile knuckling his left thigh for leverage. Emitting a slight groan, followed by a sharp exhalation of air, like a weightlifter, he achieves a standing position and straightens his back.

Around the parking lot, everyone stares.

A skinny kid with freckles, standing by the rear of a mini-van, slaps his fat brother in his jiggly stomach and points. A young Asian guy lets his mouth drop. "Dios mio!" exclaims a gray-haired woman, poking her head out the window of her Chevy for a better view.

Charlie closes the door of the Toyota with a surprisingly gentle click—it is, after all, the last surviving vehicle in the Van Dyke's fleet of vehicles—and aims himself toward my full-size Chevy Caprice, waiting nearby. He's a little nervous. He's never been in this type of car before; he's hoping he fits. At Charlie's suggestion, I had requested to rent a Cadillac, a Sedan deVille. The deVille, besides being plush, easily accommodates his size. Also, the deVille was big enough we could plan an outing with some of his friends, something he never gets to do, drive somewhere in the same car with his other fat friends, a pleasure he wanted to experience. By contrast, a Lincoln Mark IV, while large and comfortable by anyone's standards, does not fit Charlie. It has to do with the cut of the door, the relationship between the seat and the dashboard—we're talking here strictly about passenger seats. Driving either vehicle is out of the question—one reason the Lincoln has been left to rust in his driveway. Oddly, Charlie's Toyota fits him better than the Lincoln. Even so, with the seat set back as far as it will go, the steering wheel still rubs his stomach. In order to reach the wheel, he has to fully extend his arms. He grips the wheel with his fingertips, works in furious tiny strokes to make a turn.

It is the nature of Charlie's life that he must accommodate and jigger, plan ahead; the world just doesn't fit. His Timex Indiglo has the largest band available, ten inches, but it's impossible for him to use the watch's light: The push button is covered by a fold of flesh where the band bites. Even with the watch off, it's a struggle: His fingertip is too large to effectively press the little button.

Charlie is required by law to buy two seats on a plane. When he eats in a restaurant, he needs a chair without arms—a fairly sturdy one. For the record, he has bent a folding chair or two in his lifetime, but he has never broken a chair and fallen to the ground like in all those stupid comedy bits people find to be so amusing. Usually, at a restaurant, he is kept waiting for some time—it is clear they have an attitude about his fatness. Invariably, he is seated in the back of the house with the crying babies. Wherever he is seated, the tables must be far enough apart for him to walk between. Anything but a handicapped toilet stall is out. And though he can't sit in a booth or pass through some types of turnstiles, the chairs in movie theaters are usually no problem. "Fat flows," Charlie explains.

Sometimes, Charlie doesn't fit himself, either. Because of the sheer size of his body, his overall dimensions and proportions, the length of his arms relative to his girth, and so on, he cannot reach certain parts of himself. In the shower, he must use long brushes to wash himself. For the toilet, he has jerry-rigged an assortment of pump spray bottles—a sort of home-made personal bidet. He cannot put on his own socks, so he doesn't bother. An itch between his shoulder blades is impossible to scratch. As for sex—suffice it to say that where there's a will there's a way. It helps, he says, if your wife is five feet tall and is limber from prac-ticing aikido. As they say in fat quarters, Kathie is a committed "cellulite surfer."

Charlie's stride is short, effortful, stiff-jointed, a bit breathless, and—it must be said, with only the utmost respect—penguin-like: his dense forearms pump from the elbows, palms flat and facing backward, propelling him along. People gawk and point and laugh. He doesn't notice. Or so he says.

In medical terms, Charlie is *morbidly obese*, which means that he is more than 100 percent over his ideal weight. Charlie likes to say that if he would just lose enough to be 99 percent over his ideal, doctors would reclassify him as *grossly obese*. "Now that's a worthy objective," he deadpans.

To be considered merely *obese*, he'd have to lose 50 percent of his total body weight.

***

Charlie Van Dyke is a fat man in a low-fat world. Once upon a time, fat meant jolly, godly, prosperous—think Buddha, Venus, a Roman senator, a Medieval friar, Rubens's women. Today, in our health-obsessed culture, fat is a symbol of shame—a sign of weakness and sloth and lack of discipline, an antisocial act.

According to surveys, about 40 percent of women and 25 percent of men are trying to lose weight. An additional one-third of both sexes are struggling to *maintain* their weight. They spend $40 billion a year on everything from fat-free Fig Newtons to surgical stomach stapling. In a poll, fat people who've had their stomachs reduced—a major procedure requiring an incision from sternum to groin—said they'd prefer to have a leg amputated or to go blind than to be fat.

Scientists say two-thirds of people who lose weight regain it within the first year. Ninety-five percent will rebound within five years.

The last time Charlie weighed himself was fifteen years ago, at Weight Watchers. He weighed 550. At six feet three, he had a target weight, he was told, of 190. That was what he weighed in fifth grade, when he was five feet tall.

The first week on his Weight Watchers diet, Charlie lost twenty pounds. The second week, ten. After a year, he was down 104 pounds.

One year later, he'd gained back what he'd lost.

Plus, he'd put on an additional fifty pounds.

Charlie has been overweight his whole life. He was a twelve-pound newborn, a fat kid, a super-fat teenager. Today he wears shirt size 8XL: eighty-four-inch chest, twenty-nine-inch neck, thirty-six inch sleeve, three full feet between the shoulders. Charlie is an expert in the areas of fat and dieting. He has lost hundreds of pounds. And each time he's lost weight—each and every time he's gone on a diet—he's eventually gained back that amount, plus an average of 50 percent more.

Yes, it is true that once in a great while, Charlie will eat four of the smaller Cadbury chocolate eggs at one sitting. His favorite foods include macaroni and cheese, potato soup, buffalo wings with gobs of blue cheese, and all kinds of bread. He will leave his morsel of lobster soaking in the cup of butter for a full minute before eating it. And, yes, he drinks prodigiously—one Big Gulp-sized coffee (ten Equals, five creams) and at least four peach Snapples a day. At meal-time he cleans his plate so utterly, so completely, that when he's finished there is zero evidence of what he's eaten, not a sesame seed or a drop of sauce left behind.

But, no, he doesn't gorge between meals. He doesn't eat a gallon of ice cream at a sitting, though he will order a large yogurt. He eats regular-sized portions. His table manners are good. He does manage to soil his shirts fairly regularly, the distance between the average tabletop and his mouth being what it is—it's a long way to take a spoonful of soup. He does not eat red meat, was an early proponent of "health food." He has an extraordinarily well-developed palate, he says, due to extra nerves in his nose and mouth. Annually he is tapped as a judge for a local micro-beer brewing contest. The owners of the café around the corner from where he lives have enlisted him to help with their new menu. He can eat 3,000 to 4,000 calories a day and not gain an ounce.

Believe it or not, evolutionarily speaking, biologically speaking, fat has a purpose beyond bedeviling us with its presence. If the body can be seen as a complex factory on a twenty-four-hour production schedule, then fat is the energy supply it constantly draws upon to run the machine. People cannot eat twenty-four hours a day, so the body converts raw fuel to fat and then runs off that. Fat. It's our fuel.

Under a microscope, fat—more scientifically known as adipose tissue—looks like a bubble bath. At a slightly higher magnification, it resembles tapioca, closely packed globules held together with a stringy intercellular glue, streaked with narrow filaments of connective tissue, blood vessels, and nerves. Gram for gram, there is almost twice as much nourishment in fat as there is in carbohydrates or protein. In other words, faced with the challenge of how to power the Earth's creatures—needing a biochemical Eveready Energizer to store the most energy in the least amount of space—God or nature (what have you) chose fat as the principal form.

The problem, shared by the millions of Americans who are overweight, is that God or nature did not take into account the possible advent of refrigerators or fast food or even agriculture. Humans were constructed to be hunters and gatherers. We were set up for a life in which our primitive ancestors ate whenever they were lucky enough to find or kill something. When food is introduced, our bodies, by design, store energy to be used at times where there is no food around.

When there's plenty, and we eat a lot, our bodies make more fat cells. And once you make a fat cell, you can never lose it, except by some surgical means. You can starve and shrink the fat cells, but then they start to complain. They send out a chemical warning throughout the body: *Help! Our energy tank is nearing "E."* During times of privation, our bodies are designed to slow down and conserve fat. The heart and other vital muscles and organs will start breaking down before all the fat tissue is consumed.

But then, when there is food again, the body is designed to *replenish* fat cells at an even *higher* rate.

How much does Charlie weigh?

If you need a specific number, picture Konishiki, an American-born sumo wrestler Charlie admires. Konishiki weighs 600 pounds. That's about Charlie's weight, he figures—600, 625, maybe 650, maybe a bit more. The truth is, he doesn't know. He hasn't been on a scale in fifteen years.

During that time, however, Charlie has managed to keep his weight stable. He hasn't lost any but he hasn't gained any either. For example, for nine years, he's been wearing the same custom-made pinstripe suit for special occasions. It still fits perfectly. How many 44-year-old men can say the same?

His secret?

He gave up dieting.

***

In a three-room office-warehouse, in a nondescript industrial park fifteen minutes from his house, Charlie and his friend Elaine are hard at work.

Elaine is five feet ten, 250 pounds. She is stuffing colorful pieces of tiny technology into green plastic circuit boards, the kind found inside a computer. She works from a prototype, which is clamped into an upright model of a futuristic downtown, a functional little work of art Charlie designed, part of a revolutionary new computerized locking system for tractor trailers, to keep merchandise safe from theft while in transport. They are on deadline with an order, working furiously, even though the company still owes Charlie money for the last batch. The sooner he gets these boards done, the sooner he'll get paid ... he hopes.

Charlie sits at a custom-made drafting table, soldering the circuit boards Elaine finishes. He straddles a pneumatic task chair, his legs comfortably akimbo, his stomach dipped down between, as if he has a medicine ball adjoining his thighs. His zipper is twenty-one and a half inches long. Though he has lost his lap to his stomach, he has gained kind of permanent desk. He'll sort mail atop his stomach, rest things there a moment—an arm, a book, the remote control for his boom box. Charlie searched high and low for a box with a remote—one less reason to move around. He tires easily. His back is bad. Though he can bend and pick up something from the floor, he prefers using a pair of grabbers. He has two different kinds, one for paper, one for cans.

In anthropological terms, Charlie's body has a barrel-chested pouter-pigeon shape. His forearms and legs are solid as rocks. When you think about it, Charlie probably lifts more weight daily than Mr. Universe. Each time he rises from his chair, he is squatting 650-odd pounds. Scratching his head is like lifting a fifty-pound barbell. It is mainly his midsection that is so obviously constructed of fatty tissue. It sloshes and jiggles with every pothole in a road. Charlie's stomach is a cousin of the common beer belly, known as a Falstaffian paunch. Men tend to collect their weight in the front—truncal fat. Women collect it in back and on the sides and down below. More often than you would think, a kid will walk up to Charlie, poke him in his belly, and say "You're fat!" Usually, Charlie will ignore him. Once—fed up, having a bad day—Charlie turned to the kid and replied, "Yeah? Well, you're ugly!"

People often tell Charlie he has a handsome face buried beneath all that fat. "Thanks for the compliment," he muses. Strangers lean over and look into his shopping cart. Or they come up to him in the street and try to sell him diet products. "The problem you have—" they will begin, and Charlie will cut them off. "Excuse me," he will say. "The problem I have is *you*." Sometimes, when he is home with Kathie and feeling dramatic, he will mime one of his favorite scenes from the movie *Elephant Man*. He contorts his face, exhorts the heavens, cries out in pain (in an English accent), "I am not an animal. I am a human being!"

Behind Charlie's glasses, above his rosy Santa Claus cheeks, are sparkling brown eyes Kathie thinks are very sexy. He has a cute little pug nose, always stuffy, making him tend to breathe audibly through his mouth, past teeth that are slightly bucked. You can imagine him as a little kid with luminous skin and freckles, the son of LaVerne and Shirley Van Dyke of Moline, Illinois.

LaVerne Van Dyke was known as Chub. He ran a gas station. He carted around enough spare parts in the back of the family station wagon to build another car. Chub's expertise as a mechanic may have something to do with Charlie's aversion to fixing cars, the reason there is a fleet of dead vehicles marooned in his driveway. Chub lives in California now too, not far from Kathie and Charlie. Recently, he's been having episodes of sleep apnea. Charlie visits when he can. Chub is very busy in his retirement. Two or three nights a week, he and his second wife go to church. Two other nights, they go to Overeaters Anonymous. Chub is the only man in the group. The stories the women tell? "Better than a soap opera," he says. "X-rated sometimes, too." They have a chant at OA: Three/Zero/One! It stands for three meals a day, zero snacks in between, one day at a time. At his last weigh-in, LaVerne was 324. In his prime, he was well over 400.

Shirley Van Dyke was raised in an orphanage. She went about 250. It is Charlie's burden to know that because of his large pre-natal size, he smashed his mother's kidneys during gestation—or so goes the family lore. He remembers her having a tantrum one time when he was young, stomping around, telling him it was all his fault. It is a painful memory. Charlie tries to remind himself he didn't ask to be born, that he wasn't fat on purpose. She died a few years ago, at 54.

Charlie's salt-and-pepper beard covers his face, neck, and jaw, tangles down to the second button on his shirt, giving him the look of a prophet or holy man. From shoulder to shoulder, the material of his shirt rises and then falls, following the contours of his back, the characteristic fatty pad behind and just below his neck. In the past, there wasn't much choice about what clothes he wore. He'd find a store that carried his size and take whatever fit. Now he orders everything online from King Size, a big-and-tall-men's catalogue targeted at America's 18.7 million obese men. Not only does King Size offer more variety; it also saves him from having to go out in public to shop. In most big-and-tall-men's stores, the largest size is 60. Charlie is a 72. Even the salespeople gawk.

As a freelance electronic engineer, Charlie specializes in microcontroller design. At the moment, he and Elaine are working on a PC board that runs a computerized, magnetic truck-door lock, invented by a partner and himself. With any luck, it will be patented and will revolutionize the truck-lock business. With any luck, Charlie will realize some of the profit—he's invented a few things before and has been screwed—and he will finally be able to upgrade his life a little bit: to buy a nice new vehicle, to stop screening his phone calls for bill collectors, to repair the earthquake-and-fire damage still evident inside his house. Katie has declared their personal disaster area off limits to even the most intimate public. Since the fire, they've been holed up in the living room. There's a couch, a TV, a king-size waterbed, all their clothes in boxes, the six cats. The dachshund, who started the fire by tearing up some paper over the furnace grate, has been living in the backyard ever since.

A CD of Indian music, Gandharva-Veda, is playing while Charlie and Elaine work. (He'd brought the Jefferson Airplane CD, but somehow this disk was in the jewel case instead.) The three rooms of his office—at the back there is an industrial garage door—are chockablock with stuff. If you can say anything about Charlie, it's that his life is very cluttered. Nothing is put away. It must be the energy level thing. He can't really walk very far without resting. There are files, a microwave, a coffeemaker, a refrigerator, boxes of stuff from the house fire. The front door is locked; the windows are shaded with mini blinds. There is a meditative quality of busy stillness in the conditioned air, the two working together wordlessly to the sounds of sitar and tabla drum.

After a while, Charlie puts up his soldering iron. "Sometimes," he says, apropos of nothing, "I feel like a black person walking into a bar in southern Georgia."

"Oh, yeah," says Elaine, picking right up on his meaning. She is bending a resistor to stuff into a board. "You can't tell a black joke or a Polish joke, but you can sure tell a *fat* joke."

"And every other commercial on TV has a fat guy as a punch line."

"Remember that real nice karaoke bar we went to?" Elaine asks. "Me and Dale and Rachel and Jeff? We walked in and everyone turned around and stared. I couldn't believe it. I just turned around and *left*. People actually came outside to watch us get into our cars."

"You just gotta get used to it," Charlie says. "The Lifestyle Police. It gets to a point, sometimes, that you just want to hide. But most of the time I don't pay attention. What it basically comes down to is: they're the ones with the problem, not me. *They're* the ones who have a problem with me being who I am."

"It's good you can get to that," Elaine says.

"It's a long process," Charlie says.

A lifelong process for a kid who was born fat. When he was in the nursery at the hospital, someone asked what a three-month-old was doing with the newborns.

Growing up, the only child of fat parents (who themselves had fat parents), Charlie was tormented by his father. "You wanna grow tits like a woman?" This from a guy nicknamed Chub. Charlie's mother always had him on a diet. Shirley Van Dyke spent much of her life wondering about her origins, trying to find her two sisters, from whom she'd been separated at an early age. She was a very dark and negative person, who tried to lose her problems in baking. She was always making pecan pralines, divinity fudge, and peanut-butter cookies, dozens at a time, never only one variety.

Throughout his youth, it was made clear to Charlie that the world didn't fit him very well. He remembers the time he was riding along on his bike and decided to jump down a curb. He'd seen other kids do it a million times. When he came down in the street, the bike just fell apart—the handlebars came off, the front tire gave way.

For a few feet, it felt like he was riding a unicycle. Then he crashed to earth.

As you would imagine, he was a reclusive kid, a homebody. He read a lot and built models; the events of his childhood kind of blur together. He does remember a lot of social problems at school: being a target, kids throwing rocks at him. When he was five or six years old, a couple of teenagers chased him down and started beating him. He remembers the pummeling of fists, trying to fight back, crying, snot rolling down his face. A ring of adults and kids gathered around to watch—Why did nobody intercede? Another time, someone threw a brick at his head. He required stitches.

Over the years, using his superior mind to do research, Charlie figured out how to take advantage of his bulk and strength. If he could get hold of his adversary, he replied, he could just sit on him and start pummeling. After a few fights, kids started leaving him alone. But now he had a new problem—the teachers thought he had behavior issues. In eighth grade, the gym teacher really hated him. He made Charlie run extra laps up a huge hill. He got a kick out of putting Charlie on the "skins" team so he'd have to take off his shirt. As you would expect, the locker room was fraught. Even if you have a normal-sized penis, it's going to look small compared to your large stomach. Unlike other extremities, the penis does not gain weight.

When the Van Dykes moved to California—his mother having located her eldest sister at last—things began to change. Eligible in the more permissive state to opt out of phys. ed., Charlie joined the AV squad and discovered electronics. He found a niche among the nerds and misfits, a tiny little girlfriend named Kathie. It was weird, maybe attributable to the era of free love, but girls were always coming on to Charlie. "Some women just love the fat guys," he explains, though he hesitates to use the word *fetish*. Once, he was in the nurse's office and a girl on a cot across the room exposed a breast to him. Another girl, a hall monitor, would lift her skirt and show her panties as he went by, late to class. Another girl snuck him into the AV room and made a pass. It may have been some form of prank, but hell, Charlie didn't mind.

As a teenager, Charlie always had a job. He flipped burgers at Jack in the Box, scooped ice cream, delivered papers, made snow cones at the county fair. After a few years of community college, pursuing a major in electrical engineering, Charlie went to work as an electrical draftsman. For the past two decades, he has bounced from job to job, gaining experience as he went, moving up the ladder, becoming a supervisor, an engineer without a sheepskin. Sometimes, during dry spells, he has had to take other work. He's been a census-taker, a carpenter, a door-to-door vacuum-cleaner salesman—an interesting range of jobs for a guy with an IQ of around 140.

Though Charlie is an excellent employee, a monumental anxiety has always accompanied what he calls "the interview thing." He knows he's going in on the defensive, having to convince the prospective employers that "Hey, folks, I'm just an ordinary guy like the rest of you." But to some people, he says, "I'm a freak, something that shouldn't exist, an aberration of nature. It's like I'm their worst nightmare—that they'll wake up someday and be me." One prospective employer turned him down because the company's drafting tables were lined up too close together—he wouldn't have fit, they said. Another company that gave health-club memberships to employees told him he wouldn't mesh well with the other workers. A firm that did hire him instructed him not to sit on the new sofa in the waiting room. A petroleum company said he'd have to shave his beard. When he agreed to do that, they remembered that all employees were required to have a Nomex fireproof suit, in case of a disaster. As it turned out, they didn't have a fireproof suit large enough to fit him.

Charlie's reaction to all of this has been to go freelance. He is happy to be in his own space, eligible for the customary self-employment deductions—of course, he does his taxes himself—away from dress codes, gawkers, fat jokes, and health food pushers. Like he always says, "Don't let the assholes get you down; you gotta find your own solutions." Bobbing his head to the tabla drum, he picks up his soldering iron again and goes back to work.

"I'll tell you one thing," he says, holding the soldering iron poised above the circuit board, both of which look Lilliputian in his hands.

"Being fat teaches empathy. Blacks have had this same problem. Same as the Jews, the Arabs, the handicapped, people who have disfigurements or burns. If you think about it, almost everybody's a cripple. They just manifest it in different ways."

***

Late afternoon, a living room in Whittier, California. Charlie sits on a chair wearing a sweat suit. His eyes are closed, his hands rest upon his thighs, palms up; he looks like Santa Claus playing Buddha. Sitar music wends through the air. At his feet sit three very fat people and his very tiny wife—some of the members of their informal club, The Every Other Sunday Yoga and Potluck Supper Bunch.

To his friends, most of whom he met through the National Association to Advance Fat Acceptance (NAAFA), Charlie is known variously as the Guru, the Dean of Fat Men, and the Answer Man. This is one group that admires and respects him, looks to him as a role model, seeks his guidance and advice. He is, after all, a sagacious man, a man of many interests. He plows through a book on a different topic almost every night. Ask him anything; he knows some tidbit of information. He's like a human search engine.

This afternoon, Charlie is demonstrating a new discipline he's been toying with, something he's calling "Chair Yoga." It is designed, naturally, for people like himself, who have no facility to pretzel. Charlie believes, as the Buddhists believe, that it is important to recognize the way things really are. Having done that, you are able to work better within with your constraints, to flow around obstacles instead of trying to break them down. It's all about working *with* yourself instead of fighting *against* yourself—a kinder, gentler, more understanding form of self-control.

The living room belongs to Dale, a corporate headhunter who weighs nearly 400 pounds. Dale is dating Elaine, Charlie's circuit board stuffer. They've been together for six months. The third in attendance is Rachel. Her occupation, practiced on a contract basis, is executive relocation. Once people get their transfers, she helps arrange all the details of the move. Her boyfriend lives in San

Francisco. They switch off driving the eight hours. It's better than flying. ("Flying? On an airplane? In those little seats? Don't even start!") Her age, she says, is twenty-nine. Her weight, she says, is 129. Then she laughs—table-shaking, water-glass-sloshing, a little too jolly. You'd probably classify her as supersized.

Rachel's mom was tall, thin, and blonde—a princess in the Rose Bowl Parade in Pasadena. Her dad was an interior lineman with a football scholarship to Georgia Tech. They had three children. The two sons looked exactly like the mom—long and willowy and graceful. Rachel was built like her dad.

She started her first diet at age five. For lunch, her mom would give her a tomato and a pear. Or a lettuce-and-tomato sandwich, no bread. Her brothers would get PBJ and potato chips and a Ding Dong for dessert. She was allowed no sweets. Her mom kept the Ding Dongs and the other junk food for the rest of the family in a locked box on the kitchen counter. Rachel learned to pick the lock with a bobby pin. Mom bought a combination lock. Rachel figured out that if you listened very hard and moved the tumblers very slowly, you could crack the combination.

At age seven, Rachel was put on the Mayo Clinic diet. The first day, she remembers, she was allowed a hard-boiled egg and a grapefruit. Since then she's been on hundreds of different diets: the banana-and-skim-milk diet; the protein-powder-and-water diet; Dr. Ding's Diet—900 calories and lots of pills including amphetamines. During Dr. Ding's Diet, Rachel's room was the cleanest it had ever been. Sometimes, she stayed up all night cleaning. It wasn't until she started hallucinating that they took her off the meds. Next came Dr. Ding's Revised Diet. Five hundred calories a day, more pills, and a weekly injection of urine from a pregnant woman.

Weight Watchers, Pritikin, Jenny Craig, NutriSystem, Slim-Fast (aka Shit-Fast)—she's tried them all. She has lost literally hundreds of pounds. During all those diets, even as she was shedding pound after pound, year after year, all she could think about was food. All she could think about was everything she was going to eat when she reached her target weight. She dreamt of food. She'd cut pictures of food out of magazines and put them in a folder along with the recipes she was going to make. Cream sauces, cream soups, creamed *everything*. The day she'd hit her target weight, she'd go immediately to 7-Eleven and celebrate with a box of Ding Dongs. And so the cycle would begin again. Lose fifty. Gain seventy-five.

The book that changed her life was called *Compulsive Eater No More*. There was a story in it about a young fat girl who loved M&M's. Nothing could stop her from sneaking them. Finally, her parents took her to a new doctor. He told the mother to give the girl an entire pillowcase full of M&M's to carry around with her—to let her eat as many M&M's as she wanted.

The first month, the girl gained eleven pounds.

The second month, she gained two pounds.

The third month, she started losing weight.

And so it was that Rachel, a grown woman with a teenage son, got herself a pillowcase and loaded it up with Ding Dongs. She carried the Ding Dongs around for three months—in her car, to the office, even to the gym, and what she discovered at last was: all the Ding Dongs in the world weren't going to fill the emptiness she felt inside. She wasn't really hungry for Ding Dongs. "I had to realize: I hated myself."

What she needed, she says, was "Permission. Permission to eat all the Ding Dongs I wanted. Permission to weigh how much I weighed. Permission to be what I am: fat. When things are prohibited, you want them even more. It turns into a sickness. If you can just sample something, if it is normalized, you can control things better. Take a sample. Try some. Maybe you have too much in the beginning, but then you get over it. The mystery dissolves. You're able to better self-regulate."

This is precisely the kind of lesson Charlie has learned in his intellectual searching. He has been meditating for twenty years, practicing yoga for about ten. He is a "citizen Siddha," he says, a teacher without portfolio. He's read Baba Ram Dass, Deepak Chopra, Carlos Castaneda, the Hindu Vedas, the Buddhists' texts, much more. Without his spiritual interests, he believes, he would probably be a very angry man. As it is, he seems enlightened, one of those rare people who appear to be at home in their own skin. Sitting there on his chair at the front of the room, Charlie's voice assumes a calm, hypnotic quality.

"The postures I will be teaching are called *asanas*," he tells the assembled. "If you can't do a posture all the way, that's okay. Just picture it in your mind. If you only move an inch, that posture has been completed for you. As Professor Mohan said, 'We must always choose the hat to fit the head; we must not choose the hat and make the head fit it.'"

Wear the hat that fits.

Simple enough.

But what to do when the hat that fits is bigger than the biggest one available at any store in the mall?

***

Scientific evidence now seems to indicate some people are simply born to be fat. And if you are born to be fat, the world being the way it is, there is probably going to be a lot of attendant dysfunction, and you are probably going to end up being *really* fat. If such is the case, Charlie and Rachel and the rest agree, you must accept one thing: There is nothing much you can do about it. You are always going to be fat.

Some years ago, scientists at Rockefeller University, in New York, pinpointed and cloned a gene that appeared to be involved in a signaling system that regulates body weight. The gene, called "ob," tells fat cells to secrete a protein to signal the body has stored up enough fat to run the factory. The brain and other organs respond to the signal by altering the body's metabolism, telling it to stop storing fat. Some people are programmed to store more fat than others.

Given these findings—and studies of identical twins, which show weight as a function of genetics at least 90 percent of the time—science seems to be telling us now that fat is more the result of nature than nurture. Yes, our society exhibits a lot of pathology associated with eating, but that's another subject.

The fact is, it is not Charlie's fault he's fat. He was born that way to Chub and Shirley.

More recently, medical researchers also confirmed something that Charlie has believed all along: *dieting may actually cause obesity.* Some other interesting findings:

*Nondieters who overeat occasionally tend to gain very little weight.

*People regain pounds very easily after a weight loss, and the regained weight is mostly fat.

*Obese people gain weight much more easily than nonobese people.

*Health risks and mortality rates currently associated with obesity may actually be the result of yo-yo dieting—the stress on the body of gaining and losing so much weight.

*There is evidence that each person has an individual set weight. One oft-cited expert suggests the best weight for most people is simply the lowest one they've been able to maintain for a year as an adult without struggling.

Just a few things to think about.

***

Charlie Van Dyke was leery about doing this story, about opening his life and offering himself up "like a suckling pig on a platter with a big apple in my mouth." But with the risk of humiliation comes a chance to speak his mind. This is what he wants you to know:

"I was born fat," he says. "I've *always* been fat. I don't even know what it's *like* to be thin. It's like being born blind—you have no idea what sight is. It's like being black. You can't do anything about it.

"After a while, it becomes a quality-of-life question. Do I want to spend my life dieting and struggling and yo-yoing up and down? Do I want to end up gaining even *more* weight than I just lost? I've known people who've had their jaws wired, who've had their stomachs stapled. I know people who've had part of their intestines removed. They end up not being able to absorb certain minerals. They're on supplements for the rest of their lives. Not to mention the tremendous problems with gas. There's a sizable mortality rate on the various surgeries. Why don't they just line us up and shoot us?

"Nobody chooses to be fat; nobody really wants to be outside of society. If there was a way that I could safely be the proper size for my body, a little smaller, probably right around 250 or 300, something like that, I'd be tickled pink. But hey, you know what? They haven't found a way. They have *not* found a way. And I haven't found a way, either. I have to live my life now, as I am. I have to make the best of it. I have to wear the hat that fits."

In his case, size XXXXXL.

THE SMARTEST MAN IN AMERICA

By some account, Christopher Michael Langan is the smartest man in America, with an IQ of 195. He is certainly the smartest nightclub bouncer in America. As he likes to say, quoting Kermit the Frog, "It ain't easy being green." Welcome to the HiQ Nation, where smartest, it turns out, isn't necessarily best.

By some accounts, Christopher Michael Langan is the smartest man in America.

He is certainly the smartest nightclub bouncer in America, endowed with an IQ that has been measured at 195, a score that puts him on par with the likes of Leonardo da Vinci, Ludwig Wittgenstein, and René Descartes, three of the brightest minds in human history. Chris is six feet tall and weighs 275 pounds, a great Minotaur of a man with a basso profundo voice. A former cowboy, construction worker, and Park Service firefighter, he has a fifty-two-inch chest, twenty-two-inch biceps, a cranial circumference of twenty-five and a half inches—a colossal head, more than three standard deviations above the norm. Known in his younger days to play a mean lead guitar, he has light blue eyes, a dry-look Elvis pompadour, and a large chip on his shoulder, something you come to understand once you hear his story.

"It ain't easy being green," he says in typical fatuous style, quoting Kermit the Frog, resigned yet undiscouraged—the cocky, perverse, somewhat defensive assuredness of a person who has always been the smartest in any group, perhaps the loneliest, too. The distribution of

IQs through the population forms a bell curve, with the very smartest on one side, the severely disabled on the other. The IQ of the average human is about 100. The IQ of the average college graduate is about 120. IQs like Chris's exist among us at a rate of roughly one in one hundred million. In a world designed for average, folks like Chris don't always fit very well. Forty-two years old, he pulls down $6,000 a year. He lives in Eastport, Long Island, a short drive from the tony Hamptons..He shares his cluttered one-room cabin with his cat, Ramona, and his 1985 shovelhead Harley-Davidson, parked at the moment near the sink in the kitchen.

Thanks to the magic of the World Wide Web, over the past fifteen years, more than a dozen affinity groups for people with superhigh IQs have been formed. More exclusive than Mensa—which accepts those with a minimum IQ of 132, one of every fifty people—clubs like the Triple 9 Society, the Prometheus Society, and the Mega Society (with IQ requirements of 148, 164, and 176, respectively) provide electronic fellowship to an eccentric, far-flung population known as HiQ Society. Though the clubs, like all subcultures, have become petri dishes for ego squabbles and political infighting, they nevertheless supply the comfort of fraternity in a world that doesn't think fast enough, doesn't get the reference, doesn't grasp the point.

Chris's mom was a spirited young woman, the black-sheep daughter of a wealthy shipping executive. She frequented San Francisco's City Lights Bookstore, rubbed shoulders with the Beats. Chris's dad, the story goes, died of a heart attack before Chris was born. To this day, he's not sure if his mother was telling him the truth. She's dead now, so that information has gone to the grave. A kernel of truth: There is stuff even the smartest man in America can't know.

Chris began talking at six months of age, reading at three years. He skipped kindergarten through second grade, starting his schooling in third. Though his IQ was never tested when he was a child, he says, "it was simply recognized that I was some kind of kid genius. My schoolmates saw me as the teacher's pet, this little freak." When he was still an infant, his mother married a struggling Hollywood actor. They had two sons and then divorced. When he was five, she married "a mean, hard-drinking tyrant," Chris says. "He figured the best way to raise three boys would be to set up his own military platoon. Living with him was like ten years of boot camp, only at boot camp you don't get the shit beaten out of you every day with a garrison belt, and in boot camp you're not living in abject poverty."

At 6:00 each morning, his stepfather would sound reveille on an authentic bugle. His three little soldiers lined up at attention, heels touching, feet cocked at forty-five degrees, thumbs along trouser seams. He'd stand before each of the boys and feign a punch, usually a right jab he'd stop an inch or two shy of their noses. If one of the kids flinched, he would sock him for real. Chris's body was always covered with welts. The fresh ones were pink and red, the older ones black and blue, the oldest green and yellow. "I looked like a Jackson Pollock painting," Chris remembers.

By the time he was twelve, Chris got into lifting weights. "When you're the littlest and the smartest, and you're wearing rags, and you come to school with a fat lip and all these marks on you, you're treated like scum by the rest of the kids. I just decided enough was enough. I developed my strength, worked on my hand speed. I learned how to beat up kids who were twice my size. I got a reputation for being a tough guy. By that time, I was mostly doing independent study—they didn't know what to teach me anymore, but nobody was going to take me out and put me in college on the fast track, so I just did what they told me. I went to study hall and worked on my own, taught myself advanced math, physics, philosophy, Latin and Greek, all that. Meanwhile, all the parents were taking their kids out of study hall because they didn't want them anywhere near me. They thought I was going to beat them up."

One morning when he was fourteen, Chris awoke to a flash of white light, followed by intense pain across his eyes. Just home from an all-night drunk, his stepfather had wrapped his garrison belt around his fist and punched Chris while he slept. Since he was four years old, Chris had never once talked back. It was always, *No, sir, Yes, sir*; for all the abuse he'd taken, he'd never even said *boo*. Now something snapped. Chris went mental. He jumped out of bed half blinded and flew at his stepfather, knocked him across the room, against the wall, out the door. In the front yard, for all to see, Chris issued a merciless beating to the man who had beaten him so many times. Then he told him to leave and never return. He didn't.

Chris got into college on a scholarship. He lost the scholarship when his mother forgot to sign the financial forms. He took a year off, earned money fighting forest fires, enrolled at another college. Then his car broke down. It was the middle of winter. He had no money to fix it. He had to walk fifteen rural miles in the snow every day or face expulsion. School officials were unwilling to give him a break. "There I was, paying my own money, taking classes from people who were obviously my intellectual inferiors," he says. "I just figured, 'Hey, I need this like a moose needs a hat rack!' I could literally teach these people more than they could teach me, and, on top of that, they had no understanding, they didn't want to help me out in the least. To this day, I have no respect for academics. I call them *acadummies*. That was the end of my formal education."

Over the years, Chris developed what he says is known in social-psychology textbooks as a double-life strategy. "On one side, you're a regular guy. You go to work, you do your job, you exchange pleasantries. On the other side, you come home and you begin doing equations in your head. You kind of retreat into your own world. You make it work for you the best you can."

When Chris isn't busy working as a bartender, or training summer luminaries like the writer Tom Wolfe at the local health club, or wrestling with drunken rich people at the door of the nightclub, or chatting up the young ladies (his big weakness, he admits), he is often found hunched over his homebuilt computer, drinking tepid tea from a spaghetti-sauce jar, working on something he calls the CTMU, his Cognition Theoretic Model of the Universe. The result of ten years of solitary labor, the CTMU—pronounced *cat-mew* for short—is a true Theory of Everything, Chris says, a cross between John Archibald Wheeler's Participatory Universe and Stephen Hawking's Imaginary Time theory of cosmology.

Simply put, the CTMU explains the meaning and substance of reality. It resolves—once and for all time, he says—"many of the most intractable paradoxes known to physical science while bestowing on human consciousness a level of meaning that was previously approached only by religion and mysticism." The culmination of "the modern logics-linguistic philosophical tradition," the CTMU "reunites the estranged couple consisting of rationalistic philosophy and empirical science." Though Chris has invited criticism of his theories from all quarters, he has yet to hear anything approaching a valid argument against any of his conclusions or computations. Neither has he found a publisher.

"Sometimes I wonder what it would have been like to be ordinary," Chris says. "Not that I'd trade. I just wonder sometimes."

***

Steve Schuessler has an IQ of 185, which ranks him higher than Charles Darwin and Bobby Fischer, around one in 10 million.

A contract researcher for a nonprofit environmental think tank, Steve studied mime for several years with a disciple of Marcel Marceau. On his Web page, Steve notes he's a Baha'i vegetarian windsurfer. His voice is thin and reedy, the words carefully enunciated. He has the sort of flighty aspect of the joyously effeminate, a tendency to flutter and float his hands to and fro, to cock his head coyly, to giggle and mug. In practice, he says, he is steadfastly heterosexual, with a penchant for supple young students of dance and yoga, two of his long-standing enthusiasms. It's been more than two years since his last sexual encounter. He hopes to break luck soon.

A recovering agoraphobic who once made a local name for himself playing blindfolded chess, Steve enjoys setting odd goals for himself; one time he set for himself the goal of going to a party and seeing whether he could be the last one there at the end of the night, dancing the craziest. In his spare time, he runs websites for two of the HiQ societies. He is looking forward to an upcoming appointment with a psychologist who wants to do a PET scan of his brain. Steve is anxious to find out if he has larger-than-normal inferior parietal lobes, as Einstein did. Either way, he plans to post the results on his website as soon as possible.

Though Steve responded quickly to a request for an interview, he refuses to divulge his age, explaining he is rabidly opposed to ageism. When he was six, he explains further, tests found he had the intellectual development of a twelve-year-old and the emotional development of a four-year-old. "People's expectations about one's development are pinned to age rather than to capacity," he says. "This is something I really feel bad about—people's expectations for life's little guideposts and progressions. It seems to me that HiQ people either get a doctorate at nineteen and then burn out at a young age—they become hermits and collect subway tokens or whatever—or they'll wait and investigate many, many different ideas and paths and maybe get an advanced degree at the age of fifty or sixty.

"There is a little lizard called axolotl. It's one of my favorite Scrabble words. It's a strange little creature that looks like an immature salamander throughout its entire life. But if you treat it with drugs a certain way, it will turn into what appears to be an adult salamander. There are those who view a certain lack of emotional development as being childlike. Notice I didn't use the word *childish*. I said *childlike*. There is a certain curiosity, a certain believing in the moment, that a lot of people lose by the time they're seven or nine years old. I feel like I probably never lost that. I still have a childlike sense of wonder and curiosity."

Other out-of-bounds topics include the names of Steve's parents, his place of birth, the universities he's attended and quit. When questioned directly, Steve refuses to share any specific details about his life, past or present, preferring to respond with streams of intersecting factoids and well-informed opinions, giving the impression he is not so much a complex human personality as he is a walking amalgam of disparate bits of information. He prefers to explain his life experience by way of elliptical anecdotes from his three favorite movies about young geniuses: *Little Man Tate*, *Searching for Bobby Fischer*, and *Good Will Hunting*. The scene in which the young genius is lonely and alone in a crowd. The scene in which the pre-med girlfriend becomes upset because her genius janitor boyfriend understands organic chemistry better than she does. Ask Steve a question he doesn't like, and he freezes for painfully long minutes, squinting his gray eyes intensely, staring into the unfocused middle distance, the muscles in his jaw clenching and relaxing. One detail he volunteers without prompting: He colors his wispy, elbow-length hair with Clairol's "Lightest Auburn." He carries a ponytail scrunchie in the right front pocket of his pants, a comb and a round brush in the right rear.

Steve lives illegally in med-student housing near the University of Houston—a two-bedroom apartment. There are boxes and random pieces of furniture and computer parts all over the living room and dining room. Steve's bedroom is a dim study in timeless utilitarian order—the blinds drawn, the space dominated by a futon, some overweighted bookshelves, and a pair of networked computers that carry 26 gigabytes of memory—he calls it his TAN, his Tiny Area Network. Because he does not own a car, he relies on friends to get around the sprawling city. His most steady ride is named Bill, whom he met while working at Kinko's.

Steve has studied subjects as diverse as quantum physics, classical philosophy, Latin, Greek, electrical engineering, communications theory, and the history of exploration. Even so, he has never earned a college degree. This makes him feel somewhat inadequate and defensive. "The blessing part of high intelligence is that it seems that you're equipped with a telescope and a microscope, and other people have binoculars and a magnifying glass. The curse part is probably when you have a feeling that there is so much that you could be doing but haven't lived up to the possibilities.

"It's easy, when you're interested in lots of things, to get sidetracked. You start studying one thing, and that leads to the next thing, which is also interesting. Before you know it, months have gone by and you're very far afield. I enjoy the sharp upward learning curve associated with new knowledge, but, frankly, I often become bored with the tedious plateau associated with expertise."

Unfortunately, Steve says, expertise is far more marketable. "You want to find work where you can utilize your talents," he says, "but how do you put on a resume that you're probably going to see things more clearly, have better ideas for strategies, have a better overall view than anybody else in the entire company? And do people really want somebody like that? Highly intelligent people are not seen as team players. They're seen as loners with their own ideas, as people who are difficult to deal with. Some people get more despondent and isolated as they age, and it's very, very difficult. Others take that as a challenge—how to interact with other people, how to talk with other people. I kind of took that route. I took a lot of drama courses, read a lot of things. If you become actively hostile against the environment around you, that's like a certain kind of hell."

***

Gina LoSasso is a short, garrulous woman with a heavy Brooklyn accent and purple eye shadow that matches the satin bra strap peeking out flirtatiously from the shoulder of her floral blouse-and-shorts ensemble. Though she is by no means the smartest woman in America—that title goes to Marilyn Mach vos Savant, the *Parade* magazine columnist—she is way up there, with an IQ around 168, higher than that of Mozart or Thomas Jefferson. Since men with extremely high IQs (and men with extremely low IQs) are fifty times more plentiful than women, Gina estimates, the incidence of females in the population with an IQ similar to hers is about one in 3.4 million.

Gina is forty-three years old, twice-divorced, the mother of two—a twenty-year-old daughter and an eight-year-old son. She recently received her Ph.D. in clinical neuropsychology from Wayne State University in Detroit, having completed her bachelor's, master's, and doctoral programs in just under five years. She earned a great number of her undergraduate credits through something called the College Level Examination Program. She'd pick a test that seemed doable—marketing, management, literature, computer science, biology—get one basic textbook on the subject, study it, take the exam. She averaged about two tests a month. She scored in the high 90s on all the exams except biology, which she still managed to pass.

In her first e-mail to me, Gina opined that highly intelligent women make the best lovers. She believes her high libido and her high intelligence are both related to a higher than normal percentage of testosterone in her system. When she was young, in fact, she wanted to be a boy; she refused to answer to any name other than Billy. These days, she thoroughly enjoys being a girl, especially given the man-woman ratio in her circles. Gina is currently the only female on the list of the top fifty American players in the International Correspondence Chess Federation. A former member of the U.S. Chess Olympiad Team, Gina lived in Brussels for many years as a professional chess player, traveling the European circuit. Her second husband, an international master whom she married when she was thirty-two, was fourteen years her junior. Before she found chess—through a correspondence league associated with Mensa—Gina managed a weight-loss clinic, flunked out of three colleges, attended computer-programming school, sold copiers, made sand-art terrariums, and sold candy behind the counter at a movie theater. As soon as she played in her first chess tournament, she realized two things. Number one, this was what she wanted to do with her life. Number two, her marriage to her first husband—a construction worker from the old neighborhood in Brooklyn—was over. She felt the same way when she was accepted into her doctoral program; she informed her second husband she wanted a divorce. Gina has never had a problem letting go, forging ahead, concentrating on her own needs, making tough decisions—like leaving her daughter behind with her father while she pursued her dreams of playing chess. She abhors hanging around.

Though she tested off the charts in standardized examinations as a child, she hated school, often refused to go, barely graduated. Because she liked to talk and goof around a lot, and because she was good-looking—not to mention the thick Brooklyn accent—people always mistook her for an airhead. She liked it that way, because she was self-conscious about being too smart and didn't want to be thought of as a nerd. In fact, in her youth, she was somewhat of a hellion. As a young teenager, she frequently hitchhiked to Greenwich Village. She'd pick an apartment building, gain entry, listen at doors for the sounds of a party in progress. If one sounded interesting, she'd knock. She spent much of her fourteenth year in a residential drug-treatment program.

Gina's mom worked as a civilian employee of the police department. Her dad was an electrician and an alcoholic who left the family when she was sixteen. Often he'd build elaborate wooden and electronic puzzles he'd take to work for the purpose of stumping his coworkers. When Gina solved the puzzles handily, he'd become angry. He'd storm out of the house and head for the local pub.

Puzzles and games have always been Gina's passion and forte. She loves playing Scrabble, breaking tough encryption codes. She often plays computer games like Jessball and Myst for upward of six hours at a time. One of her favorite activities is riding her exercise bike while staring at her lava lamp. It helps clear her mind, she says; it's also great for her thighs. She keeps the bike in her bedroom, beside a large four-poster bed with a gauzy black canopy and sexy silken sheets. She is skilled at calligraphy, macramé, and jewelry making. "When people like me want to do something, we just do it," she says, typically unabashed. "From learning a musical instrument to learning how to tile your bathroom. You just get an instruction book and figure it out. It's a real empowering feeling, knowing you can do almost anything you try. The hard part, of course, is trying. When I know that I can do a presentation better, with little or no preparation, than the average person can with all kinds of preparation, it's hard for me to get motivated. I can be very industrious, but I have a lazy side. Or not lazy, really. It's just, like, I wanna do what I wanna do, you know?"

Gina believes high intelligence works against you, because mundane things are very difficult, and the world is full of mundane things structured for the average person. Waiting in line, paying bills, filling out forms, taking required courses, driving her son to school, answering routine questions, following arbitrary rules—life to her can sometimes be excruciatingly dull. Another difficult obstacle, she says, is finding the patience to communicate properly with others. Though she is a people person of the highest order and has many good friends, she isn't always easy to get along with. She easily becomes impatient: Why should she have to belabor a point to make herself understood? Sometimes she feels like snapping her fingers to speed people along. *Come on, come on, keep up!* And though she hates to say it, she can't stand watching her son play chess. He's already an accomplished player, having won his first trophy at four. She is proud of him, yes. But the kids' game is so slow it annoys her. They take all year to see a move. Sometimes she just wants to stand up in her seat in the audience and scream. *Knight takes queen, fer chrissakes!*

Like many of her HiQ fellows, Gina is admittedly obsessive-compulsive. Upon our first meeting, she proffers a three-ring binder complete with section tabs—a compendium of personal tidbits, FAQs, and background readings. She likes to be in charge. She likes to be the center of conversation and attention. She has a need for order and control. Often, when she buys a pair of shoes, she ends up returning them to the store because the right shoe is not identical in every way to the left. She loves to argue but has a difficult time agreeing to disagree. She believes there is always an answer waiting to be found, and she will go to great lengths to dig it up, to prove herself right. *Maude is Edith's cousin! Muhammad Ali is more popular than Pele!* Currently, Gina is embroiled in a dispute with her new boyfriend, a ponytailed HiQ postal employee she met on the Web. The argument arose after he made an obscure joke about losing his Thomas Pynchon doll. Gina didn't get it. The boyfriend said she must be an idiot if she didn't get it. She held fast to her opinion that his joke didn't make sense. She went so far as to research her position, telling the joke to her doctoral colleagues—clearly not idiots—carefully noting their reactions. They didn't get it, either. She is very proud of her new credential: Ph.D. Those three letters appended to her name are very important to her, partially because it is a label everyone can see. It says, with little need for interpretation, that she is *certifiably* smart. When you're special, you want people to accord you that extra bit of deference and respect. It's hard when they don't know you. Those three little letters go a long way. It helps explain how she was able to endure the tedious process of earning a doctorate in the first place.

Since her boyfriend lives in Virginia, they communicate mostly by e-mail and phone. Gina also has a torrid ongoing e-mail correspondence with America's smartest man, Chris Langan, the bouncer/cosmologist, though they've never actually met. She has printed out both sides of their e-mail correspondence; she keeps the hard copies in a three-ring binder beneath her desk—an X-rated, HiQ version of *Love Letters*. She is moving soon to Connecticut to take up her post-doctoral studies at Norwalk Hospital, a ferry ride away from Long Island. The next three-ring binder has yet to be filled.

"I'd love to clone myself, I really would." She smiles at the preposterous sound of her idea, continuing deliciously. "I would know how to raise me to reach my full potential. I think sometimes that if I'd been raised by a normal family, with opportunities to go to the best schools and stuff like that, I might have been a neurosurgeon or something by now. But then again, there's a side of me that's very creative and undisciplined, and maybe it's better to embrace that. Look at all the fun I've had. I've partied a lot. I've dined with heads of state and heroin addicts. I've lived in Brooklyn and Brussels, traveled to Moscow and Dubai. I've had a very broad, incredible life. I'm very philosophical about my whole experience growing up in the inner city and struggling and being different, because I'm here now, and I'm at a really good point. I can say that everything has worked out."

***

Ronald K. Hoeflin is a mild man with graying hair who wears his watch on a string around his neck.

Fifty-five years old and legally blind, he lives in Manhattan, in a $106-a-month apartment in Hell's Kitchen. He has three cats—Big Boy, Princess, and Wild Thing—and a collection of faux Frankart lamps, curvaceous female forms holding colorful globes, that lend a bawdy air to his tiny, ultra-neat bachelor pad, all of the furniture in which was found abandoned on the streets. Framed on his wall are three mandalas, photocopies from a series of twenty-four drawn by a patient of Carl Jung. The colorful works are symbolic of the patient's creative struggle and development. Though Ron can't make out the detail without his magnifying glass, the mandalas give him comfort in his solitary labors, he says, as does the crystal statue on his desk—Atlas balancing the world on his shoulders.

Sweet-natured and eager to please, Ron volunteers the fact that he has no friends. He seems nervous and awkward in public; he often goes days without meaningful conversation. When he does speak, the words gush forth so rapidly he sounds as if he's using a foreign tongue; understanding him takes a bit of practice. Once every two or three months—whether he needs it or not, he jokes—he goes on a date with a woman friend from Long Island. He's also begun corresponding with a woman in Florida. She has promised to come visit. "I'm looking for a bright woman who'd like to have bright children, if any such woman exists out there who can tolerate my low vision, modest income, and shyness," he says matter-of-factly.

Ron's father was an electrical engineer and ballroom dancer who worked his way through college playing violin in dance bands. His mother was an opera singer. Born and raised in St. Louis, Ron spent his youth "running around the neighborhood like a wild Indian." Due to his poor vision, he was never much of a reader; neither could he see the chalkboard in school. Nevertheless, when tested, he was found to be several grades ahead of his class, the fifth brightest student in his entire district. Though he remembers being upset he wasn't the *brightest* in his entire district, all of the adults in his sphere were pleasantly surprised. No one, including Ron, could explain how he knew so much—where he'd learned all the big words and complex theorems. It was as if the knowledge had come to him *a priori*.

Though Ron dropped out of his first three colleges, he now has two bachelor's degrees, two master's degrees, and a Ph.D. in philosophy. He modestly claims an IQ of only 164, though he says arriving at a final number is tricky. "I've gotten scores ranging from 125 to 175, depending upon what cognitive abilities they're tapping into," he says. "The fact is, nobody really knows exactly what you're supposed to be measuring when you're measuring IQ."

Ron is a self-taught expert in HiQ testing. He is credited with creating two of the world's most difficult IQ tests, the Mega and the Titan. Ron is fascinated with human potential, human limits. He is interested in world records of every kind: running times, weight-lifting records, home-run tallies, the number of digits of Pi a person can memorize. Since 1979, he has founded four HiQ societies, mostly because he was interested in the psychometric possibilities of forming such groups, given the numerical rarities involved. He makes his living by publishing monthly journals for two of the clubs and by scoring his tests for twenty-five dollars each. That he lives in one of the most expensive cities in the world with annual earnings of about $7,000 is perhaps the truest testament to his genius.

Seven days a week, at precisely three in the afternoon, Ron walks to a Wendy's restaurant fifteen blocks from his place. He orders a chef's salad and a large iced tea, then retires upstairs to the second-floor dining room, sits at his regular table by the window. After reading the *New York Times* and the *New York Post*, he reads exactly ten pages of philosophy—no more, no less—searching for examples to include in the book he's been writing for the past seven years, *Decoding Philosophy: Cybernetic Patterns in Philosophy and Related Disciplines—A Theory of Categories*. An expansion of ideas he first explored ten years ago in an essay for which he was awarded a prize by the American Philosophical Association, Ron's book offers a revolutionary new system for categorizing and analyzing all of the world's known philosophies. Handwritten on six-by-eight-inch notepaper—printed neatly in black ink; corrected with white streaks of Liquid Paper; edited with scissors and tape—the book runs about one million words. He keeps it filed in manila folders on two shelves in his apartment. Though he is aware the book is much too long to be published, he forges ahead. Within the next year, he hopes, he'll be finished.

Ron owns a computer but has never hooked it up, which adds to his sense of isolation. Though he has a reputation among fellow HiQs for being a technophobe, it's not the technology that daunts him so much as it is the idea of embarking on a whole new area of interest. Many years ago, he eschewed the notion of regular employment because he thought he would be squandering his time, that he wouldn't be improving himself in any way during all of those hours he had to work just for the sake of making money. While some HiQ types prefer to rip open a new gadge, ditch the instructions, and wing it, Ron is the kind of person who wants to read every word in every manual before he'll start anything new. As it is, he is known as a prodigious letter writer. "I've been using the mail for fifty years," he says. "Why stop now?" He feels the same about his financial position. "I'm sort of used to it. It's a trade-off. Money on one hand, leisure and independence on the other. I'm not really enough of a people-person to become wealthy, so I figure, what the heck, you know? I'm used to my condition. I have food and shelter and clothing. You don't have to be a genius to know that those are the most important things of all."

Ron's outward life is a series of comfortable routines. By putting the mundane tasks on a sort of deeply entrenched autopilot, he says, his mind is free to ponder larger questions. He always takes the same routes to Wendy's, to the post office, to the grocery, to the bank. He always goes at the exact same times, says the exact same things to the people who serve him. Every night for dinner, he buys two pieces of fried chicken, a can of corn, a can of peaches. Food is food, you know? Fuel for the body and mind. Later in the evening, while watching one of the five premium cable movie channels that are his only extravagance, he enjoys a scoop of strawberry ice cream. He loves the quiet of the dark, stays up all night watching movies, listening to classical music, writing essays. He sleeps until one in the afternoon. "I'm not saying it's a good life or a bad life. It's my life. It serves its purpose," he says.

When Ron was in sixth grade, a girl in his class invited everyone to her birthday party. When he arrived, she looked surprised. "Ron," she exclaimed. "I didn't expect you to come!" He doesn't remember now whether he stayed at the party, but he does remember the feeling he had, the lesson he learned. "Even though people invite you, it doesn't mean they are sincere about it. The truth is that people with average intelligence are a bit resentful. Throughout their entire schooling, they've had to compete with these people who seem to find it easy to get straight As, and they're working hard just to get Bs and Cs. If you were normal size, and you had to spend every day of your life out on a football field being run over by a three-hundred-pound guy, you'd start to resent him, wouldn't you? It's the same as that.

"There's a theory about genius. It's sort of like the 'tragic-flaw theory' in tragedy. You see it in a lot of cases of highly intelligent, highly creative people. For example, Sir Isaac Newton's mother abandoned him at the age of three to remarry. Her new husband didn't want young Isaac around, so he went to live with his aunt. He never recovered from the abandonment, could never achieve friendships with anybody throughout his entire life. His creativity in mathematics was really his way of saying, 'I'm a worthwhile person.'

"That's what a genius-type person, typically, will try to say through his work. He or she is saying, 'Even though you may not realize it, and even though I sometimes hate myself, I'm going to try and prove to you that I have some reason for being alive, that I have something important to contribute.' It's like you're born out of sync with the world, and you have to try to adjust. Your way of compensating is taking your greatest talent and just pushing it to the limits."

JOURNEY TO THE HEART OF WHITENESS

To some Americans—including freemen, survivalists, tax resisters, home schoolers, militia members, right-to-lifers, white supremacists, libertarians, Aryan Nations troopers, Christian patriots, Evangelicals, and even everyday citizens with jobs and kids and mortgages—America is going to hell in a handbasket. Many are flocking to Idaho.

The dog came charging out of the shadows of the little orchard by the barn, a dun-colored blur churning up leaves and sod, making a beeline for my car. He threw himself at the driver's door, rocking the fancy suspension of the rented four-wheel drive, snarling and barking and spewing foamy spittle, raking the glass with his nails.

Thankfully, they'd been considerate enough to mention Hans when I'd made my appointment. Wheeling into the driveway at the two tall, whitewashed poles that stood watch over the entrance to the compound, I'd rolled up my windows as a precaution. Juddering past a grove where a flock of turkeys pecked the grass beneath a hand-painted sign displaying a coat of arms with a crown and sword and shield, I double-checked the electric locks.

"Hans don't cotton much to strangers," the reverend's assistant had said. He'd also said the reverend was "very, very, very" busy and that before I talked with him, I should come out and pick up a press kit. The kit cost $150. Cash only, please. If, after doing the reading, I still had questions, I could request an audience with the Reverend Richard Butler himself, the 78-year-old founder of the Church of Jesus Christ Christian and its political arm, the Aryan Nations.

The assistant, a guy named Jerry, had a childlike voice, reminiscent of Lennie's in *Of Mice and Men*. He gave elaborate directions to the compound, two notepad pages full of landmarks and descriptions to get me to a place that ended up being a right turn off a major highway and two more right turns onto clearly marked roads. Jerry concluded his directions with the warning about Hans, a little story about the time they had tried to build a cage to hold the prize purebred German shepherd, imported from the Fatherland to sire a superrace of guard dogs. First they'd tried a Cyclone fence with razor wire. Hans simply opened the latch. Then they secured the gate with thick rope. Hans chewed it through in minutes. The final solution, proposed by one of the kinsmen, as the members are called, was an electrified fence surrounded by a moat. Hans tore the whole deal down, taking the full charge, shorting out the electrical system of the compound. Since then, whenever that kinsman comes to visit, Hans goes into a lather. "He remembers that guy, he knows his car and his smell, and he don't like him. He's got his number," said Jerry.

I couldn't decide if the story was apocryphal or not. (Though I would later hear about the time a prank caller authorized the vet who was treating the dog for a minor ailment to go ahead and neuter him while he was there.) Either way, I did what Jerry had instructed: stayed in the car, waited for an escort.

I lit a cigarette, turned up the radio, tried to ignore all the barking and growling, the fur and gums and yellow teeth sliming the window just to my left, the nails scratching and screeching against the glass.

It was a beautiful fall day in Hayden Lake, in northern Idaho, an area they call the Panhandle—a thin, majestic strip of fir trees and mountains and deep glacial lakes between Montana, Washington, and Canada. The sky was a color I remembered from grade school, when we mixed our own paints from powder, a pure royal blue, with thick, cottony storybook clouds and long, transecting jet trails glowing with the deep golden light of the afternoon sun. On all sides in the distance stood light of the afternoon sun. On all sides in the distance stood bristly moose-backed mountains, green and gold with the season—a little slice of heaven, Hans notwithstanding.

A half hour from the compound, north up the dual-lane highway, is the town of Sandpoint, new home to O.J. Simpson trial villain Mark Fuhrman. Detective Fuhrman's offense, boiled down, was using the word nigger, being caught on tape using the word nigger and, one supposes, possessing the feelings associated with using that word. Polite people, official people, correct people, idealistic people, believe our society has grown past that word and other words like it. Realistic people know otherwise. Many still use those words, and they mean them, too, maybe more these days than ever. In that way, those infamous Fuhrman tapes were like the Rodney King police beating video. They recorded an ugly piece of truth no one wanted to admit.

A half hour farther north, up the same highway, is Ruby Ridge, where, in 1992, government snipers killed Randy Weaver's son, the boy's dog, and Weaver's wife, shooting her in the face through a window while she held their infant daughter in her arms. The Weavers were Evangelical Christians, members of a sect known as Legalists, who believe the Bible is the literal word of God. They also believed the apocalypse was imminent. They had fled small-town Iowa to their wooded mountaintop to wait out the end time.

Today Ruby Ridge stands as a symbol to millions of white people across the nation, a precursor of the Waco Seige (1993), the Oklahoma City bombing (1995), the Olympic Park bombing (1996)—the first skirmish in the civil wars they believe will someday rage across the land. To these people—including freemen, survivalists, tax resisters, home schoolers, militia members, right-to-lifers, white supremacists, libertarians, Christian patriots, Evangelicals, and even everyday citizens with jobs and kids and mortgages—America is going to hell in a handbasket full of colored people and government regulations. They see crime, drugs, decay, disease, unchecked immigration, increasing social and economic stratification. They wish for a safer, more wholesome life, one governed and protected by traditional

American values—meaning, to them, those of the Founding Fathers, white Christians.

In northern Idaho, it seems, many have found what they've been seeking. Just in the last four years, the population has grown by about 12.5 percent. Of 1.1 million people counted in the 1990 census, only 9,365 were Asian, 3,370 black. Of all the states, Idaho is third in overall growth, behind Nevada and Arizona. About 30 percent of the newcomers are from California. In 1993, after the riots and the earthquakes, one-way U-Haul rentals from California to Idaho were so numerous the company was paying people to drive trucks back empty.

The Aryan Nations compound is a fairly rustic affair, twenty-five acres settled twenty-three years ago by the Reverend Butler and his neo-Nazi followers. Someday, if Butler's dreams are realized, pure-blooded white people—an estimated 33 million Americans who claim roots in the twelve Aryan nations—will abandon most of the continental United States to live in an all-white republic in the Pacific Northwest. Only whites will be allowed to vote, own property, conduct business, bear arms. There will be no taxation. Loans will be given without interest. Jews and other hybrids will be repatriated from the territory. Hayden Lake will be the capital.

Hans piped down after a while and retreated to a watchful position about five feet from my car. I turned off the radio, cracked the window. I was parked on a circular parade ground, beneath an empty flagpole. To my left was a little clapboard house. Inside, the reverend's wife lay dying of cancer. She'd moved here with her husband from the conventional suburban sprawl of Orange County, California. Together, they and their children and Butler's followers were among the first in the postmodern wave of white settlers. For better or for worse, it can be said the Reverend Butler was somewhat responsible for the exodus into this new promised land. That is why I was seeking counsel from the reverend. Sometimes there is truth buried at the fringe.

Behind the house were the orchard and the barn, a few cottages, some junk cars, a church, a thirty-foot watchtower. Just in front of me was a one-story frame building that appeared to be an office.

There were signs hanging all over the door: BEWARE OF DOG. WHITES ONLY. In a window hung a poster: "God has a plan for homosexuals. AIDS is only the beginning."

The wind through the pine needles made a sound like rushing water, ebbing and flowing. As I waited, wondering when the hell Jerry was going to appear and rescue me from Hans, my mind drifted to home. At that very moment, not far from my house in Washington, D.C., another man of the cloth, Minister Louis Farrakhan of the Nation of Islam, had gathered a million black men on the mall between the Lincoln Memorial and the U.S. Capitol. I'd been in the Panhandle for about a week now and hadn't seen one black face. No Hispanics, no blacks, no Asians. There were white folks working in the restaurants, even in the Thai, Chinese, and Mexican places. White folks patrolled the streets, mowed lawns, cleaned hotel rooms, played basketball in the courtyard at the county jail, walked home from high school listening to rap music on boom boxes, wearing backward baseball caps and oversized jeans. Like the sign on the highway had said: IDAHO IS WHAT AMERICA USED TO BE.

Over the past week, I'd noticed, I was drawing stares. With my olive skin and deep nostrils, my shaved head and earring, I was something of a sore thumb. People on the streets had this way of circumnavigating me. Women in line at McDonald's eyed me and hugged their purses. Kids stared at me and giggled. I shrugged it off. I wore a baseball cap. It didn't matter what they thought of me. I was here to find out about them.

Had my wife been along, I know she would not have just shrugged. Her dad is Creole, born in Morrow, Louisiana, a town named for its Klan leader. His grandparents were a Frenchwoman; the jet-black son of a slave; a half-black, half-Cherokee woman; and a full Cherokee man. My wife's mom, who emigrated from England as a young girl, is the daughter of Russian Jews. She was recently divorced from a Mexican man and is now living in a lesbian partnership. I, too, am the product of Lithuanian Jews. Both my parents grew up in the small town American South. My dad dodged rocks and epithets. My mother still bears the emotional scars of living in a town of blonde, pug-nosed 4-H queens. My son is also olive, a beautiful testimony to genetic mixture, with a halo of curly hair, his grandpa's high forehead, his mom's almond eyes, his dad's full bottom lip and talent for craftiness.

To my wife, and to many who agree, the *absence* of color in America indicates the *presence* of racism.

Proud as I am of my heritage, liberal as I am in my choice of politics and recreation and residence, I have to admit I share some things in common with the various Idaho extremists: The future scares me too. Though I live ten blocks from the White House, I can buy crack on my corner. Our hundred-year-old town house has iron bars and electric alarms, an attached garage with a mechanized door. When my wife and I go to dinner four blocks away, we drive. The wail of sirens, the staccato pop of automatic-weapons fire, the jangled arguments of street people: These are the night sounds that filter through my bedroom window. I have already begun saving money for my toddler son's education. Sending him to even a public preschool seems out of the question. Some nights I lie awake wondering: Where will he ride his bike when he gets older? Where will he play ball? Do I build a caged enclosure on my roof where he can romp unmolested?

At the Aryan Nations compound, the office door finally opened, and a big-bellied, pink-cheeked man came down the three stairs. He was in his sixties with white hair, wore a brown uniform shirt with a leather sash hooked from belt to shoulder, kind of like the SS in old Nazi movies. He took Hans by the collar stashed him in an old VW bus, then made his way back to my vehicle.

I rolled down the window, waved in a familiar manner.

He scrutinized me with watery blue eyes through thick glasses. "Are you white?" he asked.

By his voice, by his generally befuddled mien, I guessed this was Jerry, the reverend's assistant. According to Aryan Nations philosophy, white people are the true descendants of the ancient Israelites, in direct line from Adam and Eve. Jews, they believe, descended from Cain, who was born not of Adam and Eve but of Eve and the Serpent. Cain's children fled into the woods, mated with the beasts and produced the nonwhite "mud races." To Jerry, then, I was a mud person, a miscegenator, married to a mongrel, father of a mongrel. And I was a Hymietown-based liberal member of the "Jews-media," one of the conspiratorial arms of the Zionist Occupational Government that was leading the country to ruin.

I smiled and held up my palms and inspected them, and then turned my hands over and inspected some more. "Looks white to me," I joked. "What do you think?"

"Well, I don't know," said Jerry, quite seriously.

"OK, OK, I'm Italian," I said. "Is that white?"

"Oh yes, of course," said Jerry, but I knew the answer before I'd asked. The twelve Aryan nations are Holland, Spain, Iceland, Great Britain, the United States, Sweden, Denmark, Norway, Finland, Germany, France, and Italy. With my big nose and general swarthiness, I knew claiming Italian ancestry was my one shot at passing for Aryan. If I was going to learn anything, I had to get behind the lines. A little white lie to gain acceptance.

"So, what can we do for you today?" asked Jerry.

"I came for the press kit, remember?"

"Right. Right," said Jerry. "Did you bring the cash?"

***

"Why do Mexicans eat refried beans," rasped the brassy blonde woman, taking a swig from a bottle of butterscotch schnapps, leaving a beat of silence to cushion the punch line.

"Because they couldn't get it right the first time."

"Ba-da-bing," sang David Bond, miming a drumroll and a cymbal splash, wearing a bathrobe and a Greek sailor cap.

It was cocktail hour aboard Bond's vintage yacht, tied fast to a weathered slip in a no-name marina on the banks of the Spokane River, just outside of Coeur d'Alene, the largest town in northern Idaho, named for the Indians who now live south of here on a reservation, where they run a prosperous bingo operation.

"How do you know when an Israeli hits puberty? They take the diaper off his ass and put it on his head."

"Ba-da-bing!"

With cedar decks, brass and teak appointments, an air of faded opulence, *Sarah's Song* is the full-time floating home of the local bard and his new first mama, a professional bartender and amateur comedienne who goes by the name Geo, as in Georgia. A fortyish, self-professed biker chick, with a whiskey voice and Vegas cleavage, complete with Harley tattoo and a quiver of poison-tipped bar jokes to fell even the thick-skinned.

We were sitting in the salon of the boat. The pair was playing out a little piece of local satire for the visiting journalist, fueled by beer, the schnapps, and a hunk of freshly barbecued lake salmon.

"A couple of lesbians and a couple of fags are driving to Seattle. Who gets there first?. . . The lesbians. They go lickety-split while the fags are still home packing their shit."

Bond is the shoot-from-the-hip columnist at the local paper—or maybe shoot-from-the-navel would be more apt—an irreverent, bleary-eyed, sharp-tongued, grizzly-bearded 44-year-old devotee of Hunter S. Thompson and Jack Daniels who has earned his living over the years as a methamphetamine chemist, a mining-company official, a fisherman, a public-relations director for the Association of Washington Business, and, more recently, as a journalist.

Though Coeur d'Alene has a mayor and a chamber of commerce, it had been recommended I consult Bond for a social and political overview of the area. A precious, renovated city, Coeur d'Alene boasts two malls, an outlet mall, a wine and jazz club, a museum, a vintage auto and motorcycle store, an espresso shack on every fourth corner, a junior college, a two-star restaurant, and a lakeside hotel that has been named the top inland resort in the nation (owned by the man who also owns the newspaper, the radio station, and most of the downtown lakefront property).

Bond has been here since 1977, when he sailed a little sloop solo from Alaska to come to work for the *Coeur d'Alene Press*. When I met him, he'd been living aboard *Sarah's Song* for a year. Prior to that, he'd been sleeping for six months in his vintage pink Cadillac in the aftermath of a ruined relationship. The Cadillac, at the moment, was missing. Bond couldn't remember where he had parked it.

I'd been told the eccentric and erudite Bond represented, in a certain way, the once common notion of Idaho as the Land of the Free Spirit, a state that sent Frank Church and former governor Cecil Andrus to Washington, D.C.; a place where explorers, miners, loggers, hunters, hippies, eclectic loners, and rugged individualists have roamed the mountains, chasing dreams and natural bounty since the territory was first opened to white people by the French fur traders and their Iroquois scouts.

"A lot of the overview you're getting from the media is focused on the crackpots," says Bond, lighting a cigarette, slipping easily from burlesque to punditry. "The fact is, if you meet a born-and-bred Idaho native, you'll meet a pretty tolerant, fairly liberal, laid-back person.

"Redneck, yes. Racist, no. There's a difference.

"The problem is, the floodgates have been open for some time. People are moving here faster than anyone can count. You've got to wonder what views you're importing with them, you know? Years ago, when I first came, there was this legacy of 'live and let live.' It was kind of like, 'OK, neo-Nazis, do your thing. Just don't fuck with me.' In a sense you can say the intolerance here has been nurtured by the very liberalism of the area.

"My view of the Aryans is, if you kind of ignore them, they'll go away. When they had the Skinhead World International Congress in '88 or '89, you had twenty skinheads and three hundred reporters up at the compound, and downtown you had several thousand people turning out for a human rights show of support. But the press, well, you had guys here from the goddamn *Financial Times* of London, and everybody was staying at the resort, burning up a thousand bucks a day in expenses. So, of course, they needed some bang for their bucks. The story becomes not the human rights march. It's the skinheads burning crosses.

"But what happens is the idiots out there read the distorted stories. I'll bet Mark Fuhrman will, without his own intention, probably be responsible for 500 shitheads moving into this area, because they're gonna go, 'Hey man, he put it to the fucking niggers. I'm going where he's going.'

"Don't get me wrong; there is shit going down here. There's a belief around here that the currency is no good. And I'm not convinced Oklahoma City doesn't trace back here. And there are some pretty heavy right-wing leaders around here. You have Reverend Butler. You have Louis Beam, the former Texas KKK grand dragon under David Duke. You have Sam Sherwood, national director of the U.S. Militia Association. There is, indeed, a movement that extends into some of the more respectable middle-class areas.

"To many people, northern Idaho was going to be a white man's refuge. People really believe there is going to be class warfare and race warfare, that the blacks and the Mexicans already own California and most of the Eastern Seaboard, and that the Caucasians gotta hang onto their real estate just to keep their own shit together. That's what they're here for. They've circled the wagons. They've—"

"How do you know it's spring in Sandpoint?" interrupted Geo, apparently tired of her old man's lecture. She took a swig of butterscotch schnapps, leaving a beat of silence to cushion the punch line. "Mark Fuhrman is out planting gloves."

"Ba-da-bing," sang David Bond.

***

Two clean-cut white boys, both 13, sat in the backseat of a patrol car, parked in a suburban driveway on a weekday afternoon, school just over for the day.

Two deputy sheriffs sat in another patrol car, parked just behind the first. The boys had been apprehended leaving an empty house. After questioning them separately, the deputies put the boys in the car, turned on a hidden tape recorder, then left them alone awhile. A pair of motorcycles had earlier been stolen from the house, which was owned by the people on the adjoining lot. The cops wanted to see if the boys knew anything they weren't saying. Now the cops were listening to the tape.

"I heard your name over the radio," said one boy, call him Tony.

"What do you mean?" asked the other, Marshall.

"I heard your phone number and name over his intercom."

"I'm in deep trouble," Marshall said.

"But we didn't do anything!"

"The only thing we did was kick down the door."

"Whoo, the door!" said Tony. "It was only a piece of *plywood*."

"I guess we could get in trouble for that. It's like breaking and entering, sort of."

Sitting behind the steering wheel of his patrol car, sergeant Paul Watson, looked over to Sergeant Paul Middlemore, who was sitting in the front passenger seat. "We got two heavy-weight felons here," he said, snickering.

"Career criminals," snorted Middlemore. "Did dispatch reach their parents?"

"One kid's parents are at their lake house. The other kid's father is on his way. They're neighbors. We'll let the boys stew awhile."

Middlemore and Watson are both former L.A. area cops, currently working for the forty-five-man force of the Kootenai County Sheriff's Department. Kootenai is the county surrounding Coeur d'Alene. Hayden Lake is within its borders. Sandpoint and Ruby Ridge are just beyond.

A sportsman's and vacationer's paradise, Kootenai (pronounced Koot-nee) has sixteen deep lakes, fifty-four miles of navigable rivers. There are 92,000 permanent residents, 200,000 in summertime. As 67 percent of the county is federal land—national forest, Indian reservation, a submarine testing facility—Kootenai citizens shoulder a large tax burden, as do all Idahoans, the thirteenth highest in the nation. In the past ten years, property values in Kootenai have doubled or tripled, though five-acre parcels with electricity available can still be had for as low as $1,000 an acre. Wages have remained a steady 20 percent below California averages; food prices are also below California's. And while the timber and silver-mining industries bottomed out several years ago, in 1995 Idaho became the fastest-growing exporting state in the nation, selling 7.3 percent of its gross state product—not including farm goods—overseas.

Both officers say they were attracted to Idaho by the beautiful scenery, the low crime rate, affordable property, available work and—a bit consciously, a bit subconsciously—the comfortable homogeneity of the place.

I'd spent the past week riding shifts with these deputies and others. For a quick survey of an area, in my mind at least, nothing is better than a police ride along. You meet the criminals; you meet the citizens. You see life in all lights. The drunk couple on a Saturday night with a pair of (legally) loaded rifles in the backseat of their vehicle. The pregnant mom whose car was rear-ended on her way to work; I ended up pitching in and directing traffic for twenty minutes in the driving rain while the deputy, a father himself, held the mom's hand as we awaited the rescue squad. The harried homeowner in his two-story Quonset garage, behind his restored antique house, trying to get his hunting Jeep ready for elk season. As a public service, the sheriff's department responded to his house to register the car so he didn't have to trouble himself by going to the Department of Motor Vehicles. The widow living in a retirement condo with a view of the lake whose watch was possibly stolen by a repairman. She offered cookies and coffee. The deputy ended up re-setting all the automatic timers on her lamps so she'd feel more secure now that the days were shorter.

And, as hosts and guides and social interpreters, there are the cops themselves—middle-class white men in their late twenties and thirties who, like everyone else, aspire to the American Dream. Many, like Watson and Middlemore, uprooted themselves and their families from well-established lives to start over somewhere new. Somewhere, they hoped, that was better.

Sergeant Paul Watson is 34, wry and understated, with a flattop haircut. He worked ten years as a San Bernardino County cop before he "called in well" and escaped to northern Idaho two years ago with his wife and three young kids.

Back there Watson and his wife had built a house at the north end of Rialto. It was a nice area, a "white-picket-fence kind of neighborhood," Watson had said earlier. "And then there was this imaginary barbed-wire fence at Highland Avenue that separated our development from absolute black—gang country—I mean, the toughest you can come by.

"After about five years, the fence started getting holes in it and the dirtbags started moving in. Now, I'm no white supremacist or anything. The people in my neighborhood weren't all white. But they were all upstanding citizens. But now the neighborhood was changing. A neighbor's daughter was going out with a drug dealer. My wife was afraid to go to the store, and the store was only three blocks away. My kids weren't allowed on the streets after dark."

Sergeant Middlemore is a laid-back string bean of a man, 36 years old, with six children, five of them boys. He worked for seven years for the Southgate P.D., right next door to Compton, south of South-Central L.A. By the end of his stint, he was a motorcycle patrolman, "the ultimate in jobs, one of my dreams," he'd said. "They paid me money to ride a motorcycle all day. We were showpieces, man. My boots were like glass."

It was Middlemore's wife who engineered the move. After learning there was a Catholic school up here affiliated with the one the kids were attending in Pasadena, she cleverly gave her husband brochures from the local ski resorts; she got him up here first for a little vacation. Before they left, they'd almost bought a house. Three years ago, they returned for good.

"I always felt that I was destined to live in the hills or the mountains," said Middlemore. "Most people just visit a place and fall in love with it, and that's it; they go back home. But I went back to work, and the traffic was terrible and the smog was like soup, and I just said, 'Man, why am I here? This is ridiculous.'

"Why we don't have a diverse population up here is beyond me. Maybe I'm being ignorant of the facts or something, but I don't see anyone keeping anyone out. There are no blacks here, so they don't tend to want to come here. People want to be with their own. I do think things are easier here because there isn't any diversity. Without diversity there is more agreement, I would say. When people are different they hold different beliefs, so I think we're always gonna have race conflict. I'm not racist by any means, but I do think that when people are different, they don't get along as well. They don't have the same values or goals.

"What I wanted out of life was a better place. I didn't want my kids to have to walk down the street and get jostled by some gang-banger. Here they can fish and hunt and learn the outdoors. It's quality of life. I'm sorry this place is all white. I don't know what that means. But if it means a good quality of life, I'm not that sorry."

Meanwhile, in the patrol car, Middlemore and Watson switched off the tape of the two boys. The deputies knew what they had here: good kids, maybe a little spoiled, riding their bikes after school, getting into mischief.

"Here comes the father," said Deputy Watson.

The two deputies got out of the car.

For the next twenty minutes, the boys would be sternly lectured by the deputies, the owner of the abandoned house, Marshall's father, Tony's brother. And the boys were made to agree to come back, at the homeowner's convenience, with their fathers, to replace the plywood door they'd broken down.

After everyone had shaken hands, the boys loaded their expensive bikes into Marshall's father's Suburban and drove off. Then Middlemore drove off. Watson would get into a comfortable country dialogue with the homeowner and his wife about recipes for cooking sour apples, like the ones growing on the tree in their yard. The owners would press sour apples on Watson. Though he could taste the pie, the applesauce, the baked apples with heavy cream, he politely took just one.

***

The Coeur d'Alene Resort rises eighteen stories above a deep, sapphire blue lake, surrounded on all sides by mountains robed in cedars and ponderosa pines. A modern architectural jewel that towers over the city's quaint downtown (founded in 1878 as an army outpost), it is known hereabouts simply as the Resort.

An ambitious structure with 340 rooms, it is built of tan concrete, with myriad gables and peaked copper roofs. The floating boardwalk, three-quarters of a mile long, was designed specifically to be the longest in the world. Also built for the record books was the golf course, which features a floating green. Golfers, who pay upwards of $125 per round, are shuttled to the carefully manicured island on quaint little ferries. Rooms go from $80 to $2,500 a night.

For the last two nights, the Resort had been booked solid for a conference entitled "Educating for Virtue: The New 'Values Revolution.'" The event was sponsored by Hillsdale College, a private school and think tank in southern Michigan that accepts no government funding. Its mission, according to its literature, is to train America's young "to become leaders worthy of their Judeo-Christian, Greco-Roman legacy . . . [in a place] where we can openly talk of love for God and country, or pride in the good things that this nation has achieved, and of little heard concepts like honor and patriotism."

The featured speaker this afternoon was Ralph Reed, the 34-year old leader of the Christian Coalition. Handpicked by Pat Robertson to lead the grassroots Evangelical political movement, Reed has gathered an estimated 1.7 million souls into his flock over the past three years. Political experts say the next Republican candidate for president will not be anointed without Reed's blessing. Gramm, Gingrich, Dole: They have all come to call.

Now, at the end of the second day, just after lunch, 700 radiant white people waited politely in their folding chairs for the main event.

"The thing that really impressed me about Ralph Reed," the moderator said, by way of introduction, "was the time I watched him take on Jesse Jackson on TV. Reed was polite and unflappable. He was quick and informed. Jackson tried to get to him and could not. Ralph's a very disarming figure when the enemy is trying to tear him apart. He's just a very nice guy with an awfully good message. Ladies and gentlemen, Ralph Reed." Three large viewing screens across the front of the conference room tracked him to the podium. He has clear blue eyes, a youthful face, a winning, toothsome smile. In his suit and tie he looked like a summer intern on Capitol Hill. On his wrist, he wore a very big watch. It sparkled beneath the lights.

"We are gathered here at this conference to speak about who we are as a people, what we value as a culture, and what we believe to be true enough to pass on to our children. That is truly the highest, the noblest, and the most difficult endeavor in which we can be engaged in this critical time in our nation's history . . .

"We are a nation held together by a common bond and by a common vision, rooted in faith and in the fundamental belief that all men are created by God. That was the first and the foundational principle of the American experiment. And the second was this: that they should be free, unrestrained by the sinews of government to pursue the longings of their hearts and the yearnings of their souls."

Quoting Ronald Reagan, George Washington, Alexis de Tocqueville, Noah Webster, and John Adams, tossing in a joke here and a pun there, Reed calmly, convincingly, cited facts and figures from a multitude of sources: a cover story in U.S. News and World Report that said the United States, with the possible exception of Israel, is the most devoutly religious nation in the entire world. A survey that found that 83 percent of Americans believe that the Bible is the infallible and inerrant word of God. A study that showed that 130 million Americans go to church every single week. "It gives all of us encouragement," said Reed, "that there are more people in church on Sunday morning than watching *60 Minutes* on Sunday night."

Speaking of a "Fourth Great Awakening" that was dawning upon our nation, Reed continued: "In the place of timehonored values and faith in God, we have replaced it with a different kind of value system, based not on the relevance and the benevolence of God but on the relevance and benevolence of government. And that welfare state that they have erected—which we once measured by the height of its aspirations—must now be measured by the depths of its failures. My friends, if our inner cities resemble Beirut, if our children pass through metal detectors into schools that are war zones, and if high school graduates can't read the diplomas that they were just handed, then we will have failed ourselves, failed our children, and failed our God. And we cannot and must not fail in the task that is ahead.

"The Declaration of Independence said that we are endowed as a people by God with inalienable rights, and if the government ever violates those God-given rights, then not only do people have the right but, more importantly, they have the duty to engage in an act of revolution, to throw off that government. If that was true in 1776, then it is still true in 1996. We still have that right, we still have that duty, and we still have that obligation."

Huge, sustained applause. A standing ovation.

***

As soon as I passed the empty guardhouse, Hans was at it again. By now, having been in the Panhandle for almost two weeks, having heard the story of the conspiracy against Han's manhood, I felt sorry for the hapless German shepherd. Snarling and raking and spewing foamy spittle—all bark, you could say, and no bite.

This was my third trip to the compound.

After I'd read the $150 worth of material, I'd pressed for further access and was invited to attend the Aryans' regular Sunday worship service. After I'd wheeled in, endured Hans, and waited for Jerry, he finally appeared. This time he said the kinsmen didn't want a reporter attending their worship service. As before, the place seemed almost deserted. I could see one skinhead standing on the porch, drinking a cup of coffee. Jerry agreed to let me return at a later time.

In the intervening days, I drove the Panhandle. In Naples, the crossroads below Ruby Ridge, my first encounter was with a man on a horse trotting in front of me on an old single lane bridge. When he reined around to let me pass, I caught a glimpse of him beneath his cowboy hat. He seemed to have no face, as if it had been burned away. Just two eyes staring out from scar tissue. Pulling up at the general store, getting out of the car, I spied a guy coming from the Laundromat. He waved, said *hey*. His right eye was sewn shut.

Inside the store, normalcy returned. Microbrewery beers, hunting gear, beef jerky, staples, a little post office. I met the proprietors, Earl and Linda Berwick, a former Orange County accountant and his wife, who had come up ten years ago to start a simpler, more self-determined life. They couldn't have been happier with their lot. Except, of course, for the hundreds of nosy reporters who'd been swarming since Ruby Ridge. I encountered a similar, though considerably less friendly response on a treacherous, muddy road not far from the former Weaver residence. The man never raised his shotgun past his waist, but then again, I didn't argue when he said it would be nice if I turned around.

In Sandpoint I found the fabled residence of Detective Fuhrman, a rancher with a white picket fence. Though I'd heard Fuhrman was lying low near Coeur d'Alene, I went up and knocked. You never know, right?

Just outside of town, I dropped in on a former Chicago business executive, Melissa Donohue, at her organic sheep farm. I met her sheep and her chickens and her watch-mule, Peaches, and I also took a look at the newsletter she edits about architectural accounting software. Visiting her that day were two women friends, one of whom was a former philosophy professor from Philadelphia. After years in the ivory tower, she was living now in a tiny solar cabin overlooking the lake with a Jewish man from Long Island, a former car salesman.

And in Coeur d'Alene, I met press people and businesspeople and even the main man himself, the richest guy in town, Duane Hagadone. I also managed to meet two of the three black people who live in Coeur d'Alene. Phil Wilson, a bear of a man who runs an auto-repair business, had been profiled once by the local paper. He looked at me for several moments after I introduced myself. Then, very slowly, politely, he backed away, into his shop. Inez Anderson gave me a long interview. She was facing a court date on several counts of abusing teachers and enticing students to leave school; her son and his friends at the junior high had held a two-day sit-in to protest the use of the word nigger by some other students. Her point of view was, Why should I leave? The people suck, but the place is great. She and her white husband could probably have a much easier life elsewhere, but her point is well taken.

Now, finally, on my third pre-arranged trip to the Aryan Nations compound, with Hans once again snarling and clawing at my driver's side window, Jerry came out of the office, went down the three steps, and approached the car.

"What can I do for you?" he asked. As he did the last time, he was acting like he'd never seen me before in his life.

"You said I could talk to the Reverend Butler today."

"OK. Right. Listen. Have you got a copy of your magazine, *Gentlemanly Quarter*? Because it's the general consensus of the people up here that it's a gay magazine."

"No! Not at all!" I protest. "It's a general magazine for men."

"Well, what about your earring?"

For a second I considered pulling out the picture of my wife and kid to prove my standing as a breeder. Then I remembered the poster from the press kit. The headline read MULTICULTURISM [sic]. Beneath was a picture of two baby gorillas. "Say hello to your grandchildren!" read the caption.

"Do I seem like a fag to you?" I asked.

"I don't know if you seem like a fag," said Jerry. "Look at these guys: football players, track stars, the father in *The Brady Bunch*—you can never tell."

Jerry reached down and picked up an orange cat that had been nuzzling his leg. He cradled it in his arms, stroked it tenderly.

"You're quite an animal lover, aren't you," I said.

"Yep, I rescued this little thing when it was just a baby, and now the darn things's gonna have babies itself."

"Pets are nice."

"We have dogs and cats and gerbils and . . . Okay, *look*," he said, snapping back from his reverie. "I can't take time for this stuff." He threw the cat onto the grass. "I have to get back inside. There's nobody to answer the phones."

"Well, what should I do?"

"Oh well. Well, um . . . Heck, why don't you just come inside?"

***

The original angry white man of the Idaho Panhandle, the Reverend Richard Butler, didn't seem very angry at all. A little tired maybe. A little smug. He had a vision for the place. It hasn't happened exactly his way, but it is happening. The white people are coming. More wagons arriving every day.

He was sitting at a paper-strewn desk, surrounded by Nazi memorabilia, Hans snoozing on his feet. A tall, rugged, lean man with a full head of white hair and liver spots on his hands, he was on the phone trying to order more of "those square-type pins," haggling over a balance due. A young blonde named Jennifer was working at a computer. She had signed my receipt for the press kit with a circle over her name. The skinhead from outside the church last Sunday was running a printing machine. The walls were covered with little bins full of white-supremacist pamphlets. Jerry scooted from bin to bin, stuffing envelopes.

Not so long ago, Butler and his Aryan Nations kindred struck fear into many hearts. In 1983, when Butler called for a "racial holy war," a more proactive splinter group called the Order was born. Members of the Order ran a counterfeiting ring and committed armed robberies, netting over $4.1 million—most of which was never recovered. The Order was also responsible for the murders of a Missouri state trooper and the Denver radio talk-show host Alan Berg. Its leader was killed in December 1984 in a shootout with federal agents. More than two dozen followers were eventually arrested and convicted. Many more were acquitted of conspiracy in the case, including Butler. In 1986 members of another Order offshoot, the Bruders Schweigen Strike Force II, were arrested on charges of bombing four buildings in Coeur d'Alene. They, too, were brought to justice.

More recently, the Aryan Nations has changed its tactics, moving into propaganda, recruitment, consolidation. It has reached out to skinheads to bring in young blood. The Sunday services are now billed as "Youth Worship"; rallies feature skinhead bands. Today the Aryan Nations has chapters in twenty states, most created within the past two years. Butler's network is said to be vast. Leaders of numerous white-supremacy groups gather periodically in Idaho: the Klan, the various militias; every important leader of a far-right group has been spotted here at one time or another, according to both the Jewish Defense League and Jane's Intelligence Review. The Reverend Butler's printing machine, he says, runs eighteen hours a day.

"Why have people come to northern Idaho?" asked Butler, repeating my question. "Plain and simple. Because it's white.

"Now, most people are so brainwashed and intimidated by politically correct propaganda that they won't say it that way. They'll say, 'Well, it's because of the traffic or the smog,' or something like that, but they come up here because they want to be with their own kind.

"It's nature. Say you have horses and cattle in the same field, and maybe a few elk or a few deer, all grazing. But when a big storm comes, the horses go together, the cattle go together, the deer go together. Nature is that way. Schools of fish are all the same fish. When ducks migrate, they go together as one species.

"It's a genetic thing. The genes of our race are special. The white race feeds the rest of the world. It has brought civilization to the rest of the world. It built the greatest countries on Earth. But the white race is only 7.3 percent of the people on the planet. The other races are jealous. There is a conspiracy to eliminate us.

"Ultimately, if our race is to survive, we must establish a territorial imperative. Biology, you know, says that every species has to have a territorial imperative in order to live. Up here in the Northwest, they had the spotted owl, and they wanted 11 million acres set aside so the spotted owl would have a territorial imperative in which it could breed and hunt and do the things the spotted owl would do in order to preserve the species.

"Well, the same thing for the white race exists as it does for the spotted owl or the horny toad or anything else the stupid environmentalists come up with. For us to live, we have to have a territorial imperative.

"See, a country is like a house. You have walls and doors and windows for protection from the elements. If you are the man of the house and you allow everybody to come in and sleep on the floor and in your wife's bed and so forth, pretty soon it won't be your house anymore. Well, that is what's happened with America. And that is why people are leaving the cities and coming to places like this.

"The thing is, you can have a lot of money and bars and gates and alarms and so forth, but when the hammer comes down, they aren't gonna protect you. The only thing that will protect the white race from the storm is being with their own kind. Take my word for it. Northern Idaho is just the beginning."

***

Home at last in the nation's capital, I paid the cabbie, climbed the hundred-year-old iron staircase to my brick row house. There are iron bars on all the first-floor windows. It takes two different keys to open the locks on the iron gate.

In the entryway, there is a key pad for the alarm, which is hooked to a monitoring station. Finally, another key, for the deadbolt of the thick wooden door. Home at last.

I was met by the blinding glare of every single light in the house: My wife gets scared when I'm gone, says she hardly sleeps. My son came toddling from the kitchen, followed by my wife, a crooked grin on her face. She pulled her hand from behind her back. She was holding a VCR tape.

"It's time for your re-education," she said, walking to the TV, putting in the tape.

In a few moments, Minister Farrakhan was on the screen, taped footage of his speech to the throng of black men at the Million Man March; the tape was wound to a point near the end of his two-and-one-half-hour speech, a rambling, impenetrable diatribe that had most of white America changing the channel long before its insightful conclusion.

"White supremacy," the minister was saying, "is the enemy of both white people and black people. Because the idea of white supremacy means you should rule because you're white. That makes you sick. And you in turn produce a sick society, a sick world.

"Mr. Clinton, we're gonna have to do away with the mind-set of the Founding Fathers. You don't have to repudiate them. . . .You don't have to say they were malicious, hate-filled people. But you must evolve out of their mind-set. You see, their mind was limited to those six European nations out of which this country was founded. But now you got Asians here. How you gonna handle that? You got children of Africa here. How you gonna handle that? You got Arabs here; you got Hispanics here. You can't harmonize with the dark people of the world, who outnumber you eleven to one, if you're going to stay in the mind-set of white supremacy. White supremacy has to die in order for humanity to live."

Later I was reading in bed when it occurred to me: I had not set the alarm.

I tiptoed down the stairs, punched in my code, watched the light turn from green to red.

And then I stood there for a few minutes, lost in thought, worrying as befits my own cultural heritage, wondering where my son would go to school, where he'd ride his bike, where he'd play.

My little mongrel: Where will he go if the big storm hits?

GQ, 1996

THE ICE AGE

Rick heard Samoan war drums. Connie thought her body was crawling with bugs. Robert believed the DEA had planted a tiny speaker in his brain. Derek also thought he had a DEA implant—he used his to contact famous men from history. Carol hit the pipe to become the perfect Super Mom. A report from Hawaii on the ravages of crystal meth.

One night while he slept, special agents from the DEA entered Robert Li's bedroom and planted a tiny speaker in his brain. The device was top secret; it transmitted and received. It read his thoughts, broadcast voices, tracked him by satellite everywhere he went.

At work in the produce department of the local supermarket, he'd notice now and then that certain shoppers would stop their carts and spy on him. Men, women, teenagers, he could hear them talking. They'd be saying stuff like, "He's spraying the lettuce now."

At home he'd hear noises. He'd look out the window, but no one was there. Sometimes, if he looked quick enough, he could catch a glimpse of a shirt collar in the bushes, the bill of a baseball cap behind the fence. Once he saw a man with a walkie-talkie standing near his car. "I know what you're thinking," the man said into his handset. Li rushed outside. The man was gone.

After that, Li stayed in his room. The broadcasts got louder. He dug around in his ear with a paper clip, but he couldn't find anything. Neither could the ear, nose, and throat doctor who patched him up on three different occasions. "Then I started thinking maybe things were planted in my walls, planted in my radio," Li says. "I took apart everything in my room you could think of. I'd spend hours—ten, twelve, fifteen straight hours—just taking something apart, looking for a mic or something similar. Do you know how many parts a TV set has? I couldn't find anything. Then I had to put it back together, which didn't always go so well."

At the moment, Li is sitting on his bed, propped on pillows against the wall, grinding his teeth. Twenty-eight years old, he is an attractive mixture of Chinese, Caucasian, and Hawaiian—dark and mop haired, with hooded eyes and a square, Dudley Do-Right chin. This is his parents' place, a modest wood-frame house on the windward side of the island of Oahu, in the state of Hawaii, nine or ten miles over the mountains from Waikiki. It's a small room, the scene of his boyhood: wood paneling, a shelf full of model cars, a collection along the window ledge of spent disposable lighters.

Li reaches into his shirt pocket and pulls out a clear glass tube with a hollow ball at one end, a fluted mouthpiece at the other. At the top of the ball is a small hole; at the bottom, a little clump of crystals. The crystals are shiny and translucent, like sea salt or rock candy. Li covers the hole with his finger, teases the glass ball with a tight blue flame. In a few seconds, the crystals melt, then bubble, then vaporize. Smoke swirls inside the ball, wispy, clean, and white. He sucks it through the tube, inhales deeply. There is no smell. He says it tastes like vanilla. Others say it tastes like green apples, star fruit, the way plumeria smells. At last, he exhales. He opens his eyes and smiles.

The first time Li smoked ice was six years ago. Before that, he wasn't a druggie; he didn't even smoke *pakalolo*, Hawaiian pot. Since high school, weekends had been a case of beer, cruising the streets of Waikiki, gawking at tourists, stopping in at clubs like Masquerades or the Rock and Roll Clinic, maybe going in with his friends to buy the services of one of the hookers strolling downtown Waikiki. Occasionally, he did a little cocaine, maybe shared half a gram, not enough to get jangled, just something to take the woozy feeling off the beer.

Then one night, he was on his dinner break—he was working the p.m. shift at a grocery store. His buddy, Ron, asked if he wanted to try something. Each smoked about four hits. "It felt different," Li remembers. "I didn't know the high, so I didn't *know* I was high. But

I noticed I kept talking more. I was more friendly towards people. Usually I'm kind of quiet. It made me feel happy, you know, and it made me want to work more—harder and faster, too. I was stocking shelves like a banshee. I was *really* stocking those shelves. Great rows. Perfect balance. I really concentrated. I hardly took any breaks."

Soon, Li bought his own pipe. You can get one at any number of head shops or Korean liquor stores on the island. At the Korean stores, you have to ask for a "liquid-incense burner." If you say "pipe," they pretend not to understand. For the next six months, Li smoked crystal before work at least four or five times a week. A week's worth cost him only about thirty dollars. It is an easy drug to do no matter where you are. You put it in the pipe, heat, smoke. When you're done, the liquid cools and recrystallizes, sticks to the bottom of the pipe. You can just stash it in your sock and go—being careful that it's cooled down first (many ice users suffer burns in this fashion). The pipe stays loaded and ready. Nobody at work could really tell Li was high on drugs. He just seemed garrulous and happy. He got his work done. He was a model employee.

Unlike cocaine, which requires a re-administration every fifteen minutes, the feeling of high-energy well-being Li got from smoking a few hits of ice lasted six to eight hours. Even so, as time passed, taking hits off the pipe became his main preoccupation.

Smoking is a sensual exercise: the flame, the bubbles, the swirl. It was something he just kept thinking about, something he wanted to do again and again. At work, he started taking more and more breaks. Between breaks he'd think about the next break. Outside of work, all he ever wanted to do was smoke or visit people who smoked. In the beginning, ice makes you want to share. In time, you become increasingly paranoid and isolated.

Li would stay up for three or four days and then crash. As he was coming down, his mind would race and his heart would pound, armies marching through his brain. Then, just as he'd start settling down, an odd electric jolt would run through his body, and he'd be up again, wide awake. Finally, he'd sleep, fifteen to twenty hours at a time.

Then he'd wake up and smoke some more, usually before he got out of bed.

A year passed. Li lost thirty pounds. His eyes looked sunken. His skin turned greenish yellow. He started calling in sick at work. He stayed in his room. "I'd start thinking about what's broken around the house, how to fix it," he says. "Sometimes I'd actually fix something. Most times I'd just think how to make things. Things just for the drugs. A better pipe. Or trying to make something to hold the pipe in my car, so it only took one hand to operate the lighter and the pipe."

Sometime during his second year of daily use, Li became convinced the DEA had planted a speaker in his brain. "It's like, whatever I'd be doing, the voices would tell me what I was doing," he explains. "Like, they'd be narrating what I would be doing. It would be my thoughts; I'd hear it in somebody else's voice. Or I'd think something, and then the voices would say, 'I heard what you just thought!' It's like they were playing with me. They were always teasing me. *They*. I always say *they*. Sometimes you think it's your friends. Sometimes you think it's undercovers. Then I thought at one point that maybe it was this special agency that helped you get off drugs. I thought maybe my parents paid these people to trip me out so bad that I'd stop using."

Li was fired from his job. For the next two and a half years, he stayed home and smoked ice. When he thinks about that period of time, it's kind of like a movie he saw once, grainy and hazy, a shadow of memories. His parents knew what he was doing behind his closed door. He told them he was smoking ice because he didn't want them to think he was smoking crack—he didn't want them to worry. Since he'd worked for many years and always lived at home, he had a lot of money saved. He spent all of it on ice. He also exhausted a $5,000 line of credit he'd opened to restore an old Mustang he'd bought. He sold the Mustang. He ran his credit cards to the limit with instant cash advances.

"I heard the voices every single damn day for two or three years," Li says. "It was really bugging the shit out of me. The part that bugged me the most was thinking that my thoughts were being read. I actually thought that my parents and my friends could hear what I was thinking. I'd have fights with my parents and I'd say, 'You guys know what I'm thinking!' And they would tell me, 'No, it's just the drugs talking.' And I would refuse to believe it. I'd be like, 'You guys are playing this game with me. Just tell me how you're doing it, and I'll quit.' All my friends noticed I was weird. They said they liked me better when I was straight. I agreed with them. I knew it was true. But what could I say? I liked the drugs."

Six months ago, the voices got so bad Li finally agreed to get help. He stopped smoking, got some medication from a clinic. The voices went away. He got a custodial job. He spent a lot of time thinking about the past six years. Six years he'd done ice. It was like he'd missed this huge chunk of his life. All that time and money flushed down the toilet.

"Then you start thinking of the good times you had with your friends. You wish you could go through it again. You want to reminisce. It doesn't seem like bad memories. You can think of the hard times, but mostly it's only the good times you think of."

He managed to stay straight for three months.

Li raises his pipe and heats the bowl. The smoke swirls; he takes another hit. "I only do it once in a while now," he says. "Like maybe a couple of days a week, but not *every* day. It feels great. It's like a new high. I get the voices, but it's not strong like it used to be. I guess I've learned a lot so I can cope with it better now."

***

Ice is a smokable version of crystal methamphetamine, essentially the same drug as the pep pills and speed of yesteryear, the crank of motorcycle gangs and heartland dopers, the meth of today. What's different is the form: whole crystals; the method of ingestion: smoking; and the purity: about 90 percent. Manufactured with easily purchased, over-the-counter ingredients, ice ranges in color from translucent to milky white to yellowish brown. Fifty dollars buys one-tenth of a gram on the street, in papers or glassine envelopes. Coke sells at fifty dollars for one-half gram, but meth's high lasts much longer. Shipments of ice have been intercepted coming into Hawaii from Taiwan, Hong Kong, Thailand, the Philippines, and Korea, which law-enforcement officials say is the world's major producer. Ice is the fusion of two Asian traditions—smoking drugs and using amphetamines. It is called *shabu* by the Japanese, *hiroppon* by the Koreans, *yaamaa* by the Thais, and *batu* by the Filipinos.

Ice is not a drug that actually gets you "high." It doesn't make you drunk like alcohol or stoned like pot. It doesn't give you a rush, take you on a trip, or even bend reality. In the beginning, before the toxic effects build up, the thing ice does is make you feel bright, awake, and happy. You feel good about yourself, no matter how bad things may be. You can work and produce on ice. You don't care anymore that your job is boring or that your boss is a schmuck. You see the goodness in others. You see your place in the universe and the golden possibilities of things to come. Just a few hits of ice and all is well.

Housewives become superwomen, finding more time and energy to handle kids, job, marital duties, and still have time for themselves. Adolescents say ice makes them feel secure, well adjusted, and better able to express their inner feelings. Truckers, accountants, store clerks, hotel and restaurant workers, data processors, mechanics—mainstream, middle-class Americans—say they do it to help overcome the malaise of daily life, because it helps them accept who they are.

In time, however, the long-term effects of meth begin to kick in. Rick, a maintenance man, heard Samoan war drums and was convinced someone was out to kill him. He turned himself over to the police to avoid assassination. Connie, a messenger, believed her body was covered with bugs. She went so far as to call the health department and have her whole house fumigated. Jack went outside several nights a week and rammed his truck into the trash cans in his driveway. Derek, a data programmer, also thought he had a DEA implant. He used *his* to contact famous men like former General Motors honcho Lee Iacocca for discussions about corporate management. Jasmine, the manager of a fast-food restaurant, spent hours cleaning her kitchen floor with a toothbrush. Tommie, a truck driver, heard voices from random speakers he would pass—the PA system at a used car lot would taunt him.

The radio in his truck would be turned to the off position, but somehow it would still call his name. Auditory hallucinations, so chillingly real.

Ice affects people the way it does because of its similarity to a group of natural chemicals in the brain called sympathomimetic amines. These amines, which include norepinephrine, epinephrine, and dopamine, function as neurotransmitters, the chemical facilitators of human reactions and feelings.

Amphetamines cause the release of these chemicals into the brain and body. The physical effects depend upon the user, the environment, the dose, the purity, and the method of administration. With small doses, users experience increased blood pressure, slower heart rate, and weaker heart contractions. With greater doses, heart rate and force of heart contraction accelerate. Other effects include dilated pupils, light sensitivity, blurred vision, and dry mouth, as well as increased breathing rate and muscle tension.

Users also feel fidgety and anxious. They enjoy repeating simple tasks over and over, like stringing beads, playing darts, cleaning bathroom tiles. In the beginning, before reaching a toxic state, ice users feel euphoric and alert. They feel powerful, confident, uninhibited, impulsive, and horny. Men experience easy and durable erections. Orgasms for both sexes are delayed and intense. Often, users think their performance on the job has improved, and sometimes their ability to carry out simple manual tasks may actually be greater. Usually, improvement is delusional. You just *think* you're doing more. You're manic. You're *into* it.

After a time, the brain becomes flooded with dopamine. The resulting chemical imbalance is the same as noted in the brains of paranoid schizophrenics. In fact, researchers first began understanding schizophrenia when they applied the medical models developed through the study of "speed freaks" in the 1960s. Like schizophrenics, ice addicts can be treated with drugs such as Thorazine and Haldol; some patients continue to hear voices for as long as six months after quitting. As the acute symptoms of addiction set in, the intensity, efficiency, and euphoria vanish. Users need larger and larger doses just to feel well.

Smoking is the fastest method of drug delivery. Inhaled into the lungs, the amphetamine is absorbed immediately into the bloodstream through millions of tiny vessels. The blood then flows into the left side of the heart, where it is pumped into the brain. When injected, the drug travels from the vein through the body, to the right side of the heart, to the lungs, to the left side of the heart, and then to the brain. This way, the drug takes longer to kick in, but users experience a more intense rush. When ice is smoked, there is little or no rush.

Ice may cause the arteries in the heart and brain to shrivel. Pulmonary edema, an excess of fluid in the lungs, has also been seen, as have strokes and cerebral hemorrhages. Early reports show that ice use by pregnant women causes decreased blood flow to the fetus, resulting in underdeveloped limbs, organs, and brain. The long-term effects of ice are not known.

***

Two years ago, before she tried ice, Carol Gomez was twenty-six, married, the mother of three kids. The Hawaiian-born daughter of a hard-working immigrant Filipino stevedore, she'd married at fifteen. When her eldest child reached eleven, Carol was still young. She wanted to start a career. With the support of her husband, a hotel bellman, she got a job at a pizza restaurant. In a year she became assistant manager.

Carol loved her job, but the schedule was hectic. She was working late one night, trying to finish the books, worrying about what her husband was going to say, worrying about who was going to feed and bathe the kids. When her manager came in the office, she told him her predicament. "Try this," he said. "Just take one hit."

Carol remembers: "I was trying to be Superwoman: do the dishes, wash the clothes, raise the kids, go to work, come home, cook dinner, do the paperwork I brought home. So I started hitting the pipe. I felt really productive. I got things done. It was like an answer to everything."

Things went well for six months. Carol was promoted to manager with a salary of $40,000 a year. She worked harder, smoked more.

"We were short-handed, so I started doing all the jobs myself," Carol says. "After a while, the drug started coming into the workplace. Everybody in management was doing it. I got really frustrated with everything. I kept thinking, 'I need that pipe, I need that pipe.' But really, it was making me more confused, more frustrated.

"One thing I noticed about this drug was that it brings out the feelings—the worst part of you. In the beginning, it brings out the best part. But when you have no sleep for four days, your mind and body get out of sync. You can't function. I always had my pipe in my sock. I'd go to the bathroom, take a hit, do more work. I started to get very unorganized. Before, I was very organized, a good delegator. But after a while, my assistant manager had to take hold of me. She'd say, 'Forget this, do that! No, do this! Don't forget that!'

"When you're a manager, you hear everybody's sad story. I started feeling for those sad stories. All my employees were on the stuff. They were having problems with their husbands or wives or boyfriends. I started to counsel them. I would tell them, 'This drug is bad, you should get off of it,' and then I'd go into the bathroom and do another couple hits."

Inevitably, Carol's husband started doing ice. Her brother and sister-in-law moved into her house—they were also using and selling. Everyone they knew was smoking. There was fighting, stealing, hoarding, power play, shifting alliances. Home was a nightmare. One night, Carol called the cops and had her husband arrested. "I got to a point where I wanted to die because nobody heard me," she says. "I wanted my husband to be my friend, to try and listen to me for once. I was crying out for help in the worst way, and at that point, I couldn't even help myself. He couldn't help himself either, but I started blaming him. Blaming everybody but me.

"Then one time, my oldest kid got me real mad, and I gave him one good uppercut—I hit him right in the jaw. I don't even remember the reason. I was so hyped up, you know? I never really listened to what was going on around me. I was just lost in my thoughts, always lost in my own thoughts. This one time my son just did something, and, I don't know, this rage just came out. I plugged him."

That night, filled with remorse, Carol gathered up all the pills in her house and swallowed them. She was ready to die.

"Somehow, by a miracle, I woke up the next morning. The radio was on. The first thing I heard was this, like, public service announcement. *If you have to wake up and hit that pipe, you're an addict.* I heard it, and I got up. I looked at myself in the mirror. It was true, I was an addict. It never really occurred to me before. It just sneaks up on you."

Carol has been clean now for seventy-three days. She got help after another big argument with her husband—he'd threatened to go to court and have the kids taken away.

"A lot of people who do ice are in high-demanding jobs," Carol says. "In society today, so much is expected of you. Ice makes you feel more productive, helps you do things you want to accomplish. That's why people do ice. It makes you an achiever. It's the American way."

***

Ice, or crystal meth, is one of a family of central-nervous-system stimulants called amphetamines. Some sources attribute the discovery of amphetamines to a German scientist in 1887; others to a Japanese in 1919. What is clear is that sometime around the turn of this century, pharmaceutical researchers figured out the chemical structure of the natural substance the brain manufactures to react to stress and synthesized it in the lab. Amphetamines are copies of the brain's natural stimulant.

It wasn't until 1932 that any practical use for amphetamines was discovered. That year, the drug company Smith, Kline and French marketed a Benzedrine inhaler for treatment of lung congestion, asthma, colds, and hay fever. As people discovered the euphoriant effects of Benzedrine, the first abuse of the drug began. By breaking open the inhaler and pouring a soft drink over the drug-impregnated filter paper inside, users could extract the basic amphetamine. The manufacturer soon changed to a different chemical that did not have a stimulant effect on the brain.

Over the next decade, despite isolated instances of abuse, amphetamines became known as a kind of universal tonic. The drug industry developed a list of thirty-nine generally accepted uses for amphetamines, including treatment of schizophrenia; morphine, codeine, and tobacco addiction; heart block; head injury; infantile cerebral palsy; radiation sickness; low blood pressure; sea-sickness; and persistent herpes.

The drug was promoted as nonaddictive. Amphetamine derivatives, such as methamphetamine, were developed in both oral and intravenous preparations. A warning was included with the drug, indicating doses higher than recommended might cause restlessness and sleeplessness. Physicians at the time, according to the literature, were sure there were no significant side effects. In 1937, amphetamines were used in the treatment of hyperactive children, Parkinson's disease, depression, and narcolepsy. When narcolepsy patients reported a loss of appetite, it was discovered amphetamines also worked as an anorexic, an appetite depressant for weight loss.

World War II saw heavy use of amphetamines. According to the National Institute on Drug Abuse, 200 million amphetamine tablets were distributed to U.S. troops during the war to "increase activity in battle and to stave off hunger and sleep," according to a government report. The drug was also distributed by the British and Germans, as well as the Japanese, who also made amphetamines available to industrial workers at home to enhance output. Left after the war with large stores of the drug, Japanese pharmaceutical companies mounted a publicity campaign aimed at the general public, suggesting speed would help ease the sorrow and depression of the lost war. This led to the first documented reports of amphetamine abuse in Asia.

To avoid the need for a prescription in the post-WWII United States, millions of units of amphetamines were still sold by drug companies to shady entrepreneurs in care of post-office boxes. From there, amphetamines found their way into diners, taverns, and gas stations. Known as bennies or pep pills, the were used by college students, athletes, truckers, and housewives, in addition to the thousands of veterans who returned from the war with amphetamine habits. The earliest incidence of intravenous abuse of amphetamines was found among American GIs stationed in Korea and Japan in the early 1950s. The soldiers learned to mix the drug—then called splash—with heroin and inject the combination. This came to be known as a speedball. Over time, all amphetamines became known as speed.

In the early 1960s, doctors in San Francisco began prescribing amphetamine injection for treatment of heroin addiction. Widespread abuse followed as San Francisco pharmacies began selling injectable amphetamines without prescriptions, or with crudely forged prescriptions, or sometimes through bogus telephone orders from users posing as doctors. This era also saw the advent of "scrip-writers," crooked physicians who would write out a script for the right price.

Soon after, federal, state, and local law-enforcement agencies cracked down on speed. Drug companies withdrew their liquid, injectable products from general distribution, though the products remained available to hospitals. To capitalize on the lucrative market abandoned by legitimate producers, illegal meth labs cropped up all over the Bay Area.

The height of 1960s speed abuse began with the Summer of Love, in 1967, when thousands of teenagers left home and thumbed to Haight-Ashbury, looking to get in on a new age of sex, drugs, and rock 'n' roll. At first, pot and LSD were the drugs of choice for the masses of flower children; there was little speed and little violence. As kids arrived in increasing numbers, the original flower children— who saw drugs as a path to love, peace, and mind expansion—were overrun by the newcomers. These new kids were willing to try anything they could get their hands on. The speed labs met the need.

The popularity of speed was abetted, historians say, by the tenor of the anti-marijuana and anti-LSD campaigns that were being mounted at the time by the federal government. So bogusly *Reefer Madness* in tone, the public service announcements made outrageous claims—one ad claimed using LSD would cause chromosome damage, resulting in mutant babies. A study of the Haight in 1967 by two psychiatrists concluded, "The horrible reactions to marijuana and

LSD predicted by various authorities were virtually never seen. The runaways generally took this to mean that all the widely advertised dangers of drugs were establishment lies. This further alienated them from the social structure and made them more willing to experiment with all sorts of chemicals."

The hippie "establishment" launched its own campaign against speed, anchored by the memorable slogan *Speed Kills*. Beat poet Allen Ginsberg told the *L.A. Free Press*, "Let's issue a general declaration to all the underground community, *contra speedamos ex cathedra*. Speed is anti-social, paranoid making, it's a drag, bad for your body, bad for your mind, generally speaking, in the long run uncreative, and it's a plague in the whole dope industry. All the nice gentle dope fiends are getting screwed up by the real horror monster Frankenstein speed freaks who are going around stealing and bad-mouthing everybody."

Despite the work of Ginsberg and anti-speed warnings from the likes of the Beatles, Timothy Leary, and Frank Zappa, the use of amphetamines continued to grow. According to a report by a Canadian commission, the slogan *Speed Kills* "may, paradoxically, have carried more attractive than deterrent power."

***

Buck is seventeen, a tenth-grader. His parents are of Hawaiian descent. Danny is sixteen, a ninth grader. His parents are second-generation Japanese. Well-dressed and handsome, they are sitting at a picnic table under the shade of a banyan tree. Like most teenagers here, they speak with a singsong accent, littering their sentences with pidgin, the local dialect. They sound a little like Jamaicans, little more sing than song.

"Usually when I buy the ice, I buy 200 bucks' worth," Buck is saying. "I buy my whole paycheck, and what I do is break 'em down, make $50 papers. You sell some of the papers, make your profit. Then you get your stash for smoke, and you buy one more."

"Yeah, but some days you smoke the whole stash," Danny says.

"And the next day you're all broke," Buck says. "You're asking your grandparents to borrow money or something."

"You got to get that money," Danny says.

"What happens," Buck says, "is I'm high already, and I want more. I want to amp. I want to have a good one. Don't want to sleep for four, five days, a whole week. So you go to the other side of the island, *brah*. You rob houses. *Boom.* You pawn the stuff, you buy the drugs, you rent one hotel room, you smoke. Or, you know Levi jeans? A friend and I walk in the store, rip off five pairs, *brah*. You walk back in and return them. You don't even need the receipt."

"No *shiiit!*" Danny says.

"Especially around Christmas," Buck says.

"Really?"

"Then you get, like, one eight ball," Buck says, meaning 3.5 grams of ice. "If the three of us were smoking it, it would last one whole day and one night, and till the next day, *brah*, like until twelve o'clock, when you'd be needing more. You'd be scraping the pipe, using the Q-Tip, the piece of metal, anything you can think of to scrape out the pipe to get another hit."

"Drugs is *fucked*, man."

"You be doing it *every* day."

"Every *fucking* day."

"Me and my radio, my six-pack, my pipe," Buck says.

"Everything all set, then you enjoy," Danny says.

"You cruise."

"You call up one *chick*," Danny says. He grins large.

"Let's party," Buck says. He is grinning too.

"And then, when you're up for a couple of days, a week, you can't even move."

"You sit down and phase."

"You can't walk."

"You don't want to do shit," Buck says. "You just want to smoke some more and smoke some more and just stay awake. You want to sit there with a gun and watch the windows."

"You think, 'Fuck this drug. I can quit, I can stop.'" Danny says. "But then you jus' don't want to. You like it too much."

"Everything is drug-related. All you talk about is getting it, dropping it off, getting money, finding a safe place."

"You stop going to school. You neglect your family. It's like you have no morals."

"Just to get that high."

"It's your life, *brah*, and you don't even give a fuck."

Rolling Stone, 1990

KOBE BRYANT DOESN'T WANT YOUR LOVE

Basketball great Kobe Bryant approached his work as an art and as a calling—he was an über-practitioner: a modern warrior able to solve any problem, able to train his way into dominance. Eight days upclose with KB24, Black Mamba, and his *mamacita*, Lady V. With a follow-up written after his tragic death.

The ball traces a high arcing parabola through the air; Kobe Bryant bobs in place on the balls of his feet, holding his pose, frozen for a split second in his brand new, Nike-issue, red-white-and-blue Zoom Kobe II's, size 16, made especially for international competition, his impossibly long, Pilates-sculpted arm, bark brown and moist and smelling of complimentary hotel lotion, still extended overhead like a kid raising his hand in class. The names of his daughters Natalia Diamante and Gianna Maria-Onore—he pronounces them with the proper Italian inflections, the *t* in Natalia more of a hardened *th* sound; the *r* rolled in Maria—are tattooed onto the meat of his right forearm, which is now facing the basket, his wrist still holding its perfect gooseneck follow-through, a gesture at once so strong and so delicate, like something from ballet, and so essential, adding as it does the ball's backward rotation, the shooter's touch, which acts as a damper around the rim, helping to ensure the

9.5-inch-diameter ball will fall with greater frequency through the 18-inch-diameter hole.

A few years ago, Kobe fractured the fourth metacarpal bone of his right hand. He missed the first fifteen games of the season; he used the opportunity to learn to shoot jump shots with his left, which he has since been known to do in games. While it was healing, the finger just adjacent to the break, the ring finger, spent a lot of time taped to his pinkie. In the end, Kobe discovered, his four fingers were no longer evenly spaced; now they were separated, two and two. As a result, his touch on the ball was different, his shooting percentage was down. Studying film, he noticed his shots were rotating slightly to the right.

To correct the flaw—or really, to learn to accommodate this tiny change in his anatomy that had upset the precision of his stroke, honed over countless hours over the course of his twenty-nine years, on countless courts and playgrounds from Italy to Philadelphia to Los Angeles—Kobe spent the summer in the gym, making one hundred thousand shots. That's one hundred thousand shots *made*, he explains: He doesn't practice *taking* shots—he practices *making* them. If you're clear on the difference between the two ideas, on the ramifications of the differing mindsets, you can start drawing a bead on Kobe Bryant, who may well be one of the most misunderstood figures in sports today. It is a tragic misunderstanding, for his sake and for ours. You can blame it on the press. You can blame it on the way the world revolves around fame and money. You can blame it on Kobe himself.

Unbelievably, the youngest-ever all-star in the NBA is about to begin his twelfth season. Lately, somewhat grudgingly, people are beginning to acknowledge him as the greatest all-around player still active in the game, mentioned as a peer of Wilt Chamberlain, Larry Bird, and Michael Jordan. This year, Kobe will make upwards of $45 million from salary, endorsements, and business ventures. He is constantly in the news, usually on the wrong side of public favor as he continues to play for a once glorious team, the Los Angeles Lakers, which is working its way back again into prominence.

Spending five days with Kobe—a dozen hours, really, spread over five days—is to glimpse the life of a highly skilled craftsman. He sees his work as his art, his calling. Like Jason Bourne and James Bond, two of his cinematic heroes, Kobe sees himself as an über-practitioner: a modern warrior able to solve any problem, able to train his way into dominance. He is the self-styled Black Mamba, the name borrowed from the largest venomous snake in Africa, known for its speed, aggression, and striking ability. All those sweaty commercials for Sprite and Nike? Those were his ideas. *Film my workout*, he suggested, *that is the essence of me: the guy who guts it out on every rep.* Kobe's logo, which you will hear more about in the coming years, is called the Sheath. It is drawn to resemble the sheath of a samurai's sword. Like everything in Kobe's life, the logo has symbolic meaning. The sword stands for the raw talent, Kobe explains, the sheath is the package it's kept in—everything you go through, your calluses and your baggage, everything you learn. A man as the sum of his journey.

On the home page of his website, KB24.com, he proclaims: "*Scito hoc super omnia... Tempus neminem non manet... Carpe diem.*" He learned to speak Latin in elementary school in Italy, where he lived from age six to thirteen while his father played pro basketball. "Know this above all else... Fully use every point, moment, and hour you have. Time waits for no man... Seize the day."

He wakes up at 5:30 every morning to work out. He eats five times a day, a special diet, stressing not just the ingredients but the preparation. He studies tape of players around the world, past and present, with the curiosity of a scientist in the lab. (As a kid, he used to study bubble-gum and basketball cards in order to see which moves the players were showcasing and "which of their muscles were firing to make the moves happen.") He can look at a random still photo of himself making a particular shot from a game and tell you exactly when and where and what happened.

Kobe has spent hours at a time chasing tennis balls along the floor, running the same patterns again and again on an empty court to get his cuts right for the triangle offense, running up and down steps, running suicide sprints, running long distance.

After his first season as a pro, 1996, when he was the Laker's sixth man, his summer workouts stressed ways to keep himself mentally involved in the game while he wasn't playing, so he could come off the bench ready to contribute. Before Phil Jackson was even mentioned as a coach he might possibly play for, Kobe contacted Jackson's guru, Tex Winter, the godfather of the triangle offense, just because he was a student of the game and wanted to learn *everything*.

In his first season without Shaq on the Lakers, 2005, Kobe added fifteen pounds of muscle to handle the heavier workload he expected. The summer of 2007, he lost eighteen pounds, partially due to his need to watch his cholesterol (a family history of diabetes and heart disease) and partially to take some strain off his body in general and his knees in particular, which have been operated on several times, including once in Colorado—an ill-fated trip undertaken with life-altering results, more on which later.

According to his specifications, Kobe's shoes have been designed with a special alloy band inside the arch in order to cut hundredths of a second off his reaction time. For the same reason, he's asked Nike to design a sock-and-shoe system for him, maybe something like pro soccer players have. That fraction of a second he loses when his foot slides inside the shoe is the time it takes him to blow by a defender, he says. When he ices his knees, he ices the backs as well as the fronts, something that is usually not done because it takes more time. He has also asked Nike to design a new kind of warm-up that will wick heat way from his knees and thus enhance recovery time; recovery time, he says with conviction, is the most important element of working out.

With one ball and one rebounder, shooting his usual 80 to 90 percent in practice (with no defender), Kobe can make five hundred shots in about sixty minutes. In 2004, as a result of all the practice, all those hundreds of thousands of makes, Kobe scored at least fifty points in four consecutive games and led the league in scoring for the second time. In 2005, he turned in an electrifying eighty-one-point performance at home against Toronto, the second highest total on record, after seven-footer Wilt Chamberlain's hundred-point game (unlike Kobe's, all of Chamberlain's shots came from within fifteen feet of the basket). The reaction to Kobe and his achievements has been puzzling, as it has been since the beginning of his career, when he was voted into the All-Star game as a second-year player (he was the sixth man on the Lakers at the time) and then criticized for inciting an electric duel with the reigning king, Michael Jordan. Perhaps no figure in NBA history has been at once more respected and more reviled than Kobe Bryant.

Now, in the gym, the ball falls perfectly through the center of the iron rim, ripples the bottom of the net with a distinctive, thrilling *swish*. Kobe nods his head once, almost imperceptibly, as if to say, *That's what I'm talkin' about*, an expression he uses with exuberance when he's in private, when something catches his fancy, when something he believes is borne out.

And then there emerges a picture of Kobe Bryant seldom witnessed: his perfect white teeth bared in the large carefree smile of a young man who loves watermelon and those yummy ice cream Kahlua drinks he and his wife had the other night for dessert at the restaurant in Las Vegas before seeing the show *Ka*, and who is lately in love with the Harry Potter series, which he read at a breakneck pace, trying to beat out his wife, the first books he's read since twelfth grade, when he became obsessed with the sci-fi thriller *Ender's Game*, about a specially bred boy-warrior who suffers greatly from isolation and rivalry but triumphs in the end.

***

The doorbell chimes musically. Kobe and his party have arrived, a contained but complex weather system of youthful energy and expensive cologne.

We are in a borrowed suite in the Wynn Tower on the Strip in Las Vegas, where Kobe is playing in a summer tournament with the U.S. National Team, attempting to qualify for the Beijing Olympics. The Wynn is booked solid the entire month with basketball royalty— between the National Team and Michael Jordan's annual Dream Camp, anybody who is anybody is in town. The scene in the exclusive Tower lobby—stone Buddha, mirrored ceiling tiles, seven-foot men on Blackberries, pampered women on overstuffed sofas surrounded by shopping bags—is something to behold.

Leading the way is the bodyguard, Rico, a soft-spoken man of unremarkable size. A former LAPD SWAT team member with a background in martial arts, it is said that Rico (his first name is Cameron; nobody thinks it fits) is trained to hold off a surging crowd long enough for Kobe to flee to safety. In a few days, Kobe will be off on a Nike-sponsored tour of Asia, six cities in seven days, where his apparel sells through at almost twice the normal rate and where surging crowds are actually a threat. Worldwide, Kobe apparel outsells that of all other NBA players: The undisputed fact of his statistical dominance seems to outweigh the perceived negatives of his personal history—the aloofness and selfishness of his earlier career; the Colorado sexual-assault case that was dropped by prosecutors and the civil suit that was settled out of court; his pissing match with America's beloved clown-giant Shaquille O'Neal; his on-again, off-again insistence on being traded from the Lakers.

Jerry Sawyer is Kobe's marketing manager, six foot two with Malcolm X-style black-frame glasses and an enviable collection of vintage sneakers. His father managed boxers; one of them was Leon Spinks. Jerry carries two different communication devices in the pockets of his oversized shorts. He's one of the four pillars of Zambezi Ink, Kobe's mixed-media ad agency. Like record labels owned by rappers, Zambezi is Kobe's attempt to harness the means of production.

Jerry also does a lot of other things for Kobe, from screening press contacts (like me) to dealing with charitable causes, like the After-School All-Stars, an enrichment program for needy kids in L.A., which we visited together one day with the predictable uproar. (Snapshot: a large cooking class of middle-school-aged black and Latina girls learning to make potato salad, wearing hairnets and plastic gloves and holding knives, screeching at the top of their lungs as Kobe makes an entrance.)

Jerry was also charged with the responsibility of making sure Kobe's black-and-white polka-dot polyester sport coat, custom-made for him by Gucci (as are many of his clothes; he sits at the dining room table with his wife and chooses swatches), was pressed and delivered for this photo shoot, which is finally about to happen.

Clutching tight to Kobe's hand is the former Vanessa Urbieta Cornejo Laine, twenty-five, she of the infamous $4 million purple makeup diamond. Kobe met Vanessa—and her mother, who was along as a chaperone—on the set of a video shoot for his rap album, an experiment in cross-marketing that came and went with little fanfare. (Note: Try Googling the lyrics of "K.O.B.E.," performed in duet with the model and TV personality Tyra Banks.)

At the time, Vanessa was still a seventeen-year-old high school junior. Kobe himself was only twenty-one, a four-year veteran of the NBA. (You will recall, perhaps, that he took the pop singer Brandy to his own senior prom.) Criticized early in his career for holding himself separate from his teammates—while they were playing cards, going to clubs, and discussing child-support payments, Kobe was playing pay-per-view Nintendo and ordering room service—Vanessa seemed more his speed. A sheltered Catholic school girl from Orange County, she was as close to her family as he was to his; after residing with his own parents for two years, Kobe had only recently started living on his own. Vanessa had only recently begun booking jobs as a dancer and an extra on videos; she'd been discovered outside a hip-hop concert by a music producer, who'd been struck by her head-swiveling looks. Kobe tells me unabashedly that when he met her, it was love at first sight. They've been together every possible moment since. The first week, he flooded the administrative office at her high school with flowers for her; he'd pick her up after the bell in his black Mercedes, causing a stampede of lookie-loos.

Vanessa's dark beauty and silken, coal-black hair bring to mind the kind of idealized Mexicana frequently seen in tattoos sported by Latino gangbangers. She is known by some as Kobe's Yoko. I have seen her, purring and demure, at Kobe's side in her four-inch heels, her makeup and wardrobe obviously the work of someone with ample time and money on her hands, bringing to mind the image of a tower-kept princess before her mirror, primped to the last eyelash, the last curl, the last bangle. In public, she patiently endures the endless cell-phone pictures taken by all comers—who seem to be lying in wait around every corner, all the time—graciously thanking each person who tells her how beautiful she is: "You're so very kind," she will say, her smile royal and Splenda sweet. "Thank you so very much." And, I have seen her go *off*—like a mother bear, like a cornered cat, like a streetwalker on D.C.'s notorious Fourteenth Street strip, zero to sixty in a snap of her manicured fingers, hurling a string of expletives outside the Lakers' dressing room at a fat guy she perceived had been looking at her daughter in an inappropriate fashion. She might well own the record for the most *motherfuckers* in one sentence.

Kobe calls her *Mamacita*. He holds her hand everywhere they go. Sometimes he speaks to her in Spanish. Later this afternoon, when his fruit plate finally arrives, Kobe will ask her; "*Quieres un poquito de fruta, Mamacita?*" Kobe and Vanessa are teaching their kids Spanish and English. Sometimes, Kobe throws in some Italian, too. He'll say *manga*, for instance, telling them to eat. Natalia, four, known as Nani, will look at him like he's crazy. "You're not saying the *Spanish* word, Daddy," she will chide. Nani, of course, is tall for her age. Kobe's older sister, with whom he is very close, is six two. Kobe's mother, Pam, as long as we're doing this, is five ten.

Kobe's father, Joseph Washington "Jellybean" Bryant, is six nine. A product of Philadelphia and La Salle University, he left college early for the NBA through the "hardship draft," after showing financial need. He was nicknamed for his love of sweets. (He named his son after the pampered Japanese beef: Kobe Bean Bryant.) The rap on Joe is that Kobe didn't get his work ethic from Joe's side of the family. Joe was known as a showboat. He played eight years in the NBA, four with his hometown Philadelphia 76ers, who stuck him under the basket in their old-school, East Coast-style offense. Jellybean thought of himself as more of a Magic Johnson-type playmaker who was being held back from achieving greatness. In Italy, he finally became the player he dreamed of being, high scoring (he had two fifty-plus point games) and beloved; Kobe remembers the fans singing songs about his dad.

When Kobe was a toddler, he'd put on his little Sixers uniform and watch his dad on television. At home in the living room, Kobe would pretend to play in the game, mimicking his dad's moves, taking time-outs for water when the team did. As Kobe got older, he would end up playing for the same Italian club team as his dad, only in a younger division, wearing the exact same game uniform for real. Frequently, Joe would bring Kobe to his own practices. At age eleven, a team from Bologna tried to buy Kobe from his parents, or at least the rights to him. By thirteen, he was beating his dad's teammates in games of one-on-one. Kobe's daughter is athletic, he can already tell. Nani is playing soccer; a game Kobe still loves. (He picked his U.S.A. team number, 10, because it was the number of his favorite soccer players: Pele, Maradona, Ronaldinho.) Usually, when he plays games with Nani—the younger, nicknamed Gigi, is only eighteen months—Kobe lets her win. Occasionally, he goes ahead and beats her at something. He's noticed she plays a lot harder the next time around. His daughters' all-time favorite game is something called Tickle Man. As you might expect, it involves Daddy.

This weekend, with the Tickle Man in Vegas playing his own big boy game and Mamacita here to keep him company, the girls are home in their big house in guard-gated Ocean Ridge, near Newport, California, being watched by Vanessa's mom, Sofia Laine. Vanessa's mom and dad divorced when she was a baby, after which he returned home to his native Baja, Mexico. Sofia and Vanessa moved into her sister's spare room; she went to work as a shipping clerk at an electronics firm. Eventually, she met and married Stephan Laine, eight years her junior, a middle-manager at the firm. That began Vanessa's middle-class upbringing in Orange County.

Not long after Vanessa learned she was pregnant with Kobe's first child, Sofia Laine filed for divorce. Her estranged husband told the L.A. Times Kobe and Vanessa had lavished his wife with so many surprise gifts—a house full of furniture; a Mercedes-Benz S-500; $125,000 in cash; payment of phone, dental, and credit card bills; payoff of their mortgage—he began to fear his wife's respect for him was crumbling. Robert Laine, Stephan's elderly father, told the Times, "All of a sudden, it wasn't 'What does Steve want for dinner?' It was, 'What does Kobe want?'"

In Kobe's estimation, his mother-in-law "is the best. She's a huge sports fan. We can sit down and watch basketball, boxing, football—she loves all that stuff." Kobe and Vanessa have lived in the Newport house since their marriage in 2001. It is not publicly known whether it is still decorated, as was earlier reported, with his *Star Wars* memorabilia and her Disneyana. Presumably, it is big, with a lot of kids' stuff everywhere. The Bryants are proud to say they do not employ a nanny.

After much discussion with the hotel's management, the photographer, Nigel Parry—an affable Brit known for his stunning black-and-white pictures—managed to secure this suite for a photo session. Once the date was set with Kobe's people, Jerry e-mailed *Esquire*'s photo editor, saying Kobe needed to have his own stylist for the shoot and that Vanessa Bryant would fill the role. *Esquire* assented, offering Vanessa its standard $250 payment for stylists. Jerry countered with a request for "a more typical" rate, somewhat higher. After a bit more back-and-forth, a compromise was happily achieved.

Now, upon arriving in the suite and making everyone's acquaintance, Kobe and his crew set about their first order of business: ordering the aforementioned fruit platter. For her part, Vanessa, who has asked to be identified as Lady V in the photo credits, dives right in, voicing her concern with Nigel's choice of black and white for the photos. As it happens, she has picked out a wardrobe of black-and-white clothes—prints on prints, everything custom Gucci, even the lizard-skin shoes—all of it to be dramatically offset by the red paisley on a Neiman Marcus one-hundredth-anniversary tie. "The brown seamless has gotta go, too," she tells Nigel, referring to the backdrop he and his three assistants have so painstakingly raised, the particular shade no doubt an important element of his art. She turns and addresses her husband. She is obviously livid. "Did you know this was going to be black and white?"

For one long moment, the room becomes very still. We all look toward the big man. At six six and 207, Kobe dwarfs most of us by nearly a foot. On the court, however, next to the rest of his U.S.A. teammates—huge specimens like Dwight Howard, six eleven and 265—he appears to be somewhat small and wiry, almost delicate.

Kobe regards his wife intently. "I didn't know that," he says, a neutral tone. "I did not know that."

"It *needs* to be color," she says with conviction. "Otherwise, we can't see the *red* in the tie."

"Can you shoot both?" Kobe asks Nigel. His voice is deep, up from subbasement. The accent is a blend of foreign vowels and put-on Ebonics (he was brought up speaking proper English and Italian in wealthy Italian housing enclaves).

"We can shoot both," Nigel says.

Lady V is not convinced. "You do *have* color, right?"

"Ain't no big deal," Kobe says, sweet but preemptive, raising his chin, exposing the large escarpment of his Adam's apple just beneath. "It's all good," he sings.

And so it is. With help from Vanessa and Jerry, Kobe gets dressed and into a seated position in front of the brown seamless.

Nigel and his assistants go to work. The flash pops, followed by the electric whine of the recharger. Lady V chooses a couch off to the side. I stand next to her, so as to be close. I don't think Nigel likes us being in Kobe's line of sight, and for that I apologize. My first duty is to my audio, the little tape recorder in my hand, sprockets turning.

"That looks really sexy," Lady V says. *Pop. Whine.*

"I only have two facial expressions," Kobe muses. "Smiling Kobe and Intense Kobe."

"Look smack-dead on to me," Nigel says. "Bring your eyes down." *Pop. Whine.*

"Not so fierce," says Vanessa.

"Fierce is good," Nigel says. "I like fierce."

"He's fierce in every photo! A little softer."

"She don't want me to be intense all the time," Kobe explains.

"Yeah, it's the same picture in every magazine," Vanessa says. "And at Nike. I love when he smiles."

"We're changin' it up over at Nike this time around," Kobe tells her. Yesterday, he had a meeting with Nike designers, his player rep, and his agent, Rob Pelinka, who played college ball with the NCAA Division I-champion Michigan Wolverines, on the same team as the Fab Five. (He was open on the wing at the moment Chris

Webber called the fateful illegal time-out, or so the story goes.) At the meeting, they previewed Kobe's new fall line of apparel. Per his suggestion, it had a retro, old-school theme.

"You should see these shirts they made," he tells his wife. "One of 'em looks like it comes with a complimentary *bong!*"

"Yeah?" she says, a little unsure.

"It's got some pink-and-green checkerboard and shit." Big smile—he's actually telling the truth.

"That's it," says Nigel. "That's awesome." *Pop. Whine.* "You *do* have a great smile."

"This is the Kool-Aid smile," Kobe says, adjusting the jellybean-sized ruby he is wearing as a solitaire in his left ear.

"*Awwww,*" Vanessa coos. "That's like the pictures we have at home. I love it when he smiles." The look on her face says she has been smitten all over again by her man.

"By the way," Kobe says, keeping the game going. "They made me a pink tracksuit."

"Oh no, they did *not,*" exclaims Vanessa, her tone straight out of the O.C., her head swivel straight out of Compton.

A deep voice, musically: "Oh yes, they *did.*"

"What *shade* of pink?" she challenges.

"I don't know. Pink. Dusty pink."

"Like mauve? Or like bubble gum?"

"Bubble gum," he declares, enjoying himself. The Nike rep had sold it to him as a manly "dusty-gray-pink." He flashes a huge and untroubled smile.

"That's nice, excellent," Nigel says. "Now: No smile. Intense."

"Like when you're looking at Nani and Gigi," Vanessa says.

"But I can't help smiling when I look at them."

"Like when you're fixing one of their boo-boos."

"That's right," says Nigel. *Pop. Whine.*

"I forgot to tell you," Vanessa says. "Nani spilled some Kool-Aid on the couch today. She told me when I called. She said, 'Mami, I have to tell you something. Grandma gave me Kool-Aid and I spilt it on your couch.'"

Annoyed: "The white couch?"

"My mom says she got it out 'cause she was quick. My mom was like, 'I *told* her not to.' You know, she's not allowed to take any juice in there. But give her credit. Nani told me herself what she did, thank God. I'm like, 'I appreciate your honesty, Nani. Don't do it again.'"

"Man, I wish they were here," Kobe says wistfully. "They'd be running around this whole place. Nani is such a poser," he tells Nigel proudly.

"Yeah?" Nigel asks, a bit distracted. It's easier to take portraits when people aren't talking so much.

"She'll do a million different poses for you," Kobe says.

"That's nice," Nigel says. *Pop. Whine.* "Now, would you mind taking your jacket off?"

"Nope," Kobe says without hesitation.

"Nope," Lady V reiterates.

"Huh?" Nigel asks, taken aback. He looks from Kobe to Lady V and back again.

"No go," confirms Kobe, a command tone. He cuts his eyes to his wife, who nods her head once, as if to say, *That's what I'm talkin' about.*

And then the doorbell chimes musically. The fruit plate has arrived.

***

Two days later in Kobe's suite, the thirtieth floor. Mamacita is gone, whether out shopping or gambling or back home with the girls, it is not for me to know. Kobe drags a barstool over to the living room, where there are two plush sofas and a coffee table, so as not to have to bend his knees so acutely when he sits down. When you're six foot six and chronically suffering pain, low grade or otherwise, the world can be a very cruel place. "Ain't gettin' any younger," he explains.

Yesterday, a Sunday with no scheduled Team U.S.A. practice, Kobe went to the gym and made five hundred shots. With two balls and two rebounders, he managed to do it in one hour, stopping only long enough to chat with Indiana's legendary coach Bobby Knight. They'd never met before; Kobe was overjoyed. By all accounts, Knight also looked like a kid meeting Kobe for the first time. Then last night, in another Tower suite, Kobe spent two hours signing nine hundred autographs for the Upper Deck company—a feat made all the more difficult by the heavy "camera pen" that documents the execution of each numbered signature. (Among the items offered: a limited edition of 124 Kobe-inscribed, laser-engraved basketballs for $699.99 each.) This morning, he was supposed to be up early working out and doing Pilates, but he canceled.

"You get to the point where you learn to listen to your body and make adjustments from there," he explains. He speaks of his physical self in terms of a finely tuned machine, which of course it is.

I sit on the sofa. He is on the barstool. It is awkward; I feel like I'm sitting at the foot of the Lincoln Memorial. I drag another barstool over to the living room. Now I feel like I'm doing a talk show, with Rico the bodyguard as our audience, sitting quietly in a corner. Kobe is warm and chatty. I've been around awhile; he has become accustomed to me—though I was still not allowed to ride in a car with him or to be with him alone or to spend any unstructured time with him at all. But at least now he's *feelin'* me, as they say in the L. The other day, at the photo shoot, by way of jocular greeting, Kobe's big open palm suddenly whipped down from on high and slapped me pretty hard in the solar plexus. "What up, Mikey?" he said playfully. Luckily, I'd reflexively flexed my slightly aging stomach muscles in time to avoid getting the wind knocked out of me. It did throw me back a couple of feet, I won't lie.

For the next ninety minutes, we talk. About how he loves sharks and would like to go down in a shark cage, and how he would like to skydive, both after he retires. How, as an adolescent, he grew so fast he had horrible Osgood-Schlatter disease—it was so bad it hurt when someone even so much as breathed on his knees. How he just bought an Akita to go with his two Pomeranians. How having untrained dogs should be a crime, a form of abuse. How Michael Jordan has become a confidante and how his advice "is like getting advice from that Buddha that sits on top of the mountain, who has everything figured out and passes on some of his knowledge to the next guy who's trying to climb that mountain." How awed he felt one time in Taiwan in this big arena with five thousand screaming kids who had come just to see him run a little clinic. He remembers standing there thinking, *This is weird. This is just insane. I'm goofy. I'm silly. I play basketball.*

We talk about the philosophy of his logo, the Sheath. We talk a bit about baggage, how it's the place you store your energy. We also talk about his image in the league, how he got off to a bad start and never recovered. "When I first came into the NBA," he says, "I was one of the first to come out of high school. I was seventeen years old. At the time the NBA was much more grown-up. It wasn't like now. I was naïve. I thought that when you come into the NBA, you just play basketball all day. The thing I was most excited about was not having to worry anymore about writing papers or doing homework. It was basketball all day, this is awesome.

"The aloofness thing, honestly, I didn't really hear about it until later. A lot of it was just my youth again, because I didn't read the papers. I didn't watch, like, the news. I had no clue what was going on, what people were saying about me. It sounds silly to say, but it's true. And I think because of that, a lot of people looked at it like, 'Woah, he must be arrogant.' But I didn't know what the hell was going on. I had a reporter one day come up to me and ask me about it, you know, 'People think you're arrogant. What's up with that?' And it absolutely just seemed to come out of left field. I was just like, 'What are you talking about?' And he was like, 'Haven't you read the papers?' From that day forward, I started reading the papers."

I ask him about Colorado, about the young woman there, the alleged rape. He starts to say something, and then he stops himself, like maybe he wants to talk but knows he shouldn't. I push him a little bit. He laughs and shakes his head. "I'm not sure I can dive into that one without really *diving* into that one."

"Can you dive into some of it?" I ask.

There is a long silence.

"I . . . uh . . . hum," he says. "I don't know how to touch on that without really sayin'—you know what I'm sayin'?"

What about the whole thing with Shaq, about the whole thing with wanting to be traded for the Lakers?

"If I had to do it all over again, I just never would have said *anything* in the press," he says. "Some things need to remain behind closed doors. Do the fans really need to know everything? Do you need to know everything 'bout what goes on in your neighbor's house? Do you even want to?

"I just want to continue to push. To just become as good as I possibly can be, to see what other aspect of the game I can get better at. It's fun. I just enjoy doing it. When you enjoy doing it, you wanna find out new ways to do it. Like the eighty-one game? I had worked extremely hard the summer before that. That game was a culmination of days and days of hard work. But the most important thing about that game—and I know it's going in the history books and all that—the best thing about that game is it feels good because we won. It was a tough one. We had lost, like, two or three games in a row; it was just a rough patch. And it was my grandfather's birthday, who had passed away not too long ago, and my grandma was at the game, and my wife and daughter were at the game, so it was special, yes. But to me, winning is everything. That's the challenge, the ultimate challenge—how do you get to that elite level as a *group*? Right now, I don't care about points or any of that stuff. It's how do you get to that elite level and remain at that elite level as a unit. What are the things you need to do?

"You have to be open-minded and not be rigid. If you're rigid, that's weakness. All you can do is forget about the bad stuff and then move on. You just kind of roll with it, you just kind of learn. I will not make the same mistakes in the future that I have made in the past. I will make new mistakes, I am sure. And I will learn from them, too. You have to be fluid. Your body changes. As that happens, your moves need to change, your training program needs to change. You have to be able to adapt.

"I am going to work extremely hard. I'm not going to cheat the game. I am going to take all the steps and do all the work necessary. It's like, God blessed me with the ability to do this. I'm not going to shortchange that blessing. I'm going to go out there and do the best that I can every single time."

At that, Kobe excused himself to leave for Vegas's Thomas & Mack arena, a tune-up game for the impending twelve-day international tournament.

Over the coming two weeks, Kobe and his U.S.A. team will outclass all comers, winning by an average of more than thirty points, clinching a berth in the Olympics, earning the once-proud U.S.A. basketball team its first gold medal in international competition in seven years.

And while Kobe will go off for twenty-seven points in the grudge match against Argentina, which won the gold in the last Olympics, throughout the rest of the series, he will distinguish himself with his leadership, his tenacious defense, his artful passing. In every game, he will ask to be assigned to play defense against the opponent's best scorer. He will hold Brazil's NBA standout, Leandro Barbosa, the tournament's leading scorer, to just four points.

Kobe will also be among the leaders in minutes and assists. He will be the heart of Team U.S.A.

That's what I'm talkin' about.

Esquire, 2007

RIP: KOBE BRYANT

**An appreciation written on the night of his tragic
death, January 26, 2020.**

Kobe Bryant spent the greater part of his adult life in one of
the most heavily trafficked areas in the country. He lived
in Orange County and worked in Los Angeles—the Lakers'
practice facility is near the airport; the Staples Center is
downtown.

Sitting in a classic Southern California traffic jam—it has at times
taken me up to three hours to drive the forty-odd miles between
Staples and Kobe's neighborhood—I have often thought wistfully
about owning a helicopter.

Kobe looked at life as a skill set to be mastered, a mountain to
climb, a list of problems to solve. A man who thought: It makes no
sense to waste your life in traffic if you can fly right over.

Kobe was the kind of man who actually got the helicopter. It tells
you everything you need to know.

***

The year I moved to Southern California, 1997, happened to intersect
with Kobe's first season in the league.

As a husband and father of a toddler, with a few career aspirations of my own, I had little time for personal diversions. The
televised Lakers games became my clubhouse and safe haven. I taped
the games on VCR. I opened the old-fashioned newsprint newspaper
on my dining table with relish every morning to the Sports pages,
where I caught up on news and story lines, insider tidbits, and quotes
from the guys.

And Kobe. You just couldn't keep your eyes off him.

Love him or hate him—from the beginning the fans' attitude about him was polarized—Kobe played with an intensity, a focus, a desire for mastery that rose to the level of art. Like a painter or a musician or a writer, he seemed to be in thrall to his creative spirit.

He wanted to be the best at something. He understood in intricate detail how and where he had to push himself.

But for the longest time, he didn't understand other people very well.

And that's why nobody understood him.

***

I first met Kobe in 2007, when I was assigned to write a profile about him for *Esquire*. At that time, he was not the beloved figure whose tragic death we now mourn.

From the beginning, the reaction to Kobe and his achievements was puzzling—or predictable, depending upon your take on human nature. America has always loved an underdog. Kobe was distinctly not that.

Early in his career, Kobe was criticized for holding himself aloof from his teammates. He seemed to have zero sense of humor. When the rest of the team was playing cards or going to clubs—talking about wives and children and alimony—Kobe was more interested in reading *Harry Potter* or studying game tapes, or doing other things befitting a teenager, like going to the prom. He was seen as a selfish player who only thought about himself, whose pursuit of basketball excellence outweighed all else. There were a lot of haters.

An early galvanizing moment was his selection to the All-Star game as a second-year player (he was the sixth man on the Lakers at the time), the youngest player to ever be selected to an All-Star team. Rather than sit back and have some fun among the other stars, like the rest of the players, Kobe decided to make a run for All-Star MVP, inciting an electric duel with the reigning king, Michael Jordan, in a game where nobody usually played any defense. (In the years since, "going for" MVP has become a thing. Just another small way Kobe changed the game.)

Then came 2003, a disheartening season in which he suffered multiple injuries. After flying to Colorado for a secret procedure on his knee, a hotel worker alleged the married superstar choked and raped her. Although criminal charges were dismissed, Kobe offered an apology in which he acknowledged, "I now understand how she feels that she did not consent to this encounter." He eventually settled a civil lawsuit.

At the same time, Kobe's ongoing feud with Shaquille O'Neal, his partner in three NBA championships, led to the decision by Laker management to trade L.A.'s beloved big man in 2004. By the time I met him he was disillusioned with the state of the once-ascendant Lakers. It was reported that he was asking to be traded.

All in all, by the time we met, Kobe had come to a place where he was seen around the league as a one-dimensional basketball machine, a guy who lacked a soul.

***

I spent parts of eight days and nights with Kobe and his wife Vanessa in the summer of 2007, which is a lot for a celebrity profile. I saw him in real time, unguarded in LA and in Las Vegas.

He was 29. Not surprisingly, the man I found was very much different than the one portrayed every day in newspapers and on TV, where a lack of real access and good information has begotten the culture of gross generalizations and nasty adjectival prefixes that renders every celebrity and public figure into a caricature—an exaggerated likeness upon which we tend to base the uninformed personal and moral judgements that we make about the people who are paid large sums to entertain us.

What I found in Kobe was a young man who loved yummy ice cream Kahlúa drinks, soccer, the *Harry Potter* series, and the sci-fi thriller *Ender's Game*, about a boy who suffers greatly from isolation and rivalry but ultimately saves the planet.

Following his fall from grace, Kobe was by all appearances a devoted family man. He called his wife Mamacita, held her hand everywhere they went. The names of his first two daughters, Natalia

Diamante and Gianna Maria-Onore, were tattooed on his right forearm. GiGi, the younger, was 18 months old when I met the girls with Vanessa at a Lakers game. Nani was already tall and into soccer. She called Kobe "Tickle Man," after their favorite game together.

One afternoon, deep into a scheduled interview (one of three in different venues, all chaperoned by his manager), I asked him about the rape allegations. Shifting his long legs uncomfortably, adjusting himself in the tall bar chair he was sitting in, he looked uncomfortable and pushed aside my questions. "I . . . uh . . . hum," he said. "I don't know how to touch on that without really sayin'—you know what I'm sayin'?"

At the time of our visit, I'd been covering crime for nearly thirty years. I *did* know what he was saying: The answer was complicated. It was messy. It was real life. And I would never have the opportunity to conduct truthful interviews with the two people who participated in the actual events that passed between them. So, like everyone else but those two, I would never really be able to characterize what went down in that hotel room. By this time, I was willing to at least put it aside and give him a chance to explain.

I went on to the next question. In the same negative vein—it pained me as fan to do my work as a journalist, but so be it—I asked him about the charges about his difficult personality, his aloofness. Was he even aware how he came off?

He looked at me with a frustrated expression. A face as much disappointed in himself as anything. "The aloofness thing, honestly, I didn't really hear about it until later.

"A lot of it was just naive, because I didn't read the papers. I didn't watch, like, the news. I had no clue what was going on, what people were saying about me. It sounds silly to say, but it's true. And I think because of that, a lot of people looked at it like, 'Woah, he must be arrogant.' But I didn't know what the hell was going on. I had a reporter one day come up to me and ask me about it, you know, 'People think you're arrogant, what's up with that?' And it absolutely just seemed to come out of left field. I was just like, 'What are you talking about?' And he was like, 'Haven't you read the papers?' From that day forward, I started reading the papers."

After he said that, I began to understand him better.

***

The last day we met, Kobe was all smiles—Vanessa liked to call it his Kool-Aid smile, like the cartoon pitcher of sweet drink pictured in the old commercials. That's the Kobe she loves most, she'd said, the guy seen in "the pictures we have at home."

Before the start of our last sit-down interview, I asked him if he'd sign one of his size-14 Kobe-signature Nikes for my son, Miles, whose birthday was coming up in a few weeks. Miles had grown up watching Kobe and the Lakers, sitting on the sofa right next to me. During that time, Miles himself had become something of a ball player; for a while I was his coach, and then his manager, and almost always his driver, provider of food and beverage, and one of his two biggest fans. Basketball was in our blood, just as it was in Kobe's. You don't have to be the best to love a game. Some of my most cherished memories are playing one-on-one with Miles. Our love of Kobe and the game was something we shared, game after game, season after season. It was woven into the fabric of our relationship.

After Kobe signed the shoe, I took it from him reverently and put it safely with my things. Then I turned back to the business of doing our scheduled work.

Kobe held up the other shoe. The Kool-Aid smile. "You want me to sign this for you?" he asked.

***

While his last years in the league were hard to watch, the years that followed were different.

Just as Kobe had remade his body and his shot time and again throughout his career, just as he'd evolved and adapted through the seasons, he did the same in retirement. As we watched, Kobe transformed himself into someone quite different than the young Kobe of old, becoming an Oscar-winning Renaissance man—a doer of good deeds, an unparalleled basketball analyst, an enthusiastic coach of his own children and others', a much-sought-after pro-basketball-player-whisperer. A distinguished new elder statesman for the league, he was eternally a star among the stars.

When the news of Kobe's death first came across the transom—the first thing I saw on my phone was an alert from TMZ—my son and I were driving home from a boys' weekend we'd enjoyed with his best pal, Ziad.

Miles is 25 now. As it happened, the night before, the three of us had watched the Lakers game together as Lebron James surpassed Kobe's NBA scoring record. Kobe's tweet of congratulations was shown during the TV coverage. It was a class move, we agreed, with a certain pride of ownership. Kobe. We knew him when. And thanks to the magic of video, what he did on the court will always be.

As I write this piece, that second shoe, the one he signed for me, is sitting on a shelf here in my office, the place where I have always pursued my own craft. Like Kobe, I have spent a lifetime of effort and dedication trying to be the best I can be. And like Kobe, I have endured my share of ups and downs.

Often, I remember something he told me.

"You have to be open-minded and not be rigid," he said. "If you're rigid, that's weakness. All you can do is forget about the bad stuff and then move on. You just kind of roll with it, you just kind of learn. I will not make the same mistakes in the future that I have made in the past. I will make new mistakes, I am sure. And I will learn from them, too."

The Atlantic.com, 2020

GENERATION H

At twenty-eight, Mark is bored with his music, with his nagging girlfriend, with the whole poseur scene in the funky East Village of New York City. Only his ten-bag-a-day heroin habit is keeping life interesting. He's beginning to start thinking about quitting—again. Maybe this time he'll actually do it.

"**F**ive minutes," lisps the sidewalk diva, a caramel-colored Puerto Rican boy wearing eyeliner and a hooded sweatshirt on a deep-downtown corner of Second Avenue.

"Wait over there." He vogues his loose wrist toward a grimy brick wall riotous with graffiti, his long, varnished fingernail glinting beneath the streetlight, indicating a line of customers waiting to be served, a dozen white kids in their twenties—nose rings and goatees, a couple of rep ties.

"A fuckin' line?" Mark asks, incredulous, annoyed, surveying the group queued up earnestly like ticket holders outside a midnight showing of a foreign film. Mark's eyes are big and blue. His pupils are pinholes. There is a hard kind of beauty to his face, a slight concavity like a model's or a rocker's. He sniffles, blots his nose with a knuckle. He's not sick yet but he feels a little clammy, a little bit ill at ease—the way he always feels when it's getting to be that time. "Gimme a break," Mark implores. He's been copping Hammer brand heroin on this corner for longer than he cares to remember. "I ain't waitin' in no line."

"Then get the fok outta here!" the boy trills, his neck unhinged, his head bobbling from side to side, his tapered finger waggling back and forth, scolding. "And don' lemme see you back here for at least two days!"

For one brief moment, Mark sees himself pummeling the smartass little jerk—a quick right cross, a smashed nose, blood all over that pretty teenage face. Mark may have grown up in the suburbs, he may have been cut from a fresh loaf of white bread, but he's twenty-eight now, he's lived in New York City for six hard years. He's been robbed, evicted, disappointed, shortchanged, jailed. He's walked in on his girlfriend going down on another woman. He's pounded the sodden chest of his best friend, trying to bring him back to life. He snorts ten bags of heroin a day. He doesn't need this shit.

Mark reels away on his heavy boots, his need to cop over-whelming his need for vengeance. He heads up Second Avenue. *What's the world coming to?* he wonders, and then he frowns, thinking what a prosaic thought he's just had, what a cliché. *Christ, I sound like my father.* Mark loves his father; don't get him wrong. It's just that his father is like everyone else. They talk in clichés. They never achieve their great dreams. *Is there nothing new to say?*

Mark has been in this frame of mind lately. It probably began four months ago, when his friend OD'd, taking their band's recording contract to the grave with him. Since then, everything has felt futile and boring: his friends, the clubs, his whole life. Nothing is fulfilling. No one he knows is happy. Everyone seems to have a kind of psychic slash mark bifurcating their lives. Waitress slash sculptor. Bartender slash musician. It's like the whole world is on hold, phone cradled to ear, Muzak playing.

His girlfriend isn't helping any either. She's a secretary slash actress. She has turned into Oprah. She calls him an abuser, a co-dependent, a victim of low self-esteem. She wants him to join some group or to begin seeing someone.

But Mark doesn't need any group. He's not in a group. He's an individual. He can't be classified. *I am not everyone else. I am me.* What does Oprah know? What does his girlfriend know? She became his girlfriend only because they both needed a place to live; the piece of paper holding them together is a joint lease. They've been together for two years, about the duration of his habit.

The night is steeping. It's getting cold. He pulls the collar of his jacket closer to his neck. If he was properly high, he wouldn't even feel the cold, he wouldn't care. He considers his options. *Think.* Seventh Street—the most obvious spot in town, East Village poseurs. Ludlow—the near-fatally hip from Max Fish, the Pink Pony, and the Hat. Clinton and Delancey—the bridge-and-tunnel crowd. Second and Avenue A—young execs at the southeast border of their courage.

Passing a bodega, Mark hears two men in a doorway speaking urgently in Spanish. He brightens, remembering a trip to Spanish Harlem he once made. He went with an older guy, a little field trip, a little dope-fiend anthropology. Uptown, the spots have been the same for forty years. The dope is purer; the people are nicer. There are no lines, not a white face for miles, certainly no earnest young ones with carefully sculpted facial hair. *That's it! Spanish Harlem. I can cop in Spanish Harlem!*

He steps off the curb, raises his hand to hail a taxi. Abruptly, he lowers it. *What am I thinking?* East 117th Street is a $20 cab ride away. You can get two bags for that price, if you can find them. Mark has spent almost $15,000 in the past few months, an inheritance from his grandma. Most of it wasn't on cabs.

What time is it? Only eight? How about Bowery and Third? Mark hangs a left on Second Street. The wind blows, an arctic gust. Trash skitters. Tenements and factory lofts lean in over his head. His pace quickens. He thinks about the book *Junky.* His friends call it the Bible of Dope. Mark has read it four times. In the preface, William S. Burroughs lays down something he calls the junk equation: "Junk is not, like alcohol or weed, a means to increased enjoyment of life. Junk is not a kick. It is a way of life." For a while, Mark had the quote taped to the fridge. His girlfriend ripped it down.

Mark had planned not to be in this position tonight: pockets empty, on a wild-goose chase. He was going to wake up early and see a guy at a record company, then go score some dope. But he ended up sleeping until his girlfriend came home from work and started bitching, and by then it was Friday afternoon—in glitzy office towers all across the city, the work whistles had blown, and all the poseurs and dabblers and weekend warriors were hailing cabs to the kingdom of Somnus.

Every Friday lately, it's the same. Demand outstrips supply; the weight is down, the quality is down. *Wait five minutes,* they tell you. You wait a half hour, standing amid mountains of green plastic garbage bags, each of them with chewed holes in the sides, the entry and exit wounds of foraging rats.

Mark started doing heroin six years ago. Now, to his great inconvenience, dope is de rigueur: the fuel behind the music, the route to the sunken cheeks of the waifish models, the chemical prop in films and clubs, the self-administered antidote to diminished expectations and sensory overload in an era of ennui—180 channels and nothing on, nothing new anyway, and nothing to look forward to. *It's a bitch when something you're into gets cool and everybody starts doing it,* Mark thinks. You find something on your own, you think you're pioneering, living in some rare space. And then you pick your head up one day and it feels like you're in one of those chic clubs, in a bathroom full of mirrors—hundreds of fractured images of yourself, glaring at you from every corner, fading into tiny horizons.

What a time to be young: war, famine, pestilence, plague, all of it in your living room—some of it, quite possibly, in your bed. So much input, so much reference and noise, so much news and film and product. Images and ideas from every era, past and present, rerunning at the same time. No wonder everything seems like one big cliché. This simulcast of greatest hits has rendered history irrelevant. There is no vantage point from which to see the long view. There is no time to understand evolution, the way new things build upon old. It just appears that everything's been done before, that anything you do or say or think is prosaic. Prosaic. Contrivance. Derivative. Cliché. The words of choice among Mark and his friends, these children of the nineties, call them Generation H.

Mark sometimes feels his whole culture, his entire milieu, is beginning to seem like the beer commercial where they bang on the TV and reality gets shuffled. Hip TriBeCa clubs like Don Hill's mix seventies clothes with fifties music, Beat antiauthoritarianism with punk nihilism, grrrls taking back the night by running their own amateur striptease show, standing off in the shadows in their kitschy lingerie, tongue-kissing boys in full drag. Punch the remote. Change the channel. This is what you see: *Dazed and Confused.* Attention deficit disorder. Been there, done that. Why bother. Ho Hum. Fuck it. Kurt Cobain blowing his head off. River Phoenix convulsing on a sidewalk. Kristen Pfaff nodding out in a tub of lukewarm water.

Mark stops at the corner of Bowery and Second Street, rests his hands on his hips, catching his breath. He squints across the intersection, sees some hooded sweatshirts. *Is that them?* He bolts across four lanes of traffic, feinting around a passing car, his stride reminiscent of the high school flanker he was ten years ago. Back then, he surfed and skateboarded and played three varsity sports. He was an alcohol or weed man; drugs were a means to an increased enjoyment of life. But now he has found dope, or it has found him, cozied up and moved in gradually over the course of four casual years, until he woke up one morning two winters ago with the fever chills and diarrhea of a serious habit. Now he understands what Burroughs meant. Junk is not a lark. This is not fun. He's down on himself. Extremely down. He's begun to reevaluate. He's thinking about quitting. Thinking about getting ready to think about quitting. Turning over the possibility. It would be his second try.

Twenty feet from the northwest corner, Mark pulls up, downshifts to a cool saunter, eyeballs the action. Some people hanging around, but no dealers. Nothing happening. *Fuck!*

He squints northeast, across the intersection toward the corner of Third Street. *Is that them?*

He takes off at a run.

***

"Hey, Brian, Brian," Mark repeats into the telephone. "Pick up. Pick up . . ."

Mark rolls his eyes. *He's probably nodded out,* he thinks. Brian prefers shooting up to snorting. Mark did too—for a while. Shooting up is more economical than snorting, you need less dope to get you where you need to go. And when you shoot up, you get an orgasmic rush. But using needles, you also develop abscesses in your arms. They fester and smell. It was all too sordid for Mark. Snorting is cleaner, easier, faster. Yes, it hurts your nose, makes it burn and weep, but it's easy to regulate your dosage, one little snort at a time. There's a lot less chance of dying.

"Gimme a call when you get this," he says glumly into the voice mail, then he tosses the phone onto the bed. Over the headboard hangs an ornate, empty frame he found in the garbage. He calls it his self-portrait. It is Saturday, eleven or so in the evening. Mark's girlfriend is out of town; he has five dime bags stashed in the cavity of his right glove, which is stashed inside of his coat pocket. The night is ripe with potential.

If only he could think of something to do.

He picks up a pen and a pad of paper. "Bored bored bored," he writes, the beginning of a poem, or maybe a song. "Bored beyond belief / Belief beyond bored / Beyond belief / Beyond believing."

Mark works two nights a week, 4:00 p.m. to 4:00 a.m., tending bar in a trendy club. He makes $400 a night. Enough to cover the rent and the expenses. Not enough to keep him busy. Up until his friend died, it looked like their band might make it big and he would never have to bartend again. The group had formed during college: two English majors, an art major, and Mark, econ-poli sci. They weren't great musicians, but they each felt a need to make art, to express things buried inside. They considered themselves artists whose medium was music. For one glorious year, Mark didn't work any job other than music; his band toured the United States and Europe. It was a shoestring kind of deal in small clubs, but hey, it was a tour. Mark felt like a winner that year. Someone who'd defied the odds.

Mark opens his Casio digital phone book, begins scrolling down through the entries. When he got the Casio, he actually sat down and read the directions. You can rig it so it automatically gives the time zone for a specific city. He set it to Santa Fe, where his mom lives. His parents divorced when he was thirteen. She sent him the robe that is being used just now as a window shade. He hasn't seen her in a while. He picks up the phone.

"Scott. You home? Gimme a call when you get this message."

"Hey, Donovan, Don. *Hey!* You there? I'm watching Oil Can Boyd on the tube. Gimme a call."

He sighs and rises from the bed, shuffles out into the living room. It is a third-floor walk-up near Delancey Street, within sight of the

Williamsburg Bridge. Over the past hundred years, his building, his neighborhood, has been occupied in successive waves by European immigrants, gangsters and performers, Beats, hippies, punks, denizens of the rock scene and the art scene, Puerto Ricans, Dominicans. These days, the Lower East Side is a frontier of sorts, a patchwork of renewal and decay, trendiness and squalor. The newest wave is the people like Mark, artsy 20-year-olds, piled together in railroad flats with bunks in the bedrooms and bathtubs in the kitchen.

Mark looks over at his bass guitar, leaning against the wall. He walks over, picks it up, puts it down. He was supposed to have a practice tonight, new people for a new band, but nobody showed. He stands motionless for a few seconds, preoccupied. He starts toward the sofa, then stops, then starts again. He picks up his coat, reaches into the pocket for the glove with his stash.

It's gone!

He wheels around, scans every surface in the room.

Tiny beads of sweat appear at his hairline. He skates on stocking-clad feet across the ruined parquet floor toward the kitchen, looks on the table, the counter, the floor. He opens the refrigerator. He unlocks the front door and peers down the hall.

He rests his head against the cool metal door frame. *Think. Think.*

At last, he finds the glove on the bed, next to the phone, where he left it.

He plops down, exhausted and relieved. He removes the rectangular bags and counts them, *Onetwothreefourfive*. He puts four of the bags back into the cavity of the glove, lays the glove back on the bed. He opens one bag: Rips the heat-sealed plastic with his teeth, spits it onto the floor, unfolds the wax-paper packet, places it on the nightstand. Reaches into his pocket, pulls out a short length of drinking straw, retrieves the open bag. There is a line of white powder along the bottom, about an inch and a half long, a tenth of an inch thick. Dips the straw and snorts. Once in the left nostril, once in the right.

A burn in the nose, a medicinal scent, like a gelatin-cap vitamin from a natural-food store. His heart, his head, his limbs fill with a magnanimous swell of well-being. His body lightens, buoyed by a sudden absence of aches and pains. An odd, tranquil alertness sets in, a sense of being cut loose from the program, of floating in a dreamy place all his own.

Fuck it, fuck it, fuck it, Mark thinks. *Fuck it*. He lights a Camel, lies back on the bed, closes his eyes. His lungs feel wide open. He draws deep; the ember flares. His left arm rises, as if free of gravity, levitating absently in the air above the bed.

Dope is cool, removed, placid, faintly erotic. It is warm and fuzzy, itchy, a little distracted, a few steps off the pace of real time. It acts on the central nervous system, blocking receptors called opioids, which register feelings of pain. By a curious quirk of nature, the shape of the heroin molecule resembles the body's own natural painkillers, the endorphins. When pain is registered—when you burn your finger or break your leg—the brain releases endorphins to ease the hurt, to brighten your humor. Opiates work just like endorphins, though drug use delivers them in greater supply, to greater effect. Over time, however, you get used to the bigger kick. Endorphins alone don't really do it for you anymore. Life becomes even more depressing than before.

It takes your body time to get used to dope. The molecular fit isn't perfect, so it's not very pleasant at first. When a novice first does heroin, you initially feel energized and buzzed. Then you get itchy, and then you don't feel very good, and then, all of a sudden, your head breaks out in a sweat and you vomit copiously, the entire contents of your stomach, usually in projectile fashion. Following that, you remain queasy into the next day. It takes at least twenty-four hours for the drug to clear the system.

Soon you don't vomit anymore. Your body learns how to process the opiates. Food tastes better. Music sounds better. Your thoughts seem to be more interesting. That nagging stiff neck is gone. For six to eight hours, until you need your next fix, everything looks and feels *amazing*. If you are lonely or heartbroken, if your momma didn't love you, if your daddy took liberties, it doesn't seem to matter so much anymore. And sex becomes irrelevant. On dope you can't really get it up, though it feels good to be touched. If you can manage an erection, you get what they call a dope stick: hard for hours with no ability to climax.

High on dope, you have a euphoric feeling of being washed clean, of having intermittent sets of pleasant waves rolling through your arms and legs and dick and head, and then washing away, away, washing away sensation, hurt, memories, leaving just a warm, hollow shell of the semi-present remains of your consciousness, lubricated on every surface with sweet numb.

Most of the heroin on the streets of New York is China White, grown in vast fields controlled by private armies in Myanmar, Thailand, and Laos, an area called the Golden Triangle. China White is brought to America by Chinese middlemen—some independent, some members of gangster triads—and in increasing amounts by Nigerians. The high level of purity has rendered needles unnecessary; it can be snorted or smoked. Seeing new opportunities, Colombian coke cartels began to diversify, planting poppies on the hillsides at home and in Peru and Bolivia. The Afghans, Pakistanis, and Mexicans are also harvesting record quantities. Annual retail sales in the United States are estimated at $10 billion.

Now, in his apartment on this boring Saturday night, a bag of dope melting inside his nasal passages, Mark opens his eyes, spies his notebook computer on the desk. He has been writing a lot lately. A stream-of-consciousness novel has emerged. He is calling it *Only the Stones Remain*. He breaks out another bag, fires up the Mac.

"The tracks run through a cut in a hill. It's very muddy down here, and now I can see the train. If I stay right where I'm standing now, I will be a bug on a windshield. Once I went to a pharmacy to refill a Valium prescription. I wanted to do a mellow bye-bye. The prescription was out of date by two days. If you really want to die, there are too many very effective ways to do it. I guess I wasn't professional or at least serious enough about my career as a non-human.

"You know, it's funny. I talk about suicide and there's a shotgun in my closet. Prozac Nation my epididymis—this is the real nation. The ones who feel, think, know too much and don't want to live in the transition to perfection. I don't feel sorry for myself. I'm just bored to death and Dewar's with what's been left of me. How bad you WANT something is not important. Do you want to be a STAR or do you HAVE to make music, paint, write, act, or whatever? There is a difference. The only way you will ever find success is to know this.

"I hate advice.

"I really hate good advice."

***

On Monday night, Max Fish is filled with regulars, *Cheers* meets *The Twilight Zone*. There's a girl with a platinum crew cut and a tongue stud; a guy with an Elvis ducktail haircut, white leather jacket, and matching white belt; a hippie with muttonchops, a flag sewn over the crotch of his jeans; a Japanese couple wearing huge, multicolored afro wigs.

A guy with a ponytail top knot, the rest of his skull shaved clean, approaches Mark with a buddy in tow, a suit-type in a button-down collar. The ponytail guy screams over the loud music: "How you been? Haven't seen *you* in a while."

Though Ludlow Street is only a few blocks from his place, Mark hasn't been to Max Fish in some time. He's been so scarce lately, in fact, there have been rumors floating around that he died. One idiot even called Mark's father with condolences.

Mark shakes hands with the ponytail guy. The preppy friend turns to the bar, orders beers for all, plus a shot of Cuervo for Mark. Mark kind of knows the ponytail guy, but he has no idea of his name. The three talk music for a while. The two friends were in a band together for a short time during college in Boston. It seems like everyone Mark meets was in a band once. Either that or they're looking to join one. In the verbal style of the day, slumming upper crust, the conversation is peppered with the word *actually*. Actually, the preppy is contemplating a move to New York. Actually, he and the ponytail guy are interested in getting a band going with Mark.

Actually, fuck you, Mark thinks. He feels like wringing their geeky poseur necks. He's only here in the bar because he's looking for someone, this friend of his, a connection. Waiting: another vital component of the junk equation. The talk turns to independent record labels; who's on the bill at CBGB; the latest album review in the new issue of *Pretty Decorating*, an alternative lit-crit tabloid.

There's a lull in the conversation, that inevitable point when you need to excuse yourself and go get another drink. Mark's eyes dance around the room. The other guys follow his lead, look around, too. Then the ponytail guy cuts his eyes to his friend and gets a certain expression on his face, a kind of resolve. He puffs himself up, leans close to Mark. "Hey, uh, listen," he says. "My friend wants to try some dope. You think you can help us cop? We'll buy you a bag or whatever."

Mark looks at the ponytail guy. In the back of the bar, playing pool, are several Dominicans. Everyone in the place knows they are drug dealers. Everyone except these two assholes. Outside the bar, in the shadows up and down the street, are more dealers. Around the corner is a bodega, one of dozens in the vicinity. On the shelves are a few dusty cans of food, some sundries—neither milk nor eggs. Its main business is drugs: Beetlejuice-brand heroin, no-name crack, powdered coke, you name it.

"I'm cleaning out my system right now." Mark says. "I'm going skiing tomorrow—meeting my father and my sister up in Vermont."

"That's cool, man," says the ponytail guy, he laughs awkwardly. "Gotta clean out once in a while. That's what I do."

Mark checks his watch, looks around one more time for his connection. "I gotta go, OK? Try talking to that guy over there. His name is Justin."

Mark finishes the beer in one gulp. Justin owes him twenty bucks. Let *him* deal with these poseur assholes.

***

The truth is, Mark is *actually* going skiing with his dad and sister. That's why he went to Max Fish tonight—to try to find some methadone. He's known about the trip for a month. During that time, he kept promising himself he was going to kick, so he'd be clean by the time the trip started. And then, the next thing he knew, the month was over. He didn't even realize it. He only found out by accident. He was cleaning up the apartment for his girlfriend's return, removing all evidence of his weekend debauchery, when he chanced to flip the pages of his calendar to the right month, the right date. *Holy Fuck! The trip is tomorrow.* It was time for plan B: methadone.

That's the ticket: A few days away from the city, some methadone to help him maintain. . . . Maybe he can even get clean. It seems like a good opportunity. It's really his only choice. He doesn't have enough money right now for a four days' supply of dope to take with him. If he tries to kick cold turkey, he'll be too sick to ski and his family will know everything. Methadone will ease the symptoms.

One place to cop methadone is the clinic on Second Street and Avenue A. You can go early in the morning, find a junkie and buy "spit back," liquid methadone they stand in line for but don't swallow. To Mark, the image of collecting enough spit back for four days is disgusting. Luckily, in the city of New York, there is always another way. Mark knows a guy who gets methadone pills from a guy who gets them from a doctor in East Texas. The problem now is finding him.

Mark walks north on Ludlow, crosses Houston Street, thinking to try the Ace Bar. To be honest, Mark has never *really* wanted to quit before. Yes, he has attempted to quit, but he couldn't imagine *never* doing dope again. Now, he says, he's admitted to himself that he wants to quit. He's ready to admit he has a problem if he *can't* quit.

"In the big picture, I have kind of allotted myself this time to be fucked up. It's taken me six years to get this fucked up. But only lately have I begun to get pissed at myself. I'm at a point where my best friend is dead, I'm out of money, I'm at a crossroads. I am twenty-eight years old. I still have options.

"I hate to admit it, but dope is the best thing in the world. I swear to God, it's like cheating death. I'm a thrill seeker, I guess. I don't want to brag, but I've done a lot of dangerous things. I've surfed big waves in Hawaii. I like to drive fast; I like to run from the cops. I've gotten into a lot of fights in my time with people bigger than me. There must be a subconscious thing about being threatened and having my back up against the wall. Doing dope is like backing yourself up against death. It's the ultimate.

"But then there's the other side. Like when I was still shooting, I went down face-first one time in the bathroom. My girlfriend had to walk me around the living room for two hours. It was so embarrassing. She'll never, ever have any respect for me ever again. In one way, I feel like the closest thing you can have with a person is to reduce yourself to your most vulnerable in front of them. Then they completely know you. But then, on the other hand, it kind of puts you at a disadvantage. They lord it over you. Whatever you say is flawed to them. They can trump you with your weakness.

"For the longest time, doing dope has been a great novelty, but now it's real. I've gone through the money I've allowed myself. I've gone through the time and the people, I've burned the bridges I've allowed myself. Now it's getting serious. I can't afford to be a junkie anymore. This time I'm gonna quit."

***

Home from his ski trip, Mark starts the old Volvo he's borrowed, pulls out into the heavy traffic.

It took Mark four hours and five bars to find his methadone connection. The guy had only eleven pills left. Mark was forced to collect spit back the next morning. Like most black-market products, the methadone came with no directions.

On the drive to Vermont, he did all the dope he had, five bags. The next morning, he started the methadone. He got sick anyway. He snuck out of the condo his dad had rented, found a pay phone, called a friend who'd been in a program. The friend explained it might take a couple of days for the methadone to kick in.

Mark did the best he could. The first two days, he was feverish and had bad diarrhea. He made a valiant effort, skiing with his dad and sis, pretending the runny nose was from the cold, having to dispose of his underwear at one point. (He'd wisely brought along an extra pair to the slopes.) By the third day, Mark was so sick he couldn't ski. His dad made some comments. "What's wrong with Mark?" he asked. "Does he have the flu or is he not getting his medicine?" The way he said *medicine*, Mark felt like a piece of shit. The third day is when most junkies flee back to the streets for a bag. Mark lay in bed, drenched with sweat, chills rippling through his body. His stomach was cramped, his back was knotted. He smashed a fist into the pillow.

Then he remembered the Valium.

He rose, staggered to his suitcase, dug around. He found two ten-milligram Diazepam (*hecho en Mexico*) and swallowed them without water. He lay back down. Gratefully he slept, long and deep.

They say the fourth day is a little easier. Then the fifth day slams you almost as bad as the third. By the sixth, you get hungry. They call it the chucks. You want to eat everything in sight. By the seventh or eighth, you're home free. That's it. Physically, the symptoms subside. Your addiction has passed. Your physical addiction. From there it's a battle with your mind. You have to keep yourself from buying.

On the morning of the fourth day, Mark woke early and packed his bag. He drove home and went directly to the corner with the divas.

Now it is the evening of the fifth day. Settling into a lane in the borrowed Volvo, he takes one hand off the wheel, reaches into his shirt pocket, produces a little rectangular package. He tears the plastic with his teeth, spits it out, unfolds the bag carefully, artfully—like a cardsharp working a poker chip between his fingers.

At a stoplight, he pulls out the straw, looks around, ducks his head, sniffs.

His face ignites—a large toothy smile, the teeth yellow and stained. And then the smile slowly melts. His face becomes a mask of apology, of deprecation, of failure. This was his second attempt at quitting. Strike two.

He makes a right turn, a left, another right. He reaches into his shirt pocket. "I'm gonna do another bag," he says. "I'm just gonna suck 'em down without any remorse or guilt right now. I gave my best effort the last couple of days. I really tried to quit. I got pretty close. Now I deserve a little reward." He snorts again, once on each side. He throws the baggie out the window.

"Part of the whole problem is that you can just rationalize yourself into a corner. Now that I know I can do methadone, that I can get a prescription and I can eventually get off that way, it's giving me another excuse to put off quitting. I don't know—I guess, deep down, I've always been afraid of finding a cure. I don't want to be without it. Heroin is who I am."

He comes to a stoplight and brakes. First Avenue. A light rain is falling. He flips on the wipers, taps his fingers absently to a beat only he can hear.

And then a notion strikes. A large smile crosses his grill. "How about a field trip to Spanish Harlem?"

He turns left, uptown, into the night.

***

At precisely 11:20, same as every morning, Al the Chemist turns the corner at Irvington and heads north on Essex, muttering distractedly to himself. He is a big man, six feet, 240 pounds, in an aged corduroy jacket and dirty high-top tennis shoes. Fifty years old, he has the look of a professor—long gray flyaway hair, thick glasses, a pocket protector full of stuff.

Al stops at an artist's storefront. He rings the buzzer. The door opens. "How you doin'?" he asks.

He crosses the room, settles behind a desk, fishes a white plastic box out of his pants pocket. He puts the box on the desk and opens it, revealing a built-in digital clock and several bags of dope. From his pocket protector, he withdraws a pair of surgical scissors and a Bic pen without the ink cartridge inside. He picks up one bag, turns it to vertical, scissors open the packet. He unfolds the bag, checks the count, flicks it with his middle finger, notes the time. "This will hit me in exactly twelve minutes," he says. He takes one hit in each nostril.

Al sits a while with his eyes closed, his hands in his lap, one folded gently atop the other. Then his eyes pop open.

"Heroin restores normal physiological function for me," he says. "Without heroin, I have no sex drive, I have no desire for food, I have no energy. But when I take a snort of heroin, if you had me wired up and were monitoring all vital signs, you would find that twelve minutes after administration of the drug, all functions return to normal. When I'm under the influence of heroin, I immediately feel twenty years younger. For example, when I turned the corner from Irvington onto Essex, I felt about 70 years old. Ten minutes from now, I will feel about 30. Another bag, and I'll feel about 25."

He takes a deep breath and blows it out, as if he is exhaling the smoke from a cigarette. "I used to inject, but now I just snort. I stopped injecting heroin on December 18 of last year," he says. "That was the day my brother died of an OD.

"See, I came in the kitchen at 3:15 in the morning, and his head was on the table. I thought he was asleep, and I tried to wake him. I managed to get his eyes open, and they flickered a little bit. Then he died in my arms.

"I have no friends and no family. When my brother died, my life essentially came to an end. Technically, my heart was beating, and I seemed to be breathing, but I died on December 18, a Sunday in 1994, at 3:15 a.m. I loved my brother very much. He wasn't just my brother, my step-brother, actually: he was my best friend.

"You have to understand; my brother's death is the pivotal event in my life at this time. You would think that seeing my brother Robert die in my arms would stop me from using drugs. But I love drugs. I've been doing drugs for thirty years. Hard drugs: cocaine, methamphetamines, heroin. I've made my living studying and processing and synthesizing drugs. And doing drugs. I have a Ph.D. in chemistry, you know. And the thing is, since my brother died, I'm desperately lonely. See, he wasn't just my brother; he was my contact with the human race. He was my everything. It's like I've gone through surgery and had my right arm and my leg cut off and right side of my head. That's how I feel, like half of me is missing.

"Now, I have a plan. I'm going to purchase some prescription drugs, a few amphetamines, a few barbiturates, some Ritalin and some Dilaudid. And I'm going to purchase two kilos of heroin. I can get the money. There's a way I know. And I'm going to take my drugs and go into my apartment and clamp the door shut. And I will advise the city, state, and federal government that I'm deceased. See, a kilo would last a normal junkie fifty-four years, but my usage would be somewhat heavier. Plus, I'd like to be able to give some away. Or maybe sell some, if I needed money for food or clothes.

"Hey, let me ask you a small favor if I may. See, I'm very lonely. My friends are all dead. You know, everyone I've ever lived with is dead. If you happen to bump into anyone you think I could be friends with, I have a very broad range of interests: I'm not just a druggie, I'm interested in all phases of American society.

"Maybe some of the dope fiends you're interviewing for this article. Maybe you could introduce me. I mean, I know a couple people in the neighborhood, but I don't really have any friends. I'm sure we'd have stuff in common. I'd appreciate it."

GQ, 1995

THE GOSPEL ACCORDING TO BILL HICKS

Against all odds, Bill Hicks was a comic's comic. A critic's comic. In a class, really, all his own: Three albums, two HBO specials, a BBC special, eleven appearances on Letterman, the subject of a lengthy *New Yorker* profile. The best-known unknown in the business, he was destined for stardom, until tragedy struck.

The comic frees the microphone from its stand, charts a course across the stage, his shadow following. His right hand gropes around nervously inside the pocket of his baggy pants, puddled atop weary moccasins. The cool mesh orb grazes his lips, carries his voice over the crowd.

"Good evening, folks. It's great to be back here in good ol'—where am I again?"

He's joking, of course, sort of. That's what Bill Hicks does. Sort of joke. Sort of tell the truth. He knows perfectly well where he is, the Comedy Corner in West Palm Beach, Florida—black walls, flickering candles, glasses tinkling in the dark. But yes, every club could be the next.

Though Hicks headlines in clubs more than 200 nights a year, he's not on the marquee tonight. This is a special performance. In the back of the club, little sprockets turn, tape rolls. He wants to get this down. The exact set that was canceled.

Four nights ago, on October 1, 1993, he was supposed to appear on *The Late Show with David Letterman*, his twelfth visit to the coveted nightly network show—the mecca for all comedic hopefuls. Hicks had flown to New York and taped his spot at the afternoon performance, like always. And holy shit—he'd murdered it. The audience went wild. They were with him on every beat, falling down dead in the aisles. Even Letterman was pleased—he'd spontaneously gifted Hicks one of his fat Havana cigars.

A few hours later, Hicks was smoking said cigar in his hotel bathtub, steeping in his moment of glory, when the producer phoned.

"We won't be using your set," he said. "The material has too many *hot spots*."

"Hot spots? What the fuck is that?"

"Bill, trust me, you don't understand our audience."

"What—do you grow them on fucking farms?"

Hicks understands audiences. They're full of people. And Hicks has faith in the rest of humanity, a belief that they can handle some comedy material with ideas attached to it, something a little weightier than, "Boy, the food on airplanes sucks, doesn't it!"

So now, four nights later, after kicking up a shitstorm in the press—giving interviews to everyone from Howard Stern to the *Los Angeles Times* about the *censorship* being practiced on *The Late Show*, about the absolute outrage of his cancellation, the cancellation of a *killer* performance—Hicks aims to prove it. He wants to tape the fated set, to play it for as many people as he can. Hence this impromptu performance at the Comedy Corner.

Let the people the judge.

Bill Hicks hunches his shoulders forward as he paces the stage, back and forth, hanging his head, lips kissing the mic. It is hard to catch him all in one frame. The voice shifts from clean to rusty, innocent to foul; from a smooth, lilting tenor to a rasping, asthmatic wheeze. The face is round and rubbery, pixyish, devilish, always in motion, morphing from Sane Man to Goober Dad to Goat Boy to Li'l Willie. His eyes are deep and dark and wizened. They've been like that since birth, friends say, the eyes of a kid who seemed to disembark from the womb with his own special path in mind.

"Don't get me wrong," he says. "I've loved every moment of my 16 years of total anonymity. Every delayed flight. Every Econo-Lodge. Every broken relationship. I loved it all. Playing the Comedy Pouch in Possum Ridge, Ark. Honestly. It's been my treat."

Thirty-two years old, he's been a stand-up since 15; Sam Kinison, the comedy legend, nicknamed him the Little Prince. Three albums, two HBO specials, a special for British Channel 4. Eleven appearances on *Letterman*. The subject of a lengthy *New Yorker* profile by esteemed critic John Lahr, who called him "an exhilarating comic thinker in a renegade class all his own." Described by Len Belzer, dean of syndicated comedy radio, as "the hippest, most intelligent, cutting-edge comic of our day." Recently named Hot Stand-up Comic by *Rolling Stone*. Nominated for his third American Comedy Award.

Bill Hicks: The comics' comic. The critics' comic. In a class, really, all his own.

The best-known unknown in the business.

A man who believes that 100 percent of non-smokers will someday die. That guns really do kill people. That there's something strange about a "Just say no" commercial followed by one for Budweiser. A man who has experienced bodily levitation through the magic of Transcendental Meditation, achieved altered states in an isolation tank, risen on a wave of pure energy into an alien spacecraft, ingested his body weight several times over in psilocybin mushrooms. A man who has come to realize that our true nature as humans is spirit and not body, that we are eternal beings, that God's love is unconditional. "Heaven is here, heaven is now," as he liked to say. "To realize that is to achieve it."

To Hicks, comedy is much more than a form of idle entertainment. He believes the comic has a special role in society—the guy who says "Wait a minute!" as the consensus forms. Like Charlie Chaplin, Lenny Bruce, Mort Sahl, and Richard Pryor, Hicks is the *antithesis* of the mob mentality, a flame like Shiva the Destroyer, as he liked to say, toppling idols, no matter whose they are. A guy who stands to the side and speaks a truth. Who plants seeds.

Who tells dick jokes when the crowd turns cold.

But how much can one man take?

"Okay. Here were go," Hicks says to the audience, breaking the fourth wall. "Here goes the set for Letterman, so . . . Hello! Good evening, folks. As I said, I'm very excited to be here. This is my last live performance. I finally got my own show on TV, entitled *Let's Hunt and Kill Billy Ray Cyrus*. I think it's fairly self-explanatory. We're kicking the whole series off with our M.C. Hammer/Marky Mark/ Vanilla Ice Christmas special.

"You know, I consider myself a fairly open-minded person, but have you heard about these new grade-school books? One's called *Heather Has Two Mommies*. The other one is *Daddy's New Roommate*. I gotta draw the line here and say this is absolutely disgusting. Grotesque.

"I'm talking, of course, about *Daddy's New Roommate*. *Heather Has Two Mommies*, on the other hand, is quite fetching. You know, they *kiss* in Chapter 4! Oooh! Go, mommies, go!. . .

"You know what really bugs me these days? These pro-lifers. You ever look at them?"

A prune face, southern accent: "I'm pro-life."

"Boy, they look it, don't they! They just exude joie de vivre. You just want to hang with them and play Trivial Pursuit all night long. If you're so pro-life, do me a favor: Don't lock arms and block medical clinics, lock arms and block cemeteries!"

"I was in Australia during Easter. They celebrate the same way we do—commemorating the death and resurrection of Jesus by telling our children a giant bunny rabbit left chocolate eggs in the night.

"You know, I've read the Bible. I can't find the words 'bunny' or 'chocolate' anywhere. Where do we get this stuff? No wonder we're so messed up as a race. Like wearing crosses around your neck. Nice sentiment, but do you think, when Jesus comes back, he's really gonna want to look at a cross? Maybe that's why he hasn't shown up yet."

Jesus in Heaven: "I'm not going back, Dad. They're still wearing crosses. They totally missed the point, Dad!"

The audience roars.

"Thank you very much."

Applause. Whistles. Calls for more.

Hicks looks out over his audience. "I appreciate that, folks. Because Friday night, I did that set on *Letterman*. It was canceled because they felt you, the members of the audience, are too stupid to know that all of those things I just said were jokes. This is exactly what's wrong with this country: Networks and politicians kowtowing to special-interest groups, to some guy in a trailer with a fuckin' crayon in his hand, writing in chicken scrawl: *I saw a guy talkin' bad 'bout Jesus on your show. I ain't gonna tune in no mo'.* Come on!

"The truth is, the majority of people are very reasonable. They don't write letters when something offends them on TV. 'Cause reasonable people know that IT'S JUST FUCKIN' TELEVISION! And not only that, reasonable people HAVE A LIFE! They know I was not making fun of Jesus. They know I did not make fun of gays. What I made fun of is the double standard that exists in this fucking country.

"And, you know, the worst thing of all is that I love the *Letterman* show. They've always been very good to—well, to be honest, every single set I've ever done they've de-balled me, okay? And I put up with it because I love Dave Letterman. I'm beginning to realize: I'm in an abusive fuckin' relationship.

"And do you want to know the punch line of this whole story? At the end of the conversation, after he tells me my set has been shit canned, he says this:

"'*Bill, we really love ya. We want you back on in a coupla weeks.*'"

***

In a bedroom in suburban Houston, two boys giggled into a tape recorder.

Ladies and germs, now presenting Bill & Dwight, a.k.a. the Losers:

"We were ugly children. Our mother said that when we were born it reminded her of the time she got over constipation.

"Our parents punished us cruelly. Once, they took away our legs for a week."

Ba-da-bing!

It was the summer of 1975, the height of the oil boom in Houston, home of the largest petroleum companies in America, during a decade when the price of oil would rise from $2 to $40 a barrel. Helicopters hovered over the city's skyline, Rolls-Royces sidled up to lavish postmodern skyscrapers. Only the best in Houston, the "Golden Buckle of the Sunbelt."

West of the city was the Memorial area, an upscale Levittown for the managerial class. Bill Hicks and Dwight Slade, both 12, lived in a subdivision called Nottingham Forest. Maybe 60 percent of the fathers worked for oil companies. Almost everyone was from somewhere else. Hicks had been born in Valdosta, Georgia, and had lived in Florida, Alabama, and New Jersey before arriving here. Dwight had come from Portland, Oregon. The houses in their development were mock Tudors, Colonials, Georgian Taras with columns, all cramped together on quarter-acre lots. The high school, named Stratford, was on Avon Street.

In an era of wild possibilities and great expectations, children were the focus in Nottingham Forest. Mothers rose early each morning to plug in hot curlers for their daughters. Football began with full-contact in the Pee Wee leagues. And everyone went to church on Sunday, no exceptions.

Hicks and Dwight felt as if the clock was always ticking, as if they had to take all the lessons and play on all the teams, or their futures would be ruined. In Hicks's house, there were all sorts of rules he considered stupid. Religious rules, social rules, arbitrary rules. The grass had to be a certain height. Hicks would mow; Mr. Hicks would measure with a tape. All true.

On this July day, Hicks and Dwight's recording studio was Hicks's bedroom, just up the stairs from his parents' room, the door of which was always locked. On Hicks's wall was a single poster of his idol, Woody Allen. Hicks's dad, Jim, was a career manager at General Motors. He and his wife, Mary, hailed from Mississippi. The Hickses didn't consider themselves terribly religious. As his mom said, "We just knew to go and we went." As his dad said, "It's all written down. Jesus was resurrected. There were many people who witnessed it. It's fact."

To get to Hicks's room, you had to pass Hicks's dad, sitting in his chair near the stairs. He'd ask a thousand questions. Meanwhile Mrs. Hicks would try to feed you fruit. She was petite with puffy hair, had a certain tone of voice, high and super friendly. There was a certain tension in the house. You could feel it.

Hicks kept his door locked, too. To escape from the world, he often tied a pillow around his head with a belt. At night, you could hear him typing. Now and then he'd steal silently into the hall and slip a joke under his older brother Steve's bedroom door. There was a sister too, the eldest, Lynn.

Books lined his shelves, were piled on the floor. He always brought a book to dinner. He kept a screwdriver hidden near his bed to pry off the storm screen over the window, his exit onto the roof. To disguise his absence, he'd put a stack of records on the turntable, turn it up loud. Hicks liked Elvis Presley and Kiss, Alice Cooper and B.B. King. Hicks played guitar, too. His teacher said he was a prodigy.

Hicks's prize possession was a 13-inch black-and-white television, which he'd gotten the previous summer. He soon discovered *The Tonight Show*. *Wow!* he thought. *Stand-up comics! These guys get paid for being totally irreverent.*

Soon after Hicks and Dwight met, Hicks showed him the jokes he'd written, hidden in the locked typewriter case beneath his bed. He lent him a book on stand-up comedy. They resolved to become a comedy team.

In truth, Hicks was a little hard to be friends with. He was a great athlete, good at everything he did. Or not just good. He would wipe the floor with you. Without trying, he made you measure yourself against him. It was, in a way, even more maddening that Hicks was so sweet and humble. If you were his friend, he was your biggest fan, too.

The boys patterned themselves after Woody Allen. At first, they thought about calling themselves by their middle names: William Melvin Hicks and Dwight Haldan Slade. Mel & Hal. That their parents could choose such dweeb-y middle names seemed to sum up their entire existences. In the end, they settled on *Bill & Dwight*, *a.k.a. the Losers.* The boys worked on jokes, began creating characters, drawing material from their lives: There was Goober Dad, Dumb Jock, Mumsy, Maharishi, Fatso, and many more.

After honing their routines, the boys decided they needed an agent. They found Universal Entertainment in the Yellow Pages. The agency signed them unseen. The secretary told them to send their 8 x 10 glossies and a tape of their act. The boys rode their bikes eight miles downtown to pose for the pictures. Now, in Hicks's room, they were trying to get something down on tape.

"Finally, we got a part-time job, so our parents were nicer to us. On Fridays and Saturdays, we baby sat four abortions. It was an easy job. The babies didn't make any noise. And we couldn't hurt them inside those little jars . . ."

By Labor Day, the boys had their first gig, a 45-minute spot on the local telecast of the national Jerry Lewis telethon, scheduled for 2:00 A.M.

Hicks's parents immediately refused to let him go.

Dwight didn't even ask his.

Then, in the fall of 1978, when Hicks was in 10th grade, he spotted an article in the paper: The Theatre Workshop in downtown Houston was holding an open-mic night for comics.

By now Hicks and Dwight had started hanging out with Kevin Booth. Kevin was a year older, kind of a pot head, but also a member of the track team. And most important: he had a driver's license.

That Tuesday night, Hicks and Dwight escaped from their bedrooms, met Kevin, and drove to the open mic night at the 200-seat theater. The place sold liquor, so the manager made the kids wait outside for their turn . . .

"Our father's very lazy. He once worked in a mortuary, measuring bodies for tuxedos. But then he was fired. He was accused of having an intimate relationship with a corpse. The family was shocked. We all knew it was purely platonic . . . "

Ten minutes later, the audience was howling, and Bill & Dwight were taking their bows. The manager, Steve Epstein, a comic himself, was riveted, especially by Hicks. The kid's timing was impeccable. The faces. The accents. The characters. He was obviously blessed.

For the next five or six weeks, Tuesday nights became a ritual: the Workshop, followed by a party at the Zipper Lounge, a nearby dive with porno movies and lap-dancing. Word spread. Kids from school started taking dates to see Bill and Dwight. There were lines to get in, old and young, no one was being carded. Inside, the crowd chanted: *Bill and Dwight! Bill and Dwight!*

Home from college one week, Hicks's brother, Steve, went to see him at the Workshop. The kid who'd slipped jokes under his door! Steve was stunned.

So stunned, perhaps, that he thought his parents would be happy to learn that their younger son was a star.

Hicks was grounded.

A few months later, Dwight's family moved to Oregon.

***

Bill Hicks shuffled out into the spotlight, guitar case in one hand, suitcase in the other. This was it, the Comedy Store on Sunset Boulevard.

It was a Monday night in September 1980. Hicks had graduated high school in June. He was 17 and more than six feet tall, still skinny, with a little paunch, still baby-faced, T-shirt too tight in the armpits. Moving across the stage, he played a rube, craning his neck at the sights.

He reached the microphone, dropped his luggage in a slapstick heap. He squinted into the crowd, one hand shielding his eyes.

"Welp," he said, his doofus voice, "I'm here to be a comic."

Soon after Dwight's family moved to Oregon, Hicks's father announced he was being transferred to Little Rock, Ark. Hicks didn't want to go. There were fights. Hicks ended up staying in Houston to finish his senior year. He had the house to himself, the family Cadillac. Kevin came by when he was in town, and their garage band, Stress, would reunite and jam, but that was about it. Hicks went to school every day, then to work at a shoe store. After supper, he went to the library and studied.

At least, that's what he was telling his parents.

He was really going to the Comix Annex, a new room adjoining the Theatre Workshop. Appearing nightly: Bill Hicks.

The very first evening Hicks had gone to the Annex, Sam Kinison was performing. The gnomish former boy preacher from Oklahoma had just begun his career. He had this bit where he'd put a pair of men's bikini briefs over his jeans, sing a song called "I'm Mr. Lonely." He'd go down to the audience, pick a guy in the front row, and by the end of the song, just when he was singing "I'm a lonely soldier," he would throw the guy to the floor and start humping him.

Of course, Hicks was sitting in the front row the first night. Of course, Sam picked him.

Hicks became a regular at the Annex, great friends with Sam. By the end of Hicks's senior year, Sam was exiled from the Annex after a brawl. At the time—spring of 1980—the only true hallowed ground for stand-up was the Improv in New York and the Comedy Store in L.A.

Sam decided to move to L.A. To raise money for his trip, he rented a theater and set up a show called "Comics on the Lam." He hired locals Riley Barber, Carl LaBove, and Bill Hicks, dubbed his quartet "the Texas Outlaw Comics." The special guest was Argus Hamilton, a regular on *The Tonight Show*. Hicks killed that night at the Tower Theatre. Impressed, Hamilton told him that HBO was casting a *Young Comedians* special and that Hicks would be perfect.

Hicks called his parents in Little Rock to tell them he planned to skip college and become a comedian. Both his parents were college graduates, as were their two older children. The battle over Hicks's future was ongoing.

Then, one night when the Hickses were back in town, Hicks invited Sam to dinner. Sam may have been a wild man onstage, but he knew how to talk to church people like Jim and Mary Hicks. He told them Hicks was really funny, that this HBO show thing was a big deal.

The Hickses gave their approval. He could go to L.A. Mr. Hicks arranged for him to pick up a brand-new GM Chevette at a dealership out there. Mrs. Hicks lined up an apartment in Burbank. The Hickses would pay for food and rent.

Though the bit with the suitcase onstage was theater, Hicks actually had taken a cab straight from the airport to the Comedy Store and walked into the reception area carrying his luggage and a guitar.

Mitzi Shore and her husband, Sammy, an old-school comedian, had opened the Store in 1972, and Mitzi had turned it into a three-room comedy circus. For years, it was the only game in town for new talent. Richard Pryor, Andy Kaufman, Robin Williams, Jay Leno, Richard Belzer, and Dave Letterman had all gotten their start here. Now it was time for Bill Hicks . . .

"I grew up in what's called the Memorial area of Houston. It's a well-to-do area. My friends were spoiled. But not me. No, sirree. As a 12-year-old, I wanted a go-cart. When Christmas rolled around, all my friends got go-carts. I got a Webster's college dictionary. *Wooh!* Party! My dad goes, 'Wait a minute, Bill. *Go-cart* is in the dictionary.' 'Yeah, Dad, so is *tightwad*.'"

Mitzi had a booth off to the side of the stage, where she sat in judgment with her coterie. Often, comics would come over and try to distract her when a new act was on. But nothing could cover up the sweet roar of laughter.

The thumb turned up.

***

Hicks became a regular on open-mic nights at the Comedy Store on Sunset and also worked at the club's Westwood venue, where Mitzi sent her second team, including Marsha Warfield, Elayne Boosler and Andrew Dice Clay. Mitzi hired Hicks as a gofer. He shuttled liquor between the clubs and drove the Shores's son, Pauly, to school.

Hicks moved to the Valley, into a tiny efficiency on the second floor of a converted motel, overlooking the courtyard pool, not far from NBC Studios. It was stifling, and he had no air-conditioning. He wrote beneath a wet sheet.

"Well, I finally have my own place, hooray!" he wrote Dwight on Oct. 10, 1980, in his tiny, intense scrawl. The two had kept in close touch since Dwight had moved away.

He went on to outline his goals. First, there was his "always goal, God, please," of improving as a comedian, "ever more funny, original, hilarious, refreshing, creative, lovable, wonderful, perfect." Then there was the movie he and Dwight had conceived, *The Suburbs*.

"Our characters will appeal to people because they are people like us, hating hypocrisy, mixed-up, confused by stupid people, hating school," wrote Hicks. "We can affect movies for generations. We're original, we're hilarious, we've got something here, dammit, don't you see? This is Classic Comedy."

Though the HBO special didn't happen for Hicks, Mitzi put in a good word elsewhere. Within a few weeks, he was cast in a pilot and signed by William Morris.

The half-hour sitcom was called *Bulba* and starred Lyle Waggoner. Hicks played the grit Marine guard at a zany American embassy. The pilot went nowhere.

Dwight arrived in L.A. the next summer. They shared Hicks's tiny apartment, worked on *The Suburbs*, practiced transcendental meditation, became vegetarians. Midway through work on the screenplay, Hicks's agent called. They had a meeting with the head script guy at William Morris in one week.

He was impressed. "You guys are 19 years old? How'd you get into my office?"

Two days later, he got back to them. "You guys are gonna be great screenwriters. I want to see another one and another one, and after that, maybe we'll start talking."

***

Five in the morning in a living room in Austin, the college digs of Kevin Booth and another friend, David Johndrow, an artist and film student, Stress's newest drummer. There were books on the floor, on the couch, on the table, everywhere. The Bible; *Satan's Angels Exposed*; *Listen, America!* by Jerry Falwell; *Upanishads*; *The Autobiography of a Yogi*. In the middle of it all, Hicks and David scribbled furiously in their spiral notebooks.

Down on L.A., Hicks had moved back to Houston in the winter of 1982. By the following spring, the other Outlaws, minus Sam, had also drifted back to Houston, figuring to get more stage time themselves. Hicks's plan was to work at the Comix Annex, see what happened.

Lately, he had been spending a lot of time in Austin, a two-hour drive from Houston. He and David read, cross-referenced, made notes, trying to build new systems of belief. They felt the Church and their parents had run all these programs on them, internal things for keeping people in line, things that made people unhappy. They felt Fundamentalist religion sought to create unhappy bastards, people who never look below the surface of what society tells them is proper. To be creatively free, they believed, you had to be spiritually free.

With Kevin they joined Float to Relax, a flotation-tank enterprise, got into John Lilly, author of *Altered States*. They meditated to a tape of Guru Muk Tadanda. They tied pillows around their heads with belts. They bought books on astrology and did their own charts. They worked on telepathy, trying to send cake ingredients to one another in separate rooms. On a more terrestrial level, they formed ACE Production Company (Absolute Creative Entertainment), later to become Sacred Cow Productions, a collaboration that would last more than 10 years. Stress would record on this label, as would their later band, Marblehead Johnson. They also embarked on a decade-long film project called *Ninja Bachelor Party*. The video, a cult item, is still available in the Southwest.

As time went by, Hicks and David began to realize there are no certain answers to the big questions in the universe. Religions, philosophers, political movements—they were just trying to make sense of something way too big to comprehend. As Hicks once wrote: "No one can give you any answers. There aren't any. You have to discover for yourself. You must learn to navigate the mystery."

Hicks took an apartment in a run-down section of Houston, bought a ferret he named Neil. Soon, he began seeing Laurie Mango.

He'd first spoken to Mango on the last day of 10th grade, when he'd finally gotten enough courage to walk up and tap her on the shoulder.

"Hey, Laurie Mango," he'd said. "How'd you like to go on a big high-school date?"

She laughed. "Sure."

It was a magical date, complete with a trip to a toy store and the purchase of matching rubber giraffes. Laurie's family was from the

Bay Area. She had brown hair, dark eyes, was real smart. Like Hicks, she felt like a lost soul in the suburbs. When Laurie looked at Hicks she saw very intense brown eyes filled with a mixture of pain and amusement. She had the feeling that this guy was not 16. He was more like 130, you know?

Hicks became very close to the Mangos. Mrs. Mango felt that she could talk to Hicks on an adult level. She saw him as an iconoclast, a kid with a strong wind at his back, blowing him away from all he was born into, sailing him into the unknown.

At the end of 11th grade, Laurie began to feel that Hicks was too serious about her. She wanted to go to medical school. "We can still be friends," she'd said.

Now they'd reconnected, they were dating again. It was love. On nights he wasn't working, she'd come over and they'd prop themselves up in bed and Hicks would read to her from *The Princess Bride*. Laurie was in heaven. He cured her bulimia by feeding her ice cream and making love to her. What they had was beyond romance. Mango felt loved by someone with a golden heart.

***

Happy with his personal life, Hicks began struggling with his art. By 1983, he was working the Comix Annex and touring the South, keeping pace with the comedy boom. For a time he worked as a warm-up for Jay Leno, who would later get Hicks his first shot on *Letterman*.

Frequently, after a show, Hicks would go home and cry. "I suck, I'm not going anywhere," he'd tell Laurie. He felt he had gained all this knowledge but didn't know what to do with it. "I can't feel anything," he wrote to Dwight.

One night at the Comix Annex, Hicks approached Steve Epstein. Eppy was a big partier, as were the Outlaws. For many years, Hicks had stayed clear of cigarettes, alcohol, and drugs. He had always been a man on a mission. He never wanted to waste time. But lately, he kept wondering why the real geniuses of comedy—Bruce, Pryor, Carlin, Kinison—had been into drinking and drugs.

"I wanna get drunk," Hicks told Eppy.

Twelve shots of tequila later, Hicks stumbled out of the wings with a cigarette dangling from his rubbery lips. He was in a rage.

"You people, you're the ones responsible for Gary Coleman! You're the reason why *Diff'rent Strokes* is the number-one show on TV!"

Drunk, slurring, Hicks was angrier than anyone had ever seen him. Religion, parents, television, war, fire and brimstone. It was as if the flood of alcohol had broken a dam inside.

Ninety minutes later, he was lying on his back onstage, sweating profusely, screaming into the mic: "You people, you're the reason for war! You stupid fuckin' old people, what the fuck do you care, man, just building up your fucking pensions!"

A woman in front stood up. "I lost a boy in the war," she said, sobbing. "I don't appreciate you criticizing us. We love our country." Hicks crawled to the woman. She had puffy hair. He smiled, a big, fake goober smile. "Listen, lady, maybe I was a little hard, BUT YOU FUCKING PEOPLE . . ."

The woman and her husband walked out. Hicks lay there, ear to the floor, screaming after her: "YOU CUNT! CUNT! *CUUUUUUUUNT!*"

After the show, two Vietnam vets approached to complain. A fight ensued. They broke Hicks's leg.

***

A new Bill Hicks emerged after that night. Patrons would send drinks up onstage, and Hicks would suck them down. He'd rant on and on, something new every night. It was as if he were having a primal experience up there before the audience, chemical group therapy, breaking down his old hurts, metamorphosing onstage.

So it went for the next four years. Alcohol, LSD, mushrooms, cocaine, ecstasy, Quaaludes, Valium, crank, meth—everything in heroic doses. Onstage, he'd lecture, no jokes, just drinking and ranting, chain-smoking, on and on for hours.

On the comedy circuit, he began getting a bad rep. He'd pack his bags for a weeklong date and be back two days later. Still, there were clubs that welcomed him. Owners pressed eight balls of coke into his hand. Hicks's traveling freak show: Wasted Man.

Hicks tripped as often as he could. A strange, physical theme accompanied his trips. It first came up with Kevin and David. Hicks said that when he died they would open him up and find a giant golden cross stuck upside down in one of the organs in his left side. With Laurie one time, he went through a birth experience, recalling the pain of forceps grabbing him on his left side. At other times he envisioned a Bible in there, an alien creature, a spear wound from an earlier life. It was odd, but he never felt the pain any other time.

Soon, Hicks was broke. He and the others were spending hundreds, sometimes $1,000 a week, on drugs. By early January 1986, he was padlocked out of his apartment.

On the periphery of the Outlaw clique was a young wanna-be comic named Jack Mark Wilkes. The night Hicks was locked out, Wilkes gave him shelter. The next day, with Hicks's approval, Wilkes met with the owners of a luxury high-rise apartment building called Houston House.

Though Hicks was having some trouble on the road, he was a big name in Houston. In 1984 he'd done *Letterman* the first time. He'd finally made it—albeit as the bottom act—onto an HBO *Young Comedians* show, which had already launched Andrew Dice Clay. The local papers were writing about him; he was featured on the cover of *Houston* magazine. Wilkes pointed all this out to the management of Houston House, and he promised Hicks would mention the complex in his act.

Wilkes came away with a rent-free apartment on the 22nd floor. It had a balcony, a killer view of the city. When Hicks and Mark moved in, they found a book on the floor. It was called *Making Your Dreams Come True.* "Guess we don't need this," Hicks said.

Mark gave Hicks the only bedroom. Hicks covered the windows with aluminum foil.

Houston House became party central. The core group was Andy Huggins, Eppy, Riley Barber, Ron Shock, a lawyer-comic named John Farnetti, a chef-comic named Jimmy Pineapple. Kevin and David were in and out, as was Laurie, who was now in medical school and seeing less of Hicks. Everyone wore Outlaw black. They drank, did coke, smoked cigars, listened to Frank Sinatra. They had epic parties, lasting days. They hung out and let their egos dream, writing movies in their heads, envisioning a new era when Houston would be known as the Third Coast. They'd convene raucous late-night dinners at favorite restaurants, acting out scenes from *The Godfather*, throwing food. At one bar, after Wilkes had persuaded the management to issue them house credit cards, they ran up a $3,500 tab. To pay it off, they held a show: "The Texas Outlaws Pay Their Bar Tab."

***

Things continued apace until early 1988, when Hicks found himself in a club in Raleigh, North Carolina. As he sat in the green room before his show, a series of well-wishers came by. Every single one was a drug dealer or someone offering drugs.

Is this me now? wondered Hicks. Are these my friends? Is this what I've spent my life for?

He returned home, gave notice at Houston House. He had a lot of work to do.

"Yes, I'm drinking water tonight. It's really amazing how much your fuckin' life can change. Tonight: water. Four years ago: opium. Night and fucking day."

Hicks moved to New York, got an apartment, signed with the first in a series of managers. For the next four years, he would play almost 300 nights annually. The metaphor safari that had been his life in general—and his Outlaw period in particular—had yielded a roomful of trophies and insights, and Hicks worked at breakneck pace to tell the stories, play the characters, share the epiphanies, get his point of view across.

And along the way, he told a few dick jokes.

You gotta play to the whole room.

What he was doing by now wasn't really comedy. Stand-up philosophy, maybe, alloyed with a keen sense of mission, a feeling that his purpose in life was ministering to his audience, his flock. He thought he had found some answers; he thought he had a lot of love to give. Sort of joking, sort of telling the truth: That is how he gave.

A few months after he left Houston, he and Kevin and David collaborated on *Sane Man*, his first video. He released his first album, *Dangerous*, in 1989. Following in quick succession came an HBO special, *One Night Stand*; then the *Ninja Bachelor Party* video; another album, *Relentless*, in 1991, then *Marblehead Johnson*, in 1992; a special on Great Britain's Channel 4, *Revelations*, filmed in January 1993.

Hicks's following grew, especially on the other side of the Atlantic. He mounted two sellout tours of theater venues in England, Scotland, Ireland, and Wales. He won the Critics' Award at the Edinburgh comedy festival. On the streets of London, he was mobbed by fans. He began writing a column for *Scallywag*, the British satire magazine. Channel 4 signed Hicks and another American comic, Fallon Woodland, for a show—Hicks's concept—called *Counts of the Netherworld*.

In America, comedy was in a slump. Though Hicks kept notching the *Letterman* dates, he remained on the periphery, turning down a part in a sitcom as a truck driver, a part as a hospital patient in a movie with Dana Carvey.

During his heavy time on the road, Hicks stayed in touch with his friends by telephone. He talked with Kevin and David and Dwight, who was married by then and doing stand-up in Oregon, and to all the Outlaws, some of whom would follow him into AA, some of whom he got work.

***

In April 1993, Hicks was touring Australia, and the person he was speaking with by phone most often was his new manager, Colleen McGarr. She was based in West Palm Beach and had a partner in L.A., Duncan Strauss.

Colleen had met Hicks when she booked him into the Montreal Comedy Festival, in 1989, and they'd become friends. Colleen was a gregarious Canadian with attentive green eyes, a shock of reddish hair, a quick, throaty laugh. In a way, Hicks had always taken care of himself and nurtured others. But Colleen was also a nurturer. She ministered to Hicks.

Recently, Colleen and Hicks had realized they were in love. In April, calling from Australia, Hicks told Colleen he was feeling weak. He was eating badly, he said, couldn't get used to the food. He had this sort of malaise, he just felt crummy. And there was this pain keeping him up at night, probably just stress or anxiety. A sharp pain in his left side . . .

"Mind if I smoke? You do? Tough. I realize I smoke for only one reason: spite. I hate you non-smokers with all of my little black fucking heart. You obnoxious, self-righteous, whining little fucks.

"Ever seen that commercial Yul Brynner did right before he died? 'I'm Yul Brynner, and I'm dead now because I smoked cigarettes.' Okay. That's pretty scary, but they could have done that with anyone. How about Jim Fixx? Remember the big runner who died while jogging? 'I'm Jim Fixx, and I'm dead now, and I don't know what the fuck happened. I jogged every day, ate nothing but tofu, swam 500 laps every morning. Yul Brynner drank, smoked, and got laid every night of his life. I'm running around a dewy track at dawn, and Yul's passing me on his way home in his big, long limo, cigarette in one hand, drink in the other, two girls blowing him. Where did I go wrong?"

"Yep, they're both dead. But what a corpse you were, Jim—look at the hamstrings on that corpse. Look at the sloppy grin on Yul's corpse!"

***

In mid-June 1993, Hicks was diagnosed with pancreatic cancer. How much time did he have? The doctors couldn't say.

Hicks began chemotherapy, told only his family and Colleen, now his fiancée, of his illness. He continued to tour, with her at his side. He put the finishing touches on his fourth album, *Arizona*

Bay, which included an impressive soundtrack—his guitar, voice, and songs—something new for a comedy album. He started another, *Rant in E Minor*. He started writing a book called *New Beginnings* and wrote a screenplay, *The King's Last Tour*, about Elvis's turning up, having staged his own death. Another movie was in the treatment stage, as was a television show, *Free Press*, a sort of *Northern Exposure* set at an alternative college newspaper.

He had been living in L.A., but now he moved to West Palm Beach to be with Colleen, leaving the bad air and the black clothes behind, giving away everything else, except his Jeep, the first car he'd ever bought himself. (His dad had lobbied for the GM version.)

Hicks was happy with the work he was doing, delighted with his shows, the seamlessness he had finally achieved. All the doors were starting to open. He felt loved and appreciated, completely happy for the first time in his life. Like that book from the day he'd moved into Houston House. *Making Your Dreams Come True.*

The *Letterman* censorship incident was picked up by the press. Then *The New Yorker* published the lengthy tribute by John Lahr. *The Nation* called and asked him to write a regular column. Four publishers began bidding on his book.

It was not to be.

***

In the end, Hicks went home.

In January 1994, he moved into the room of his parents' house in Little Rock that was always meant for him. He was losing weight, growing weaker, in pain, but the mind was fine. He turned his mother on to *Course in Miracles*; he played her Elvis, John Hiatt, Miles Davis; showed her documentaries on Jimi Hendrix and the Beatles; burned incense and explained the *Tibetan Book of the Dead*. He told her death would be his greatest adventure. That he was like a drop of water reuniting with the ocean. He sat on the back deck and talked to his dad about the lawn, about the trees and the crickets, about the year's new line of cars from GM. And he tried to get Jim Hicks to take mushrooms. He bet Steve $500 that Dad would do it. Mr. Hicks asked a lot of questions and took it under consideration.

Hicks set about reading *Huckleberry Finn* again, then went to work on *The Hobbit*. He spent a lot of time with Steve, who shared his memories of their youth, dragged out photo albums, pictures of the Hickses and their cousins at the family farm back in Leakesville, Miss.

Hicks called all the friends he'd ever had—gave his advice, said his goodbyes. On Valentine's Day, 1994, he finally got in touch with Laurie Mango, now a pathologist in New York.

Then he stopped speaking.

"I've said all I have to say," Hicks told Colleen and his family. Though he lived for two more weeks, walking around the house, going for drives with Steve or his folks, those were his last words.

He died at 11:20 p.m. on Feb. 26.

***

At his own request, William Melvin Hicks was buried in the Hicks family plot in Leakesville. Five months later, following a special, hour-long documentary on Great Britain's Channel 4 and on Comedy Central, following live tributes in Houston, San Francisco, and New York, Colleen and Hicks's family signed with Zoo Records to release *Rant in E Minor* and *Arizona Bay*. His film and TV projects are also being shopped . . .

"Here is my final point. About drugs, about alcohol, about pornography, and smoking, and everything else. What business is it of yours what I do, read, buy, see, say, think, who I fuck, what I take into my body—as long as I do not harm another human being on this planet? I'm not scary. I'm basically just a joke-blower. That's basically all I am, a joke-blower on the back of some Mexican gardener, blowing jokes all over the driveway, a fairly harmless guy, believer in love and truth, antiwar, believer in the values under which this country was originally founded: FREEDOM OF FUCKING EXPRESSION.

"And for those of you out there who are having a little moral dilemma in your head about this, I'll answer it for you. IT'S NONE OF YOUR FUCKING BUSINESS!

"Take that to the bank, cash it, and take it on a fucking vacation out of everybody's life."

GQ, 1994

THAILAND'S HOME FOR WAYWARD VETS

After fighting in Vietnam, unwilling to return to America, these vets put down stakes in a place they thought would be better than home. From the sex bars of Bangkok, to the blood-red sunsets over the Mekong River, to VFW Post 10249 in Udon Thani—what happens when you follow that wild hair to the end of the earth.

The mouth at the bar is John Murdock—chopper pilot, sandwich maker, tennis pro with one student, a resident alien of Thailand, with corkscrews of chest hair and a gift for the grandiose. He's poking a hole in the air with his finger, and his quarter-pound Rolex is flashing, and his blue eyes are flaring, and if you didn't know he was in a bar in Patpong, in Bangkok, bathed in neon and reeking of beer, you'd be sure he was back in Vietnam in '68, Lieutenant Murdock, *Lieutenant Cocksure*, driving his U.S. Army Cobra down hard on a tree line, firing bursts of obscenities at some *gooks*.

"C'mon puss wad. I'll spot you thirty-love, two-to-one odds, and I'll still wipe your ass all over the court."

What he's doing is challenging Paul Jones, a British deep-sea diver, to a simple game of tennis. 'Nam comes up later, of course, after a few more Singha beers. Right now, the rap is all about green ones and red ones and purple ones, preferably purple ones, 500-*baht* notes, worth about twenty-five dollars each. Scam as art, art as life, life as "survival of the fittest, or it's on skid row for the kid," as Murdock likes to say in his too-tight smile in his eighth month without a proper job.

But not without a plan. So what if no one's hiring chopper pilots at the moment? When you decide, as Murdock has, that there's a place to live that's better than America, you hustle to make sure it doesn't blow back in your face. Sure, he can always go home to the farm in Pomfret, Connecticut. But when you're thirty-eight years old and you've been in the States for only two weeks in the past ten years—when you've been telling everyone you ever knew that life in Thailand is a piece of cake for a vet, nothing like back in the States—you don't just show up at the airport one day with your trunk. No way. *You gotta make plans, see. You use your head, you understand? You make it work.* You sell sandwiches here at the Grand Prix bar on Saturdays—you talk about finding investors, expanding into weekdays and burgers. You hear that a hotel chain is looking for tennis pros. *Shazam!* You become a tennis pro, so utterly convinced of your own prowess you're ready to play anyone who'll put his *baht* where your mouth is. *Hey, I'm thinking of the future. I'm trying to make some money here. You can make a million bucks if you got the right angle. I can do anything. Anything, you understand? You just gotta line up the suckers and let it roll.*

"C'mon," he taunts, poking the finger again toward Jones. His tight, nasal, Connecticut Yankee honk rises an octave with the challenge. "You said you've been takin' lessons, right? One thousand *baht*. Two purple ones. C'mon, ya lousy limey, ya queen-mother lover."

Jones is watching the video screen sunk into the wall above them, the 9:00 p.m. showing of *Dirty Harry*. Jones has a steady job. He makes *beaucoup* bucks. He doesn't give a shit about Murdock's challenges and schemes. He turns his head, back to the video, takes a slug of his beer. *Fuckin' Murdock*, he thinks. *Somebody needs to shut him down before he crash lands.*

Behind the bar, the owner of the Grand Prix shakes his head, an expression of mock pity. Rick Menard is a stocky ex-Army aircraft mechanic with a patch over one eye from cataract surgery. He looks contentedly bored, polishing a glass, watching three of his Thai go-go girls dancing on the stage, meanwhile daydreaming about the kind of kitchen cabinets he's going to order for his new, two million-*baht* condo. Sex sells in Bangkok, the most aptly named city in the world; Menard is one of the ones making trips to the bank. The girls range from cream to mocha, with ebony hair and a certain perplexed innocence in their eyes, spangled bikinis on their boyish little bodies. They dance to a Michael Jackson tune, humping in the back-beat with half a heart.

Next to Jones is another Viet vet; he says his name is Hamber Moody. He's on leave from his electronics job in Saudi Arabia. Black and lanky with a goatee, he goes on about "sand niggers," his exorbitant overtime pay, his growing savings account, his myriad "bitches." Next to him is a retired Air Force pilot, laying over in Bangkok on his way home to Tulsa. He also works in Saudi. One of the bar girls has her rump dug meaningfully into his crotch. The button pinned on her left bikini cup identifies her as Number 12.

The group sits together along the rail, not too far from the shithouse. Once upon a time, a man could get a blow job while taking a dump in any bar in Bangkok, or so they say. You can probably get one in the Grand Prix, too, but you'd have to arrange it yourself—there are no girls on permanent station in the loo. Then again, if that's what you really wanted, you'd probably have no trouble finding it within a short distance. This, after all, is Patpong—three square blocks of skin and sin, joints like the Pink Pig, the African Queen, the Sexy Bar.

The night streets are nuts to butts with *farangs*—the derogatory Thai term for white folk—strutting and gaping, hunting for beer and pussy, man's most essential needs. There are girls on high chairs outside the doors of musky bars; wooden racks of American cigarettes; food vendors in bamboo hats with carts full of bubbling pots of mystery food; ragamuffins begging for one *baht*, selling flowers, asking for bonbons; little old Thai men hustling, imploring, handing out show bills for featured performances of the Pussy Smoke Cigarette Show, the Pussy Write Letter Show, the Pussy Drink Beer Show.

Tinsel streamers on the lampposts, hot chili peppers, thumping disco, and nonchalant lust in the air, a lawless tide of scooters and minicars and motor rickshaws on the narrow streets—a place where any man, no matter how old or fat or pockmarked, can be Hugh Hefner for an evening, as long as he has a couple of purple ones in his pocket. There may be loneliness in Bangkok, but no one is ever alone.

This is the nightly haunt of John Murdock and the Patpong Commandos, as the local *Soldier of Fortune* magazine correspondent likes to call the regulars. The U.S. Defense Department says there are 1,100 Vietnam-era veterans residing in Thailand. Patpong is their headquarters. Here is where you drink until your face goes numb, here you find your love object of the evening. Here is your frat house, your locker room, your Elks club—Bangkok's home for wayward vets.

Here are the regulars—Murdock, Menard, and Al Dawson, news editor for the *Bangkok Post*, an Army vet who stayed on with UPI news service after his hitch. Jack Shirley is part-owner of the Tavern, another bar around the corner. Shirley says he worked, before retiring, as a "special adviser" to the governments of Thailand, Laos, and Vietnam, "attached to the U.S. Defense Department." Shirley's friend, Tony Poe, comes down occasionally from his tapioca farm. A former CIA man, Poe is said to have walked every mile of Laos on foot, to have killed uncounted numbers with his bare hands, the right of which is missing two fingers, lost in some unspeakable way. A guy called Book says he's a former Navy SEAL. A huge man, with legs as wide as an average man's waist, he is said to have bitten off a guy's ear in a bar fight. "Then he spit it out on the floor and walked back to his stool like nothing had happened," Murdock says. Lurch is ex-Special Forces. One night, the record on the jukebox started to skip. "He pulled out a .38 and drilled the fucker six times," recalls Menard, who didn't bother handing him a bill for repairs.

L.T. "Cowboy" Edwards, retired Air Force sergeant, also hangs now and then, though mostly you'll find him in the New Loretta Café, his own bar across town on Sukhumvit Road, downing his daily ration of two six-packs of beer and two fifths of Johnnie Walker Black. Not too far from the Loretta is Soi Cowboy, a street named in Edwards' honor. Edwards likes to point out that only two other Westerners have ever been so distinguished: Red Cross founder Henri Dunant and country singer Bobby Dee. On Soi Cowboy you can find another regular, retired Air Force sergeant Josh Gaines, proprietor of J's Soul Food, purveyor of the finest fried chicken and salt pork and chitlins this side of North Carolina.

Farther upcountry, in the lush flatlands to the north, retired Air Force intelligence sergeant Doug Martin lives in a tiny and isolated village, a rice farmer with ten acres of paddy, two water buffalo, a Thai wife, and three kids. Father John Tabor, a former Navy Seabee, remained in South Vietnam after his hitch to study for the Catholic priesthood. He fled the country in 1978, after being imprisoned by the communists for six months, and came to Thailand to work in refugee camps along the border. In Udonthani, 300 miles north of Bangkok, VFW Post 10249 boasts eighty members, a group of whom shows up every day to burp and fart and drink one another under the table before the sun goes down.

"Why do we stay?" repeats John Murdock, incredulous, super-animated as always, swilling another Singha beer. "It's the night life. It's the food, the climate, the lovely, lovely ladies. You gotta understand. 'Nam was a big fuckin' high. You remember what it was like. You don't want to live without that charge. You want to have something of that left. In some ways, living here, I still got it. I've stayed in the same line of work—flying choppers. I stayed in the same part of the world. 'Nam sucked, sure. But what a lot of people don't talk about is how much fun it was, too. There was a lot of good times with the bad, like when we were laying back in the hooch, drinking like hell, going downtown, sneaking out of the compound—'cause we had a little house of ill repute around the corner. Here we are. We're still in Southeast Asia—"

"We're just not in the army no more," Menard adds.

"We're not restricted within certain confines of what they call respectable behavior at home," Murdock says with a wink.

So what if Murdock sometimes hungers for a Big Mac or if Dawson would love a thick, juicy cut of prime rib? Or if Doug Martin, the rice farmer, can't plow his fields himself because his water buffalo doesn't like his smell, or if, after eleven years of marriage, he still can't get his Thai wife to sit down to dinner with him? And so what if *Monday Night Football* doesn't get to the Bangkok VFW post until three weeks later on a Thursday, or if the willing and seemingly demure Thai women have a scary reputation for taking razors to penises in fits of jealous rage? It is a fact that Bangkok boasts the world's most advanced penis reattachment clinic. So what if Menard felt like an idiot on his last visit to the States? Is it his fault a kid had to explain to him that the faucets in the bathroom at JFK airport turned off automatically? So what if Harry Reid, commander of the VFW post in Udonthani, where he plans to live until he dies, doesn't really like the Thai people he has to be around every single day, including his own wife?

Life isn't exactly perfect. So what? Whose life is? You think the guy on Long Island likes commuting into New York? You think the tractor doesn't break down in Bucksnort, Tennessee? Everybody's got his load to bear. At least it's cheaper here. At least there's opportunity. Where else but Thailand, asks Menard, could a high-school dropout aircraft mechanic purchase himself a two million-*baht* condo? Where else but Thailand, asks Josh Gaines, could the son of a mechanic and a maid have the one-and-only soul-food emporium in the entire country? Even Cowboy, a man with a healthy ego, has to admit that the chance of having a street in the States named after him would probably be slim. (He readily admits that only in Thailand could he divorce nine wives without paying a cent of alimony.) Where else but Thailand could Murdock have afforded a full-time servant on a sandwich maker's salary? Or purchase potent Thai stick at the equivalent of $100 a kilo? Where else would Harry Reid have rise to the rank of commander of his VFW post? Back in Columbus, Ohio, he settled for the number-three spot on his bowling team.

"For various reasons," Dawson says, "a lot of people here are doing much better than they could have ever dreamed in the States. Some of them aren't smart enough, some wouldn't have had enough money, or a combination of both. Some are not as frightened to try something bold in a country like Thailand. There's a bit of racism involved, maybe, a natural feeling of superiority between themselves and the little brown people running around.... Sure, there are some hard-luck stories. There's probably a good bit of escapism, too. But basically, it's a bunch of guys over here who think they just might have found a better way."

Welcome to Thailand—last frontier of the American Dream.

At least for some.

***

It was late 1966 when Doug Martin returned to the States from his first stint in Vietnam. Boy, was he ever glad to get home. He knew the war was lost before it started. He says he remembers being at a briefing in Saigon where Secretary of Defense Robert McNamara suggested the United States collect all its junk cars, ship them to south Vietnam, and pile them up along the northern border. *Enough of this bullshit*, Martin thought. It was time for family and a regular job—a normal life.

But when he got home to Long Beach, California, his wife and kids were gone. No note, nothing. Just gone. His wife had always been a runner, that he knew. But to leave him with an empty house— the way his knock had echoed; he will never forget the wrenching hollowness of that sound. "She left me at a time when I really needed her. I was coming home from war, I was determined we were going to make a go of it. I was looking forward to being part of a family again. It was all gone. I lost twelve years of marriage, my home, my wife, my children, my car, my clothes. Everything. It was worse than losing a leg.

"I don't know why, but as I was standing there in the empty living room, the first thought that came into my mind was I wanted to go back to Southeast Asia. Maybe I had a death wish. I didn't think about it. I re-enlisted."

Martin went back to Vietnam, and then to Texas and to Hawaii. In 1973, he was assigned to Rammasson Air Force Base, a huge facility in Udon Thani, Thailand, from which a great proportion of the heavy air strikes of the Vietnam War had originated. By this time, Martin had been in the service since 1953, when he'd run away from his doting mother and the family's resort lodge in upstate New York. Now he'd done his twenty. He was ready to go back to the States, maybe find a new wife, start a new family—try again.

Then his house girl announced she was pregnant. Martin was suspicious of the timing, but he decided to marry her anyway. Sumlee cooked pretty well, she didn't talk back, she kept the apartment clean. She *seemed* to be in love with him. He was forty and she was twenty, a good-looking girl for a middle-aged man. Why go home and start searching? He decided to stay in Thailand.

Udon in 1974 was bustling. Thirty thousand Americans, cheap outdoor restaurants on every sidewalk. There must have been 200 bars and clubs catering to GIs, and scores of hotels, with names like the 69 and the Coconut, which had vibrating beds and fountains and mirrored ceilings in every room. An American could have anything he wanted in Udon, from a ten-year-old virgin to a hamburger pizza. At its peak, GIs were said to be spending upwards of $400,000 a day in Udon, and some small part of that cash was going to Doug Martin, who was walking door to door in his brand new civilian suit, selling *Encyclopedia Britannica.*

Soon, Martin moved into selling Chrysler automobiles. He sold the cars to GIs, white-walls gratis, ready for pickup from the factory as soon as they got back stateside. When the Americans pulled out of Vietnam in 1975, Martin's business went with them. Next he tried a catalog export business, only to be bilked by his partner, who turned out to be a "gay crook," Martin recalls. He wandered through some consulting jobs and more crooked partners. In Bangkok he set up a travel agency in the back of a bar. His partner was a guy the Patpong regulars remember as Nick, a retired Army master sergeant who'd enlisted during World War II in lieu of serving a murder sentence. Martin and Nick did well, specializing in discount airline tickets, illegal tiger hunts in India, visa extensions, things like that. Then the business was lost. Martin is vague on the details. Around Patpong, they say it had to do with the law.

Today, Martin farms ten acres of rice paddy in a tiny village called Nongkhai, his wife's ancestral home, about eight hours northeast of Bangkok.

He is a graceful, kindly man with polished fingernails—imagine Felix Unger gone native, wearing a straw hat and drawstring pajama pants. He lives with his family in a green cinder-block house with a tin roof and a porcelain hole in the floor for a toilet, on a narrow lane of deep sand, rutted with ox-cart tracks, shaded by tall palms. During the day, children laugh and play everywhere in the village— there go four of them now, all under ten years old, riding together on the back of a water buffalo, a pair of pre-teens attending. Chickens and ducks are everywhere underfoot.

By night, the air outside his house is cool, alive with the chirps of bugs and the stirrings of the family's animals. A musical kite flies from the Buddhist temple, a talisman against lurking spirits. Inside Martin's house, the village's only refrigerator is humming, its only twenty-six-inch television is blazing Technicolor. A dozen women have gathered at the threshold of the open first-floor of the house to watch the latest installation of their favorite Thai soap opera. The three Martin children play Monopoly with some neighbors in the middle of the cement floor. All the villagers call Martin "Daddy."

Martin would love to make some changes in the village—if only the villagers would listen; they're kind of set in their stone-age ways. For instance, he's trying to convince the other farmers to grow hay instead of having to climb trees and hack up shrubs for livestock feed. He's trying to teach them to plant their rice in straight rows for a bigger yield, to use factory fertilizer, to buy cows for the milk, a scarce commodity in Thailand. An elected member of the village council, he has convinced the elders to buy xylophones and harmoniums for the children's marching brigade. He is respected by the villagers, liked by most. They all know he receives his pension check during the second week of the month. And they all know that when they run out of rice just before the harvest, he will share what he has with them.

On this night, Daddy Martin is sitting off to one side of the throng, the only one occupying a chair—squatting as the locals do hurts his back. He asks them in Thai to please turn down the volume of the television.

Martin says he has enjoyed his life in Thailand, his English a little rusty. He speaks with enthusiasm of his experimental garden by the side of the house. He has imported exotic seeds from catalogs. Unfortunately, the village kids like to take bites out of his guavas while they're still on the tree; the neighbors' ducks love the taste of the Italian basil his mother sent from the States. But his bananas and his mint are growing pretty well, and that gives him a solid feeling of accomplishment.

The water buffalo are another problem. He's never been able to solve that one. Why won't they pull the plow for him? He's tried everything; even gone so far as to sell the old buffalos and buy two new ones—but those wouldn't plow for him, either. The village elders say it's the fish sauce—the traditional Thai fish sauce everyone here uses like ketchup on everything. Fish sauce is made by burying a fish in the ground and leaving it there for several weeks to rot and ferment, a notion that is totally disgusting to Martin. Because he doesn't eat fish sauce, the elders say, he doesn't sweat fish sauce. Hence, the buffalo all think he smells bad. Or so they say. It could be they're fucking with him, but the upshot is this: His wife has to plow the paddies—and she's not one bit happy about it. She lets him know it in many ways, large and small. He has learned to endure. It all comes down to one thing, he says. "No matter what I do, I'll never be one of them."

Such is the nature of the expat life: Nothing's the same as home. Martin's imported tomatoes won't grow in the sandy soil. He misses pizza and golf. He has to take the bus eight hours to Bangkok to call his mother. When he listens to his music on his boom box—Frank Sinatra, Bing Crosby, Jo Stafford, Elvis—his head tips back and his eyes get misty. Village children are told if they misbehave, they will be turned over to Daddy Martin, who will eat them. In fact, Sumlee scarcely even *talks* to him—another confounding custom of Thai wives.

Clearly, he's kind of lonely. During my unannounced, two-day visit, he welcomes me like a long-lost brother, talking nonstop from early morning to late at night, seeming to savor our English and male conversations the way he savors a tin of sardines I offhandedly gifted him one afternoon, a favorite from home he hasn't tasted in years. Long after the TV has been turned off, the children put to bed, the bottle of whisky drained to half, Martin unburdens himself:

"If I had the money, if I had something more than my $600 pension to live on, I'd pick up everyone right now and go build a new life in the States. There wouldn't be a minute's hesitation. My feeling right now is that I've just got to get out of here. I am drying up mentally. I'm a man who likes to use his brain. It's much easier to use brain than brawn. I have a couple of books I would love to write. I just can't get anything going here. There's a mental factor involved about living here. Like the ducks that are eating my basil. Ordinarily, you'd just put up a fence. But if I did that, it would mean, in an offhand way, that I was complaining about my neighbors' ducks, and then they'd lose face.

"I have no role here. I can never be equal. No matter whether I speak the language like they do or farm the land like they do, I am still a permanent outsider. I am still a *farang*."

***

VFW Post 10249 is housed in the Golden Mountain Bar, in a suburb of Udon Thani, four hours northwest of Martin's village.

The Golden Mountain is an oasis of Americana—*Sports Illustrated* posters on the walls, a library of English paperbacks on the shelves, a menu of burgers and hash browns and creamed chipped beef on toast. The soundtrack is Jimi Hendrix, Ella Fitzgerald, and Earth, Wind and Fire. Abraham Lincoln stares down from behind the bar.

The veterans gather here each noon to order up pint bottles of Mekong beer and pass the idle time of retirement, to fight against what post member Leroy Wilson likes to call "the one thing over here that will eventually kill us all—boredom."

Wilson is a retired Air Force environmental engineer. He is sitting at the bar with John Pough, retired Air Force technician. Harry Reid, the owner of the Golden Mountain and also the Post commander, has just finished wiping down the bar. Now he's organizing the cigarette display. Kenneth Wilson, also retired Air Force, has just walked in carrying a *Better Homes and Gardens* cookbook he borrowed from the library. The mailman can be seen through the patio service window, headed toward the bar.

"Here comes your check now, Harry," Leroy Wilson says, upbeat.

"That's funny," Reid says. "I'm not due to get it till tomorrow."

"Well, I got *mine* this morning."

"Really? Maybe this is it, then."

"Maybe it is."

The postman hands over the mail; Reid thumbs through. "Guess it didn't come," he says.

"You'll probably get it this afternoon," Leroy Wilson offers.

"Do you generally get yours in the morning or in the afternoon?" Kenneth Wilson asks Leroy Wilson.

"Sometimes in the morning. Sometimes in the afternoon. It varies, I guess you could say."

The music plays. The men sip drinks and look out the window into the dusty street. They light cigarettes.

Reid pulls out a knife and a cutting board. He begins slicing limes. "I hear Sammy up in Korat had a heart attack." he says.

Pough looks up from a four-year-old issue of *Newsweek*. "I didn't think he was *that* old."

"He's been drawing Social Security for some time," Reid says.

"No," corrects Leroy Wilson, "I think he's been collecting *disability*, not social security."

"I know he's older than Woodie," Reid says, referring to another member of the post. "Woodie's been getting *his* social for two years."

Reid begins restocking the beer cooler, pulling long-neck bottles from a box. After living overseas for most of his twenty-five years in the service, going home to Columbus, Ohio, seemed "kind of dull," he says. "I'd go over to somebody's house, and all they could talk about was stuff like, this one just had a baby, the baby's got a rash, they need this toy. Or they talked about how this football team or that baseball team was going to win this or that game. And here I am; I'm international. I've been all over the world. I'm talking about this country here and that country there, and all they can do is nod their heads. It's just too dull back at home. You don't have anything in common. You just aren't comfortable there anymore."

If Reid and the boys aren't comfortable at home, they aren't quite comfortable in Thailand either. Reid doesn't drink the water or eat Thai food. He doesn't speak the language. He doesn't really even like Thai people. "I think all of us Americans who stay here feel that we don't really want to get involved with the people here," says Reid, a sleepy-eyed man with a molasses-slow delivery. "You don't get involved with their politics, and you don't get involved with their conversations. As friendly as they are, to a certain extent, they don't really like Americans. After a few drinks, they can get abusive. They resent us. They resent the things that we can do and have that they can't.

"I don't really like their ways, but I condone them. A person has to fit into his environment, 'cause that's the main way of survival. But that's also why we have the VFW Post. Sometimes you just want to be around Americans."

Leroy Wilson laughs and takes another swig. "Sometimes you just want to be around other people who don't have anything else to do, neither. It gets awful tiring sitting around the house, watching yourself get old. Your knees start knitting together, your arms break out at the elbows from leaning on the bar.

"Man, you *are* old!" says Kenneth Wilson.

"Find him a wheelchair," says Reid.

"Find him a *plot*," says Plough.

"Guys, I'm just kidding!" Leroy Wilson says. "It's not really *that* bad, I have four beautiful kids. I spend a lot of time cooking and cleaning and taking care of them. I could have a maid do it, but I like to do it myself. Sometimes I find myself just waiting for the kids to come home so I have something to do."

"Yeah," says Reid, restocking the display rack with bags of pretzels and chips. "No matter where you live, you gotta stay busy. Otherwise you're just wastin' precious time."

"Time you don't get back." says Leroy Wilson.

"Amen to that, brother," says Kenneth Wilson, holding up his beer bottle, offering a toast all around.

***

The Prince of Peace Seminary sits back from the road, next to a place that used to be called Kiddie Land, a combination amusement park, brothel, and gambling house before its Thai owner was ambushed by gangsters with M-16s.

The seminary building is constructed of brick—a long, low, Western-inspired structure standing in stark contrast to the primitive wood and cinderblock huts and houses dotting the nearby countryside. Inside the seminary, it is cool and peaceful and empty. The walls are hung with needlepoint maps of Southeast Asia, religious oil paintings, a large framed photograph of the local Bishop meeting with the Pope in Rome. At the foot of a teak stairway are two pairs of rubber flip-flops.

The place seems empty except for a young kid sweeping the floor. I ask him if Father John is around. I'd read about him in a newspaper article back in the States.

Soon after, Father John Tabor descends the steps—a beefy guy in an olive drab undershirt—rubbing his eyes like he's just awoken. He steps into his flip-flops and walks outside into the sunlight, working his neck, looking more like an ironworker just off a binge than a Catholic priest who spent years working in refugee camps along the Thai-Laotian-Cambodian border.

There is an odd, uncomfortable look on his face, as if he's not sure exactly where he is, or if he's where he's supposed to be. His eyeballs track here and there.

"Are you sweaty?" he asks me. "Are your palms sweaty? Are you cold? When I woke up, everybody said it was cold, but I didn't feel it at all. I just felt the headache. What's that in that tree?" He points to a fruit tree fifty yards away.

"It looks like a kite," I say. It is always my policy to stay within myself and go with the flow. Something is not right. I figure it will reveal itself soon enough.

Father John looks at me long and hard. He blinks a few times, as if trying to clear his vision.

"Are you me?" he asks.

I stare him in the eyes, remain calm. *Are you me? WTF?*

"I don't think so," I reply.

He looks nonplussed. He massages his temples for a bit, and then he digs his knuckles into the trapezius muscle at the back base of his neck. "This thing is like a rock," he says. "Maybe I need something to eat. You want something to eat? Come on inside."

Tabor turned thirty-nine yesterday. He enlisted in the Seabees after high school, an eighteen-year-old farm boy from Jaffrey, New Hampshire, who didn't want to go to college and damn sure wasn't going to collect eggs and shovel chicken shit for the rest of his life, either. He got to Danang early in the war. At that point, they were calling it a "police action." In fact, there was hardly any action at all. Mostly, he drilled water wells and partied and took it easy.

"You like frog legs?" Tabor asks. He is seated at a table in the seminary kitchen. He pulls a leg off a dead frog and stuffs it in his mouth. Then he puts the frog down on the plastic tablecloth, a festive red and white checkerboard. It is clear the frog is not cooked. It has not been alive for some time. There is an odor. A chunk of black decay falls out of the inside of the frog; a little red ant falls out of that. The ant scuttles across the tablecloth, past a bowl of bananas, out of sight. Tabor swigs a warm beer. "I found the frog out in the yard yesterday. It must be a gift from God to take care of my headache. I think they use frogs for headaches in Vietnamese medicine."

"What about Vietnam?" I ask him. "What happened when you were there?"

"I don't remember much. It was a long time ago," he says. "I remember that when they told us we were going there, I didn't even know where it was. I was a choirboy. I'd kind of always had a calling, but I kind of didn't want to pay attention to it back then, I guess. Do you know the old name for Indonesia? It's Sumatra, I think.

"We flew in from the Philippines in a C-130. The first thing I saw was this little guy with a big helmet guarding a plane. And I thought of—what do you call those kids? From TV? The Little Rascals. I thought of them. Here was this little guy with this big helmet. Really, it was just too big for his head. It looked pitiful, you know, and I got this big feeling of superiority because we were here to train this guy. I mean, here was this little kid with a helmet as big as a bucket on his head, and a gun, and baggy old clothes, and he was out on this runway guarding a plane. Clearly, he needed my help. I don't know— there was something about him. Something about the sight of him.

What I felt, heaven knows. But I felt something, because at that time, at that moment, it was so attractive and so moving, it hit me like a ton of bricks. I don't know if I could analyze it, exactly. Was it the hand of God? I don't know. But that was the moment. That was when I decided to stay in Vietnam, the first minute I arrived."

Tabor finished his tour and then volunteered for a second. When that was up, he wrote to the Secretary of the Navy, requesting permission to stay in Vietnam to study for the priesthood with missionaries there. This request was granted. He stayed in Vietnam after the United States pulled out its troops, continuing his work. In 1978, following his ordination, Father Tabor was arrested by the ruling Vietnamese communists and tried by a people's court. After the trial, he was loaded onto a flatbed truck, handcuffed to prostitutes and criminals, paraded around the village, and then taken away to serve six months in prison camp. Upon his release, he fled to Thailand, where he used his fluent Vietnamese and Laotian to work with refugees.

"I guess Vietnam was where I realized my calling," Tabor says. "God didn't appear to me in a vision or talk to me in a big voice. I didn't hear any voices—not back then. Sometimes I do hear voices now. I don't know who they are. I try to communicate with them, but they don't answer. I guess some of them are good voices and some are bad. They just talk to me when they want to. They told me to drown myself when I was in Rome this year. You know how hard it is to drown yourself?"

"What else do you remember about Vietnam?" I prompt, trying to keep him on track. "What did you do when you were there?"

"I remember that there was this little girl. She was something. Little Mia, I think her name was. She was like the pet for the whole little group that was drilling this well. I remember when we took her out for supper one time at this hotel in Danang. I'm trying to think of the name of it. I don't remember it too well. Somebody had made reservations, I think, and we went up there. That's where the mayor's office is now—"

Just then, the kitchen door opens. A man walks in, followed by a couple. The man is wearing a clerical collar. He looks familiar somehow. The trio wears a joint expression of extreme concern.

"Hi, Bishop," Tabor says, nonchalant.

"Hello, Father John," the Bishop says. Now I remember: He's the one who is standing with the Pope in the photograph on the wall.

"Hello, Father John," the other man and woman say in chorus. They look and sound American. "How are you feeling today?" the man asks. He sounds like he's talking to a child. Or someone experiencing an unidentified mental health problem.

"Okay, doctor," Tabor says flatly. He folds his arms across his chest, commences rocking slightly back and forth in his chair.

"John, have you packed your things?" the Bishop asks. He sounds pastoral but also slightly annoyed. "It's time for you to go."

Rolling Stone, 1984

THE SHARPTON STRATEGY

He's got Martin Luther King's dream, James Brown's hairdo, and a date with political destiny. Black folks love him. The rest aren't so sure. "I just haven't learned how to talk to white folks yet," he says. At home and on the road with the Reverend Al Sharpton during his early years, before he ran for U.S. president and became a mainstream chat show host.

"**N**o justice! No peace!"

"No justice! No peace!"

Oh no! Here he comes again, churning down Wall Street at high noon like a big black tug—shoulders back, arms pumping, hair luffing, flesh roiling and slushing beneath the silky nylon of his teal-blue jogging suit, his trademark, size XXL. Al Sharpton, Al Charlatan, the Reverend Soundbite, the Minister of Hate—a tribal chief leading a militant horde straight up the asphalt seam of America's silk stocking, hollering for justice, threatening the peace.

Lunchtime in New York City, at the business end of the dagger-shaped island of Manhattan. The air is gray, the streets are jammed, the Dow is down forty. The usual cacophony of urban disharmonies has been lifted to a crescendo this afternoon by the dozens of dump trucks and heavy machines hugging the curb two deep around City Hall park, air horns blaring solidarity with the large group of black construction workers who are protesting, a demand for more jobs.

A few minutes ago, Sharpton penetrated borough limits in a white Pontiac Grand Am. He hoisted himself out of the passenger seat, trundled across three lanes of traffic, and entered the park, where he was swallowed in a chanting, teeming mass, twelve busloads of followers, gathered as planned under the camouflage of the protest permit issued to the construction workers.

Now they head south, Sharpton and six hundred marchers, led by a phalanx of police and attended by a gaggle of press.

Along the sidewalks, the usual lunchtime crowd has frozen. WASPs and Jews, Italians and Asians—all of them stare grimly, eyes glazed with hate and fear and incredulity, mouths open, beef franks and spoonfuls of yogurt suspended en route. *It's him,* they say to one another. *Him!* The guy who called Jesse Jackson a "limp dick." Who called Mayor David Dinkins an "Uncle Tom." Who occupied the the Brooklyn Bridge and shut it down. Indicted on sixty-seven counts of fraud. Implicated as an FBI informant. Defended the Central Park jogger wolf pack.

Spends $2,000 a year on his hairdo!

His long, straighted, sweptback, James Brown *hairdo!*

The marchers chant in the tones and rhythms of a chain gang, a war party—six across, one hundred rows deep, a coalition of blacks and Latinos, jobless and homeless, gays and leftists. They are marking the anniversary, twenty-seven years ago today, of the historic civil rights march on Washington, D.C. After Montgomery, after the bombings, the dogs, and the fire hoses, 250,000 people from all over America gathered at the Lincoln Memorial. Fresh from a jail stint, the Rev. Martin Luther King Jr. told the country about his dream of racial harmony—his most famous speech. Today, in New York City, Al Sharpton's marchers carry Xeroxed pictures of Dr. King. Their signs ask, "What happened to the dream?" Their message is...

Well, it's not altogether clear yet what the message is.

Something to do with Martin Luther King. *Something* to do with justice and peace. *Something* terribly important to the state of civil rights in our country today.

They march swiftly, ranks tight, heels scuffing, sweat mingling, fists and pickets jabbing the air, a polyglot sampling of the nation's underclasses—hobo rags and cheap three-piece suits, African prints, blue work shirts with names in bubbles over breast pockets—all of them here because Sharpton has called, none of them even slightly aware of the very secret stunt he has planned for later.

They turn off Broadway and enter Battery Park, a living mass, a village on a hike. They gather in front of a makeshift stage—huddling, milling, hitting up the lunch crowd for spare change. Cameras roll. Police take positions around the green.

Sharpton pulls up behind the stage, rests his hands on his ample hips. He surveys the crowd, the police. He checks the sky.

Then, casually, he swivels his head to the left, puts his eyes on the prize.

Out there, across the harbor.

The Statue of Liberty.

***

Al Sharpton is one of the most reviled men in America today.

He first showed up in the national news in 1986, seemingly out of nowhere, in the aftermath of a racial killing in Howard Beach, New York. Since then, he's become a fixture on a present-day civil rights stage that seems devoid of visible leaders. According to polls, most Americans see Sharpton as a media manipulator, a rabble-rouser, a threat, a joke. One white columnist called him "a racial ambulance chaser"; another, a "race racketeer." A poll by the New York *Daily News* found that 90 percent of whites and 73 percent of blacks believe he is harming race relations rather than helping.

Representative Major Owens, a black Democrat from New York, says Sharpton's history "shows he has no principles. He's not to be trusted."

Andrew Cooper, publisher of the *City Sun*, a black newspaper in New York, says, "Most middle-class black people are embarrassed by him."

But the telephone poll can be read another way: One in four blacks *does not* think Sharpton is harming relations between the races.

Which doesn't account for the Sharpton followers who couldn't be polled (many don't have telephones).

To the several thousand blacks who have joined the United African Movement (UAM), to countless more across the country who have seen him in the media, Sharpton is, in the words of the *New York Times*, "an authentic, stirring leader who has challenged the city and state power structure too often to be doubted."

Rev. Timothy Mitchell, pastor of Ebenezer Baptist Church, in Queens: "He's sort of a hero here to the young people. They admire his courage."

Rev. William Augustus Jones, pastor of Bethany Baptist Church, the oldest congregation in Brooklyn: "We recognize his gift. We applaud his spirit. We thank God for the fact that he has been consistently on the firing line on behalf of our people and our cause."

Moses Stewart, father of Yusuf Hawkins, a black teenager who was killed by a white mob in Brooklyn: "I called Rev in 'cause I wanted to get me some justice, and that's what Sharpton does. He stands up for black folks like me, and if some whites don't like that, I could care less."

Al Sharpton: "I wanted to build a grass-roots movement with a little pizzazz. That's what Dr. King did. He brought *theater* into the movement. Dr. King said, 'We will close down the bus company.' It was made for TV. It was theater of the street. That's how Dr. King changed America.

"Look at this country. We went from Harvard-trained Kennedy/ Camelot to made-for-TV Ronald Reagan because of the media. So why shouldn't America go from Dr. King to Rev. Al? The times call for who's going to emerge. Let's not have no deception about why I'm in the media. We're talking ratings for you, followers for me.

"My thing is: I'm talking to the guys from Inglewood, from Brownsville, from Harlem. I'm talking to thirty million black guys out there, guys who are just like me."

***

Tuesday morning, 7:30, one week before the march.

We are in Sharpton's apartment in Park Slope, Brooklyn, his living room/office. A video tape of a speech by Nation of Islam leader

Louis Farrakhan is playing on the TV; a reporter from a black-owned radio station is sitting on a sofa covered with cat hair, waiting his turn for an interview. Above his head is a framed poster of Malcolm X—he looks defiantly out a window, an M-1 carbine rifle in his hands. "By any means necessary," it says at the bottom.

Sharpton is wearing black socks, print boxers, and a yellow wife beater. He is pacing back and forth across the shag carpet, thundering into a telephone, using his pulpit voice for an interview with another reporter. "This town is closer to exploding than ever!" he exclaims, his typical church hyperbole. Sharpton is thirty-five. His allergies keep his nose stuffy; his gravelly voice makes you think of James Brown with a cold.

Sharpton's apartment is clean but cluttered—a walk-up above a machine shop, $1,000 a month. He lives here with his wife, Kathy Jordan Sharpton, a former backup singer for Brown (more on him later), and his daughters, Ashley, three, and Dominique, four. All four Sharptons sleep in the one bedroom. This living room has no window. Lining the walls are photos, typical political grin and grabs: Sharpton with George Bush, David Dinkins, Jesse Jackson, Melba Moore.

"The violence in the minds of these kids!" Sharpton preaches into the handset of the portable phone, the whip antenna following him as he continues to pace in the limited space of the room, which is decorated with furniture that might have been inherited from somebody's grandma. "These kids think life's a fuckin' television series. They have no fear. When I was in jail after the protest, I was two cells down from that kid—the one who shot the police officer in Jersey? He said to me, 'Rev, I told 'em we shouldn't hit that dude. The car we had was too slow.' Now, I have to tell you. That rendered me speechless for a minute. Here I was, I thought the kid was gonna tell me he had a moral problem with killing a cop. I thought he was gonna tell me he was feeling remorseful. But that wasn't his problem. His problem was merely functional. 'Rev, we needed a faster car!'"

"Excuse me, Rev. Sharpton?" It's the radio reporter.

Sharpton holds up a finger, one minute. The other telephone line rings. He puts both calls on hold.

"What?" he asks the radio reporter.

Just then, the front door flies open.

Sharpton wheels around.

"Yo!" he calls to his driver, Carl. They've been together a long time. They spend more time together than they do with their respective wives.

Then Sharpton remembers: the phones. He punches the first line. "Call you back." He punches the second line. "Call *me* back." Then he turns to Carl. "Did you get the *Journal?*"

Handing it over: "I finally found it over at—"

"Don't matter *where* you got it, long as you got it," Sharpton says, grinning with excitement as he pages through the *Wall Street Journal*. At last he spots what he's searching for.

He reads to himself, his big black eyes tracking across the columns . . .

And then he throws back his head and laughs—a loud, long, phlegm-tinged guffaw that shakes his belly. "Can you believe this?" he roars.

He reads aloud for the assembled, doing his best impression of a network news anchor, albeit one with a stuffy nose:

"A trader from the New York Stock Exchange reports the following joke: 'What do you do if you have Saddam Hussein, Muammar Qaddafi, and Al Sharpton, and in your hand is a gun with only two bullets?' Answer: 'Shoot Al Sharpton twice—to be sure he's dead.'"

"Now they're advocating my *death!*" Sharpton crows, slapping his large and ashy thigh, laughing real tears.

He does his best impression of a cracker sheriff: "Shoot Al Sharpton *twice!*"

***

Wednesday, 7:00 P.M., six days before the march, a strategy session at a community center in lower Manhattan.

Eight people sit in swivel chairs. They drink coffee and take notes. The center belongs to the New Alliance Party, a coalition founded by a former Marxist who made a fortune in a field called Social Therapy. The NAP pulls its members from the scattered remains of the far Left. Its causes have included the fight against the government "roundup" of black leaders in America. The Jewish Anti-Defamation League has called the group anti-Semitic. This is denied by the NAP's founder-financier, Fred Newman, who is himself a Jew.

When Sharpton got the idea for the march on Wall Street, he went directly to the NAP. First, he wanted his demonstration to be racially integrated. Second, he needed technical assistance: planning, flyers, literature, copiers, fax machines, and phones. And, of course, he needed money, something white liberals are good for, in his estimation.

Not that Sharpton doesn't have a few problems with the NAP. They're a little too academic, a little too fey. But, hey, he's realistic. There aren't many liberals left.

And very few of them want to get involved with *him*.

"Okay now," Sharpton is saying, "I want to hand pick the arrest crew myself, 'cause I got to live with them in jail."

"You don't want anybody from the homeless?" asks the man from the shelter.

"If they want to. But nobody with a warrant outstanding."

"So how many people we need to get arrested?" asks Raphael. He's from the Latin community.

"I think we should keep it down to about twenty people," Sharpton says. "If you start getting into big numbers, it's harder for the police to deal with."

"Do we care what's harder for the police to deal with?" asks Lenora Fulani, the face of the NAP and a perennial candidate for various offices. A black woman with close-cropped hair and big earrings, she ran for mayor of New York in 1985, for governor of New York state in 1986 and 1990, and for president of the United States in 1998.

"*Yeah*, we care," Sharpton answers sternly. "See, you don't need two hundred people going to jail. You don't need to piss off the police—they're just doing their job. It's the symbolism that's important. This is the reclaiming, the *redefining* of the King movement. If we didn't do this, nobody would be discussing the homeless, which is the issue King wanted to discuss with the Poor People's Campaign and Resurrection City. They're going to say this is another showboat piece. But we're going to make them at least discuss the *issue*."

"All right," Fulani concedes.

"Right on," says Rafael.

"Okay," Sharpton says, buoyant again. "Now remember. What happens *after* we get to Battery Park is strictly confidential. *Super confidential!* Got it? It can't get out of this room! If the police find out—" his eyes budge antically.

Everyone laughs.

***

Wednesday, 9:00 P.M., Bedford-Stuyvesant, Brooklyn.

The Slave Theater is headquarters of the year-old UAM. A once-grand movie palace, the ceiling snows green flakes onto the mildewed, graffiti-covered seats. A large epic mural, *The Holocaust of the Black Race*, depicting the African-American experience from Africa to the Middle Passage to slavery, takes up one huge wall.

The microphone squeals. Sharpton pulls away, hikes his pants, waits for the applause to die. Though he has been called a preacher without a congregation, this theater is his church for now, rented by the UAM from the black judge who owns it. The rent on the building is paid with donations collected after rallies and services. In this way, Sharpton pays all of his expenses: his leased Grand Am; a headstone for Yusuf Hawkins; ad space in black newspapers; bail for two of the Central Park jogger defendants; food, salary, and pocket money for Sharpton and his three-person staff. There's no real budget for the UAM. Whatever they can collect, they spend. A year ago, the UAM was getting 200 people at rallies. Tonight, there is standing room only, 1,500.

Sharpton speaks from high on the stage, his voice strong and throaty, the edges tinged with a soulful rasp of phlegm. He points his finger at the audience, pans it slowly across the room, the upturned faces shining—lawyers and homeboys, welfare mothers and church ladies, all of them spellbound.

"I don't care whether you a revolutionary: bang-bang-shoot-em-up," he preaches.

"Go on!" the audience responds.

"Whether you a militant: just mad but ain't got the gun."

"Tell it!"

"Whether you a moderate: where you smile at white folks and then cuss them under your breath."

"My *Lord!*"

"Or whether you an *outright* Tom—"

Hoots and shouts!

"Whatever kind of Negro you are, whether you a fat Negro or a skinny Negro, a tall Negro or a short Negro, a brilliant Negro or a simple-headed Negro, you have to *understand.*"

"Work it, Rev!"

"Ain't no homes for the homeless. Ain't no health care for the sick. Ain't no education for the young. Ain't no housing for *nobody.* Ain't no goods and no services. And now, despite *allllllll* that, they tellin' you to go over to *Iraq* and defend a flag that never defended you." He points his finger around the room, a pause for dramatic effect. "I say, hell no, we won't go!"

"Hell *no.*"

"*Hell* no."

Shouts, applause, tambourines . . .

From the time he was four, when he preached his first sermon at the largest Pentecostal church in New York State, Alfred C. Sharpton Jr. has been moving people. He has moved them to God, to the offering plate, to musical acts, to prizefights, to strike lines.

He was raised in a ten-family building in lily-white Queens. His father owned the building, along with thirty houses in Brooklyn. Al senior was a contractor. He and his wife both drove Cadillacs. Young Alfred was their famous son, known on the New York gospel circuit as the Wonderboy Preacher.

When he was seven, Sharpton's father took all the money and left. Sharpton hasn't heard from him since. His mother moved her kids to Flatbush and went to work as a maid for a rabbi. Sharpton's cut from revivals went straight to family budget.

Sharpton's earliest political mentor was civil rights pioneer Adam Clayton Powell. Young Sharpton was eleven when he spied the tall, dapper U.S. congressman for the first time; he was known in the neighborhood as Big Daddy.

Under Powell's tutelage, the Wonderboy Preacher matured into the Wonderboy Activist. In 1969, at the tender age of fourteen, Sharpton was named youth director of the New York chapter of Operation Breadbasket, the economic arm of Dr. King's Southern Christian Leadership Conference. He was handpicked for the job by none other than civil rights leader Jesse Jackson. Today, with a smirk, Sharpton recalls Jesse's marching orders: "Defy and kick ass."

Sharpton generated a core of about four hundred students. They protested alongside the grown-ups for jobs and concessions from white-owned businesses in the ghetto. Two years later, Sharpton started his own group, the National Youth Movement. The NYM targeted businesses at first, then turned to politics. By 1972, several presidential candidates came seeking Sharpton's endorsement.

Meanwhile, young Sharpton was attending an all-white high school in Flatbush. He was vice president of the student council, associate editor of the school newspaper, the *Tilden Gadfly*. Many mornings before school, he would gather his followers around him and declare a boycott *du jour*. They'd protest cafeteria food quality, dress codes, any issue that mattered to the students. At graduation, the principal informed all assembled that he would *not* be missing Alfred Sharpton at all.

At nineteen, Sharpton met the already-legendary R&B icon James Brown. In time, the Godfather of Soul, aka "the hardest working man in show biz," came to regard Sharpton as his son—he said so frequently in public. Sharpton toured with Brown, working as a manager/private clergyman. Sharpton booked Brown's shows, hired his band. He even hired as a backup singer the woman who would eventually become his wife. She still sings occasional solo dates at the Cotton Club in Harlem.

Brown also deserves credit—or blame—for Sharpton's lightning rod of a hair do; never has one hairstyle caused so much ruckus. For the record: James Brown, who famously processed, or straightened, his own hair, was the one who took Sharpton to a beauty shop and got him his first wash and set. The story goes that Brown, the mentor, made young Sharpton promise to always wear his hair that way. *Your hair is your strength*, Brown believed, perhaps drawing from the Bible's Samson. Since then, Sharpton has kept his word—some say to his own detriment. Sharpton will explain no further. Obviously, it is important to him. Obviously, he is fiercely loyal. Everyone he works with says so.

When Sharpton wasn't living the high life—on the road with Brown or promoting concerts and fights with another new confidant, the infamous, electric-haired boxing impresario Don King—he would be back in the trenches in New York, fighting the continuing battle for justice and civil rights, registering voters, marching against crack, even helping at one point to uncover a nest of bad cops who were selling drugs and fencing stolen goods.

In the mid-1980s, a series of racial incidents occurred in New York that changed everything for Sharpton:

The shooting of four black youths in a subway by Jewish everyman Bernie Goetz. The death of a young black man in Howard Beach, Queens, after he was chased by whites into highway traffic. The shooting death of Yusuf Hawkins in the Italian enclave of Bensonhurst, Brooklyn.

As he has for years, Sharpton responded to each injustice with protest. Only this time, he got the idea to take the demonstrations out of the ghetto, where he had always operated, and go instead to the offending neighborhoods. Sharpton and his followers ate pizza in all-white Howard Beach, marched through all-Italian Bensonhurst, shut down the subway and the Brooklyn Bridge. In doing so, he turned up the thermostat on the bonfire of the races—and the media loved it. They played the soundbites of his most hyperbolic remarks; in short order, Sharpton began to take on nearly mythic proportions. Out of nowhere, it seemed, had come this new black leader.

There was only one problem: white people didn't consider him a bona fide leader.

Detractors point to his attempted run for state senator, which was ruled illegal by a judge, who found Sharpton was trying to represent a district in which he did not live. His bid on a Con Edison garbage contract was disqualified when it was discovered his financial backer was an organized-crime figure called Matty the Horse. There was his stint as an FBI informant, his highly publicized suit for nonpayment of rent, his multiple disorderly conduct arrests as a result of protests, and his trial on sixty-seven counts of fraud (he was acquitted on all counts).

And, most egregiously, there was Tawana Brawley—a fifteen-year-old who claimed she'd been raped over a four-day period by several white men who then smeared her with excrement and left her in a garbage bag. On the advice of Sharpton and her attorneys, Brawley refused to testify before a grand jury, which in turn ruled the whole affair a hoax—a story cooked up by a teenager who was trying to avoid her parents' wrath over a curfew violation.

Of all the incidents in his past, Brawley in particular was Sharpton's undoing.

To this day he does not apologize.

"If I'm guilty of anything, it's believing Tawana. I still do. I do not believe that a fifteen-year-old black girl knocked herself out, spread shit all over herself, drank urine, the whole nine yards, just to avoid a beating from her daddy. Whether it was six cops or two cops, she told me it was cops involved. She gave me names. She knew a license number.

"If I had any feeling that this girl was wrong, it ain't like I didn't have fifty other cases I could have represented. If I'd known, I'd have picked another. This thing so hurt me. I am willing to admit that I lost a lot of my balance arguing about it. It got very personal. But I still believe Tawana."

Tonight, at the Slave Theater, Sharpton doesn't mention Tawana Brawley; none of his bad press seems to matter here anyway. He is a masterly speaker—ironic, alliterative, moving. Frequent was the occasion, in my weeks with him, when he raised goose bumps on my flesh.

Sharpton's political sermon this evening covers a wide range of topics. How police shoot first at blacks and ask questions later. How black leaders are being selectively targeted for investigation. How black kids are being disabled by the schools. How a new drug from Kenya is curing AIDS, but the white press will not publicize it. How public defenders are puppets of the state. How the white man has a complex about the black man's penis.

He is either frightening or inspirational, depending upon where you stand. In a recent article in *New York* magazine, Edwin Diamond investigated what he called the "reverse reality" preached by Sharpton, Minister Louis Farrakhan, and the black media. In this Afrocentric view of the world, Diamond wrote, "the 'facts' no longer matter; the 'truth' is beside the point—indeed, it may impede the point.... The city's black media have helped construct a kind of anti-universe, a world mirroring the mainstream but where everything is reversed."

But, as Diamond also pointed out, a *Newsday*/Gallup poll shows 20 percent of black New Yorkers consider black-owned media their most important source of news and information. Wrote Diamond: "The audience for these black-media outlets seems to trust them and not the mainstream press."

"To a white mind," says Sharpton, "it's tangible wins and losses that count in the world. So you can look at it like this: I got people to invest money in black banks, I got a black person a seat on the MTA board; I got the protests at Howard Beach and Bensonhurst. Those, you could say, are tangible wins. Brawley and them others—they might be losses. But that's only to a *white* mind. To a *black* mind, I'm successful 'cause I'm still here. I'm a *survivor*. I carry on.

"What I've been doing is trying to use the media to talk to black people and further organize a national black movement. I haven't figured out yet how I'm gonna use the media to deal with *white* America. I will admit that publicly. I haven't figured out yet how to talk to white people. That's my next challenge."

***

Thursday morning, five days before the march.

A procession of cars eases through a Brooklyn drizzle, Sharpton's Grand Am in the lead. Carl is driving, Rev. Al is riding shotgun. In the backseat, behind Sharpton, are his assistant, Jennifer Josephs, and Moses Stewart.

A year ago today, Moses' son, Yusuf Hawkins, went to Bensonhurst to look at a used car. He was surrounded by a mob of Italian kids and gunned down. This morning, the family is laying a headstone. Sharpton is officiating. (He also paid for the headstone.)

Carl enters Evergreen Cemetery and pulls up to a dirt-covered grave. Reporters and cameramen are already there. Waiting with them, flanked by cops, is Charles Hynes, the Brooklyn district attorney, one of Sharpton's political arch-enemies.

Spying Hynes through the gloom, Sharpton bangs his hand on the dash with glee. "That cracker! Look at him, standing out in the rain. He couldn't show his face at the *trial*, but now he's here to get his picture took!" He twists around in his seat. "Jennifer, go over to Hynes and tell him that if he says one word to the press, we're gonna put him in one of these open graves."

Jennifer is nearly six feet tall. She speaks quietly to Hynes. He nods curtly.

The next day, *Newsday* reports: "The only official at the brief ceremony was Brooklyn district attorney Charles Hynes, who said he was invited by the family."

***

Monday night, lower Manhattan, NAP Headquarters, the last strategy meeting before the Wall Street protest.

"We need to sing 'We Shall Overcome,'" Sharpton is saying. "There's a certain segment of white America that really responds to that song."

"I agree one hundred percent," Fulani says.

"And we need to get a big picture of Dr. King," Sharpton says.

"We have one," the NAP woman says.

"That's the drama!" Sharpton explains. "Bring us your tired, your poor! Bring us your *homeless*. Right at the foot of Lady Liberty!"

"What if they don't let the press on the island?" Raphael asks.

"They will," Sharpton assures him.

"They may *not*," Fulani agrees.

"Don't worry about it," Sharpton says dismissively, a cockeyed grin on his face. "I've already thought of that."

***

"No sandwiches! No peace!"

"No sandwiches! No peace!"

Al Sharpton is sitting like a big black Buddha in the grass on Liberty Island, listening to talk radio through headphones. Behind him, a large orange sign eddies and shudders in the harbor breeze. It says MARTIN LUTHER KING JR. CITY. Looming above the sign is the Statue of Liberty.

After the march down Wall Street, after the speeches in Battery Park, the secret plan unfolded. Sharpton announced he was going over to Liberty Island to lay a proclamation. He said he'd be right back. Then his assistants quickly handed out ferry tickets to one hundred of the marchers.

And lo and behold... It worked!

Al Sharpton's army has seized control of the Statue of Liberty!

Now they have been here for two hours. NAP members work furiously, erecting tents. The homeless are restless. They cut up, pose for pictures with tourists, beg for money. They complain about the shortage of bologna and cheese sandwiches. They begin a new chant: "No sandwiches! No peace!"

Sharpton sees the humor in the moment. All in all, things are going well. He has engineered a beautiful telegenic panorama: the tents, the King sign, the Statue of Liberty, the harbor, the blue sky. He is proud of himself, the clever way he has managed to meld the enduring images of King's Resurrection City with the State of Liberty—Lady Liberty's promise, King's dream, and one hundred people of color, many of them homeless. King's dream revisited, twenty-seven years later. Masterful.

Unfortunately, there are no cameras on the island.

Just a radio reporter and two print journalists.

Time passes. Sharpton makes a few calls on a cell phone. A park ranger walks over. He offers a piece of paperwork for Sharpton's perusal.

"We issued a permit for a public assembly," the ranger says, "but you've got to be at the flagpole."

Before Sharpton can speak, he is joined by a short, fierce black woman in a business suit, the NAP's lawyer. She steps forward and snatches the paper form the ranger. She studies it for a moment, thrusts it back.

"This is not us," she says dismissively. "You don't have the name right. We're the New Alliance Party, not the National Alliance Party."

"In that case, I'd be happy to issue you a new permit."

"We don't *want* a permit."

"Then I'm going to have to shut this island down."

"You do what you have to do," she says, crossing her arms.

The ranger turns and leaves. The three reporters press close to Sharpton for a comment.

"I'm gonna stay," Sharpton tells them. "The last one off this island in handcuffs will be me."

Sharpton stretches himself a little, takes a look around. The ferries have stopped running, he can see that from here. No doubt the cops are on the way. He hopes they just fine and release him. He's got a lot on his plate right now. He doesn't really have time to molder in jail. There's the appeal for the Central Park jogger defendants, Tawana's book, a fundraiser for an old Movement hand in Cairo, Illinois, who's up on an arson beef. He wants to see an agent about getting a speaking tour going, and he's working on a deal to make a record with James Brown and an all-star team of rappers—a rap against illiteracy. There are also plans for a UAM chicken franchise, a grocery store too. Economic self-determination is one of Sharpton's new big themes.

And in his future, who knows. Mainstream politics, perhaps? Privately, he jokes about running for president. "Just kidding—" Is that statement ever really true? (He will do so in 2004.)

Whatever he does, he knows he's going to piss off a lot more people before he's through. He knows his disapproval rating will always remain high. Maybe he just likes it that way. Maybe it's just his style. Maybe he likes to be the one who shakes everyone up.

"What I'm sayin' needs to be said. I ain't makin' no apologies. I ain't puttin' on no Brooks Brothers suit. This is how we are. But we can still deal. We can negotiate on any level you want to negotiate on. But I'm still gonna be the same Al—Big Al from Brownsville. I didn't come out here to Liberty Island to be liked. I got plenty of homeboys that'll like me just because I'm me, and I'm more comfortable with them anyway. I like it at the Slave Theater. I like it on Fulton and Bedford Streets. It's cool. It's where I been all my life. I know that crowd. And I'm gonna make sure they get the best shot, 'cause they been good to me. It's what's right."

Now the ranger is back. He informs Sharpton and the lawyer that the island is officially closed. "The last ferry leaves in twenty minutes," he says.

"What about the press?" asks the lawyer. "They have a right to gather news."

"Be gone or be arrested," the ranger says.

With that, the press and most of the demonstrators walk over to the ferry and board. As it pulls away from the island, a police boat ties off at the docks. Three dozen cops, nightsticks drawn, file onto the island.

Over on the grass, beneath the orange sign invoking Dr. King, beneath the Statue of Liberty, Al Sharpton and thirteen volunteers circle up and hold hands. There is no press left on the island; no cameras bear witness. Just Big Al from Brownsville and his people, waiting to be arrested, wondering what happened to the dream.

They sing another chorus of "We Shall Overcome."

***

Epilogue: "We've been saying serious things this week. But the press puts us on the Style page. Not the black press, the *other* press. The white press puts us on the Style page while we're talking about our *humanity*."

It is a month after the Liberty Island takeover. The speaker is Congressman Ron Dellums, the august black leader with the long, salt-and-pepper beard, from Oakland, California. The occasion is the twentieth annual gathering of the Congressional Black Caucus in Washington, D.C.—the biggest mainstream black political event of the year. This is the gala of the weekend, the awards dinner. Three thousand people are in attendance—every black luminary in America, from Jesse Jackson to Quincy Jones, from Louis Farrakhan to Miss Black USA. Dinner is tournedos with béarnaise and salmon, $10,000 a table.

Yesterday, the caucus officially convened meetings on the "systematic harassment" of black public and elected officials. A gathering of hundreds heard stories of surveillance, wiretaps, videotaping, attempted bribes and trumped-up indictments.

"The President is threatening to veto the civil rights bill twenty-six years after the first one," Dellums says forcefully, banging a hand on the podium. "Is that progress?"

"No!" yells the crowd.

"The world is rushing toward democracy and we're running to fascism!"

"Yes we are!"

"How long can we put up with this?"

"How long?"

"Not one minute longer."

Cheers, applause, shouts!

Over in the corner, at a donated table with Jennifer and Carl and some others, Al Sharpton listens, hands resting peacefully on his belly. His mouth is shut. He is smiling.

Esquire, 1991

DEATH IN VENICE

Back in the day, when gangs fought for turf and respect, V-13 ruled the streets of Venice, California— proud *vatos* in their Pendleton shirts and hair nets. They drove shiny low-riders and sold heroin to the *miatas*, the poor blacks across the street. Then crack arrived in the neighborhood and the tables turned. Life inside an L.A. gang.

Lil' Sleeper and Margarita are hanging out at Yogi's, all three sitting on his bed. The room is dark, narrow, smoky. A towel is jammed against the bottom of the door.

"I forgot to tell you," Yogi says. "Sleeper called."

"Yeah?" asks Lil' Sleeper.

"He asked what have we done to pay back Culver City."

"Pay 'em back for what?"

"You know, man. The drive-by at the park. Those *vatos* who shot at us. Remember, *ese*?"

Lil' Sleeper chews his thumb and thinks for a minute. The TV flickers, the radio plays rap, a table fan moves air back and forth. He turns to Margarita, his girlfriend. "When this happen?"

Margarita's eyes pan slowly toward his face. They've been dating for a year. She is wearing a black miniskirt and a necklace of hickeys, a pair of three-inch heels she bought two weeks ago on her four-teenth birthday. Her hair is shoulder length, crowned at the front with a stiff pompadour—a four-inch tiara of bangs combed skyward and encased in Aqua Net hairspray. She blinks. She shrugs. She don't remember, either. One day be like the next.

Lil' Sleeper chews his thumb some more. The skin at the tip, just below the nail, is burned and crusty, a condition the homeboys call Bic Thumb. Like Yogi, he is nineteen. He is wearing a nylon sweat suit and high-top Adidas. His hair is black as tar, clipped short and oiled straight back from a widow's peak. His lashes are long and curly, his eyes are bloodshot, one of his front teeth is missing. The first time he was arrested he was six years old; he stole a TV from his grammar school. Last year, he was arrested eleven times for being under the influence of heroin and two times for being under the influence of PCP, a drug he likes because "when you do it, it be hard for you to walk and think."

As days in the neighborhood go, this one started off pretty well. At 10:00 this morning, Lil' Sleeper and Margarita ran into a crack dealer they know. He kicked down some love, gave them some free drugs, the dregs of last night's stash—a couple of five-and ten-dollar rocks and a bunch of crumbs. The pair went immediately to Yogi's place and smoked it all in fifteen minutes. Now they need more.

Sitting on the edge of the bed, Lil' Sleeper is a ramrod. His mouth is pulled back in a tight grimace. Above his lip, among the faint stirrings of a mustache, are little drops of sweat. His teeth are clenched; you can see the strain in the muscles of his jaw and in the cords of his neck, upon which is tattooed, in big blue letters, the logo of his gang, V-13.

He plucks an ice cube from his glass, holds it up, regards it in the light. "Wouldn't you like a rock this size?" He sounds like a kid wishing for a pony for his birthday—which in fact he did when he was ten.

"*Yea-ah!*" Yogi enthuses.

"How big would you say this was, a fifty?" Lil' Sleeper asks.

"A righteous five-oh," Yogi opines.

Lil' Sleeper loses himself in his daydream; hope pops like a flashbulb in his eyes, and then the light recedes. His attention drifts to the carpet. There are lots of little white pieces of paper and lint and cloth and cigarette ash down there. To him, each piece looks like a rock. Could be a rock. He has an urge to reach down with his index finger and feel around for *pedasos*, little pieces of crack cocaine. That he *knows* there are no *pedasos* on the carpet, that he's way too methodical to have dropped anything, doesn't matter at all, because something strong makes him want to get down on his hands and knees on the filthy rug in the dark, musky, narrow room and touch each little piece of paper and lint and cloth and ash and test its composition. There are no crumbs. He knows that. It doesn't matter. A few minutes ago, he tried to smoke a sesame seed. It tasted like burnt toast when he fired it up in his pipe, which is really a piece of broken-off car antenna stuffed with Choir-boy brand copper scouring sponge—the kind without the soap. A recent letter in a local weekly paper complained about the recent epidemic of broken car antennas. Now you know.

"So what are we going to do about Culver City?" Yogi asks. "Sleeper say that if we down for the neighborhood, we gotta pay them back."

Lil' Sleeper looks up from the floor. He and Yogi are members of the Venice Gang, among the oldest and most proud of the 400 gangs in Los Angeles. For more than thirty years, Chicano homeboys have claimed this neighborhood, one square mile of palm trees and poverty in the middle of Venice, California, a little piece of ghetto encrusted in the heart of the California lifestyle like plaque in an artery—long established, nearly impossible to dislodge. Ten years ago, when Yogi and Lil' Sleeper were still playing with toys, war was raging in the neighborhood; V-13 was locked in epic battles with all the gangs surrounding—Santa Monica, Culver City, the Shoreline Crips, the black gang with whom they share Oakwood, the official name for the section of Venice in which they live. At the time, the *Los Angeles Times* devoted a special section to the unrest. "DEATH, DAILY VIOLENCE BECOME WAY OF LIFE FOR NEIGHBORHOOD," said the headline, one of twelve screamers in the twelve-page pullout. The Los Angeles police department's now-infamous CRASH unit (Community Resources Against Street Hoodlums) cut its teeth in Venice; the National Guard walked the streets for a period, too. A whole generation of Venice homeboys went to jail, became addicted to heroin, or died.

These days, Venice still gets its CRASH sweeps: low-key Tuesday and Thursday night affairs. The *pop pop pop* of automatic-weapons fire is still part of the everyday soundtrack of squealing tires, cursing home-boys, laughing children, and thumping rap. But aside from Popo—a homeboy who lost his cool during a burglary and slit the throat of L.A. city councilwoman Ruth Galanter—Venice hasn't been in the news at all lately. South-Central Los Angeles is where the action is now. There, black gangs have adopted the gangsta lifestyle pioneered by the Mexican *cholos* of yore; they have begun a reign of entrepreneurial terror that has turned the L.A. gang culture inside out. For generations, the poor and the powerless of Southern California—as in every urban center across the world—banded together to form neighborhood self-protection societies. They fought for the safety of their streets and for some measure of self-respect. Back in the day, in Los Angeles, the Chicanos were ascendant. Gangs like V-13 were strong and proud.

Today, gangs are no longer about turf and respect. Instead, they are about drugs and money. Crack has done to V-13 what the police and the National Guard and other gangs have been trying to do for years.

Now, in Yogi's room, Lil' Sleeper grinds his teeth some more. He looks beseechingly at his homie: "You think you can get twenty bucks from your moms?"

"*My* moms?" asks Yogi. "What about yours?"

"I asked her yesterday, *ese*."

They both look at Margarita.

***

The drive-by happened two nights ago.

Yogi, Lil' Sleeper, and Margarita were there, and so were Wormy, Linda, and a couple more *vatos* and *heinas*, dudes and chicks. They were kickin' it on a grassy field behind Broadway Elementary, hunkered in the middle of their own neighborhood, their home turf. Someone had brought a couple *pistos*, big bottles of Colt 45 malt liquor. Someone had some *yeska*, Mexican marijuana, ditch weed. Four of the homies were *shermed*, high on *frios*, which are menthol cigarettes dipped in a bottle of liquid PCP—two of them were crawling around on all fours, unable to walk. Yogi, Lil' Sleeper, Panther, and a white guy named Mike, your reporter, were taking turns crouching behind a wall, doing blasts, taking hits of crack.

Right around midnight, Wormy was smoking another *frio*. Loud and grandiose, he was telling everyone about the time in jail he was stabbed in the head. After that, he began talking about his father, a white man who had abandoned his mom. When the *frio* was finished, he got very quiet. His face assumed a strange, tortured expression.

And then he went *off*.

He smashed a bottle on the sidewalk, uttered incantations to the devil, danced around in the grass. He locked his focus on the white guy who was among them, and stood over me and shook his fists. "Prejudice!" he bellowed, over and over. I tried to remain calm and still. At last, Yogi and Lil' Sleeper tackled him. No matter how fucked up they were, during the six weeks I was with them, my guys always had my back.

After a few minutes, things got mellow again. Everybody was chillin', smokin' out, drinkin', having a laugh.

And then, out of the darkness came a souped-up '65 Chevy, white on blue with mag wheels. It squealed around the corner. Shots rang out: quick loud pops from a semi-automatic. From the sound of it, a .22-caliber.

The rounds sizzled the air above our heads. Small bullets can do a lot of damage; they get inside your body and ping around, tearing up organs. Yogi rolled on top of Linda. Margarita rolled on top of Lil' Sleeper. Everyone else hit the dirt.

And then it was over.

A single tail light receded from their territory. In the nighttime stillness, you could hear hoots of laughter coming from the car.

"There go those motherfuckers from Culver City," somebody said.

"Cheese eaters!" Yogi yelled.

"*Putos!*"

Margarita pointed in the opposite direction across the field.

It was Sleeper. He did not look pleased.

Twenty-seven years old, Sleeper is an OG, an original gangsta, one of the leaders in the 'hood. There are no elected officials in V-13; in a gang, a leader makes himself. Rank is bestowed naturally, over the course of time, by dint of service, reputation, and personality.

Sleeper has a thick scar across this cheek, two bullet holes in his side, another in his shoulder. To this day, he carries a shotgun pellet in his penis. He calls it his Mexican tickler. "What the fuck was that?" he screamed at his young homies.

"Just some of those cheese eaters from Culver City," Yogi said matter-of-factly.

"*Those* motherfuckers? Again?"

Nobody said a word. The two who had earlier been nonambulatory were now passed out on the grass.

Sleeper shook his head sadly.

Lately, he thinks, everything is fucked up in the neighborhood. Everything has changed. These younger homeboys know as well as he does what the code is: If someone disrespects you—if he calls you a name, if he mad-dogs you, if he owes you money, if he shoots at you, if he talks shit about your old lady, if he makes you angry about anything at all—there is only one thing you're supposed to do. You go get your gun out of its hiding place, you hunt him down, you cap him, you bust a grape. Or, if you can't find *him*, you cap one of his homeboys. You don't drive by—that's for cheese eaters, something else new in the picture. For years the homies from Venice and Culver City have been shooting each other, but it was always done face to face. That was always the rule. Yes, there were *rules*. A code of honor if you will: You don't shoot from a car. You don't shoot at a house. You don't do things to jeopardize innocent children or family members. A few years ago, one of the Venice homeboys took a shot at a rival gang member who was standing outside a church. A mother and her child were killed. As soon as they heard what happened, the Venice homeboys beat up their own *vato*. He was banished from the neighborhood.

Sleeper looked off in the direction the Chevy had retreated. He hocked a fat lugie on the ground. "Somebody better do something soon—or *all* y'all gonna have to deal with *me*."

***

Since 1990, when "Venice of America" was built, complete with canals, as a sort of residential theme park by the Pacific Ocean, the

territory just adjacent, called Oakwood, has been poor and predomi-
nantly nonwhite, a little patch of blight along the pricey Southern
California coast. The older families living in Oakwood date back four
or five generations, though the notion of generations can be decep-
tive here. Many of the women become pregnant at fifteen or sixteen;
thirty-year-old grandmothers are not difficult to find.

The neighborhood claimed by V-13 is a ramshackle collection of
bungalows with front and back yards. Invariably, there will be one or
more older-model Chevrolets around the properties, in various states
of repair, and maybe an old stove in the back yard. Women who work
outside the neighborhood tend to drive small Japanese imports. The
walls of all the buildings and fences are covered with graffiti, colorful
and riotous tags that identify the gang and its members by their
street names—each gang and each man has, in effect, his own logo.

Inside, the houses are tidy and clean; the furnishings and knickknacks are inexpensive but lovingly kept. Wedding, graduation, and
post-boot camp military portraits of family members are displayed
high on the walls, above the typical sightline, lending the pictures
an iconic air. The television burns twenty-four seven; the electronic
hearth is always on. Typically, there is a large living room with lots
of sofas and chairs. The seating is plush and comfortable—in general,
the dwellers are a substantial lot, owing to a diet heavy with lard and
tortillas and sweets; in the eat-in kitchen, there is always an iron
skillet of beans on the stove, fresh tortillas on the table. Every other
room, including the back porch, is used as a bedroom. People will
also sleep at night in the living room.

Typically, four or five generations of relatives live in one house.
Great-grandma shares a bedroom with Auntie. Grandma and an
orphaned great-niece will share another room. A high-ranking
daughter—often the one with the best job—will have a room to
herself. A young couple will also have a room. If they have a small
child, the child will often sleep with the ranking female. The females
of the clan share an elaborate and interwoven network of responsibilities. Everyone cooks, cleans, and takes care of the kids. Young
couples have the fewest responsibilities. They are encouraged to
sleep late, to make more babies. The older children take care of the

younger children. They grow up taking care of one another. One sixteen-year-old mother, when asked about her status as an "unwed mother," knit her brows in puzzlement. "I been taking care of babies since I was five or six," she giggled. "I love babies. I don't see it as a *bad* thing."

The women run the household with a loving but firm hand. Grandma or great-grandma holds the lease; all the women work in some fashion or another, some off the books so they can still collect various benefits from the government. Because the homeboys live at the pleasure of their wives' or girlfriends' mother or grandmother, and because many have no job and no prospects, they are low in the family pecking order—treated not so differently from the children. Not much is expected of them, either.

Until recently, the word *gang* wasn't used in connection with V-13. Gang was something the police called them, something the newspapers called them. To themselves, they were, and have always been, simply a *neighborhood*: people who live in a place where they've lived all their lives, where their parents have lived all *their* lives. To the Chicanos of Oakwood, this one square mile is their village, their home, their world, a society within society. Everyone knows everyone, and they have known each other since they were born. When somebody disrespects the neighborhood—when somebody from Culver City hits Lutie's mom on the head with a bumper jack, or takes a knife to Beaver, or a bat to Tavo, or shoots Gato in the back—the neighborhood is supposed to make sure somebody from Culver City is bumper-jacked or knifed or clubbed or shot. It is the job of the men to protect the honor of the neighborhood. This is the meaning of the expression "down for the 'hood." Either you is or you ain't.

Lately the youngbloods of V-13 have been eatin' cheese. Three times over the past ten days, gang members from Culver City, Chicanos from the projects in the town next door to Venice, have driven through the neighborhood and taken potshots at Venice people. Unfortunately, Yogi and Lil' Sleeper and the rest have been too fucked up on crack to continue their four-generation cycle of violence. Even the social workers have begun to notice.

"I remember the Venice from when I was gang banging," says Marianne Diaz, 29, a former member of the Compadres, another Chicano gang in Los Angeles. She is now an outreach worker with Community Youth Gang Services.

"Venice is such a big, old gang," she says. "Even back in the day they had, like, maybe a thousand homeboys. They were down. People respected them. Venice, Lennox, and South Los, and Eighteenth Street. Those are your four big gangs. Everyone has heard of Venice. I mean, if you got busted, you were gonna see twenty or thirty of them down in the pen, and they were the ones running things. Just about every older Venice homeboy I meet is a *veterano*," an ex-con.

In Venice, she says, a high percentage of the males over fifteen have been to jail or to juvenile. "He figures the system is against him, that no one wants to give him a chance. And he also figures there's a good chance he will die tomorrow. It is a very live-for-today society." In his nineteen years, Lil' Sleeper has done a total of four years behind bars; Yogi is about to go off and serve a one-year sentence. He says he's innocent of the actual crime for which he was found guilty, but he's taking it like a man: "I figured I'd already done about thirty or forty *other* burglaries. They had to get me for one of them."

Being respected in the neighborhood for being an ex-con is only one aspect of a curious system of beliefs in Venice. Take the Gonzales family. On a typical Saturday night in the living room there is popcorn and a video, adults and kids. Three people in the room, of varying ages, are nodding out from heroin. A joint of *yeska* is being passed around. The daughter's boyfriend and two of his friends are bustling in and out from the back yard, smoking crack. At one point, great-grandma looks up from the movie. "Oh, Sleeper, I *know* you are doing that shit again." She laughs heartily, setting her chins ajiggle. "You are sprunger than a motherfucker!" Everybody in the room guffaws.

Over the years, one homeboy's father, a $22,000-a-year city employee, has borrowed a total of $40,000 to bail out and defend his son for various crimes. Another's father took a week off from work to help his son kick his heroin habit. "I just love my boy," the father says. "What would you do?"

By the time gang members reach the age of twenty-five—if they live so long—they usually move toward a more settled life. Many work in city sanitation and maintenance. Delivery services are another good shot for ex-cons. Almost all of them have children; their culture puts a high value on the young; they want to see their *niños* grow up. War is a young man's game. The OGs rest on their laurels.

"The older homeboys are saying that the younger guys, all they care about is getting high," Diaz says. "They're telling them, 'You like to wear Venice on your hat, you like to write your name on the walls and throw up a hand sign and get tattoos all over your body, but you won't bust a grape on nobody.'"

Back in the 1940s and 1950s, says Diaz, the Chicano gangs that emerged in Southern California were "more or less derived from the Hispanic culture." Descendants of the Mexican *banditos*, and later of the zoot suiters, they inherited a macho culture dedicated to the preservation of territory and respect.

"Now," Diaz says, "things are changing. The rock cocaine has come in, and the blacks have taken over the gang thing. My partner, who is black, he always tell me, 'My people took your idea of gangs and totally bent it and turned it around and took away any of the pride or the respect.' I think that's true. It's like before, in the old days, the leader of a gang was the homeboy who was downest. Now it's the homeboy who is richest. In Venice, nobody's got nothing anymore. It's all about getting high."

***

Lil' Sleeper and Yogi are back in the room, both of them siting on the bed. It's morning. Or maybe it's afternoon. They've been smoking a few rocks.

"*Pssssst. Psssssst!*"

Yogi starts. His eyes go wide. "What was that?" he whispers.

"What?" asks Lil' Sleeper. He looks up from the carpet, where he's been searching for crumbs.

"That noise," Yogi says. He turns down the radio, switches off the fan, cocks an ear.

"What noise?" Lil' Sleeper repeats.

"Hey, *Yogi!* Lemme in, *ese!*"

Yogi pulls back the curtain on the window over his bed. Outside there is daylight. The palms rustle in the breeze. Into the room waft the scents of salty sea, pink hydrangeas, refried beans, blue exhaust from souped-up cars. It is Panther. He holds up a dove, a twenty-dollar rock, about the size of a marble.

Yogi's bedroom is the unofficial clubhouse for the members of the Little Banditos, a twelve-member *cliqua* within the V-13 gang, which numbers roughly 300. A *cliqua* is an age-affinity group of homies who were all jumped into the gang at the same time—sort of like a pledge class in a fraternity. Like a soccer or basketball club, the Venice gang has a number of *cliquas* for different age groups, ranging from early teens to late twenties. There are the Banditos, the Little Banditos, the Tiny Banditos, the Midget Banditos. Likewise, within the gang, there are *cliquas* of Locos, Winos, Chucos, and Dukes, all of them with subgroups ranging from Midgets to Bigs.

Whenever the Little Banditors come by Yogi's crib, they follow the same procedure. They check first with Yogi at the window, then they go around to the front of the house and knock politely at the door. Permitted entrance, they exchange pleasantries in the front room—like so many brown-skinned Eddie Haskels, talkin' polite shit to Yogi's mom, his grandfather, and his little sister. Then they walk down the hallway to the back room, Yogi's crib. His mom thinks they're watching television and videos all day long. Or maybe she doesn't. Over the past month, since he got his tax-refund check (he worked for his uncle's landscaping company last summer), Yogi has not been away from his room for longer than an hour. The more crack you do, the harder it is to leave the pipe and sally forth.

"First hit!" Yogi calls, in the same manner he calls "shotgun" if you're driving him somewhere.

"It's *my* rock," Panther protests.

"Yeah, but it's my *room.*" There is nothing worse than having a rock and nowhere to smoke it. You need somewhere cool and quiet. Somewhere nobody will bother you. If you don't pay attention, you can fuck off your high, which means you don't take advantage of the rush. It's only there for a little while. You can easily miss it. And then, all you're left with is the jittery need for more.

Panther hands over the rock.

Yogi slices it with a razor blade, puts a piece the size of a small aquarium stone into his car-antenna-pipe. He melts it some with a Bic lighter, blows out all the air in his lungs, takes a blast. You can't hit it too hard or the hit will liquefy, and you'll lose it; later you'll have to scrape it out of the pipe. The resin is like the mint after dessert.

As soon as Yogi finishes his hit, Lil' Sleeper snatches the pipe from his hand; he and Panther begin to argue over who's next.

Yogi sits back and closes his eyes. Finally, he exhales—a light, clean smoke that smells of ether. Upon his next intake of fresh air, there is a supercharge effect—an instant explosion of pleasure inside his head, an orgasmic body rush. It drills a hole from the top of his scalp down to his groin, and then it drills another between his ears—an ecstatic, physical, electric sign of the cross. The music from the radio comes flooding into his head. His brain buzzes. He smiles cherubically, eyes slightly crossed.

Then the smile recedes, the feeling starts to fade. He begins thinking about the next hit.

One more hit.

More.

That's *all* he can think about. All he cares about.

His teeth clench, his jaw muscles stand, his throat tightens. Everything inside tightens. His veins constrict, his dick shrivels, his heart pounds. He lights another cigarette.

With each subsequent hit, the rush is less intense, but the desire for the next hit becomes *more* intense. With heroin, you have a twice-a-day obligation. You fix the morning and night and forget about it. Crack is different. It's moment to moment. You do a hit, feel the rush, start obsessing immediately about the next hit. About getting more. And more. One more hit. If you can stop yourself from thinking about it for thirty minutes, the urge will pass. You'd be jittery and speedy, but you can ride it out.

But you can't *not* think about it. Your every thought is focused on the next hit.

And the next hit is never as good.
You don't care.
You keep going.
You are *sprung*.

***

"So what are we gonna do?" Yogi asks. He is sitting on the bed in his narrow room. It is noon on another day. The drugs are gone, again. Lil' Sleeper is here, as usual. Panther is out trying to get some money some *vato* owes him.

"Let's go get a rock," Lil' Sleeper says, as if it's a new idea.

"You got any *fedia*?

"No."

"You do *so*."

"I do not."

"Don't bullshit me, *ese*."

The way you find rock in the neighborhood is this: You walk outside of your house.

Day or night, rock is always for sale. You can buy it from men or women, boys or girls. You can buy it on corners, in alleys, through windows, inside apartment buildings. The dealers here don't even bother with packaging—no glassine envelopes, no vials. They sell the *pedasos* loose. The rocks are hard, white, crystalline, irregular. Cooked down from powder cocaine, using baking soda to trigger the chemical changes, they are pure and insoluble. The dealers stash the *pedasos* in their socks, in baggies, in pockets, beneath their tongues—a place the cops haven't yet learned to look; it won't be long. In the coming years, to frustrate the chain-of-custody considerations of the law, a more elaborate sales system will have to be developed: one guy to take the money, one guy to monitor a stash nobody physically possesses, an underage kid to deliver the actual rock. For now, though, things are simple. The dealer has the rocks. He works the curb. He *slings*.

There is constant commerce. There are businesslike slickers with theme raps ("I'm Billy D./Stick with me"). There are hot babes, cold gangstas, skinny rock dawgs—by five in the morning, they are scrapping and arguing like extras from the set of *Night of the Living Dead*, trying to sell another rock to go score more. Besides the members of V-13 and their families—one night I partied with a group of women in their thirties and forties, all of whom were gainfully employed; they smoked *way* more crack than the homies could ever even afford—the customers are a steady stream of *gavachos*, white people in nice cars, residents of nearby Marina Del Ray, Santa Monica, and Beverly Hills. The dealers rush aggressively into the street, surrounding the cars, sticking their hands inside, jockeying and fending for position . . . vibrating, clenching, exhorting, "Take mine!" "Me!" "I got you!"

Most of the dealers are *miatas*, derogatory Chicano slang for African-American—in this case members of the Shoreline Crips, whose families have coexisted with the Chicanos in Oakwood for years. Lately, there has been peace between the two gangs. The Shorelines have no beef with the *vatos* smoking up all the product they can sell.

Sleeper remembers the days when things were different.

"Nineteen seventy-seven was the first I remember somebody getting killed that I actually knew," he says. "And then, *bang*, all of a sudden there were like ten shootings a week. Homies were dropping left and right on both sides. It was all out war. When we walked down the street, we carried a gun. We wore the whole outfit, the khakis and the Pendletons, the hairnets, the bandannas, the hats, the overcoats, the whole bit. We was clean, five creases in every shirt, and we ironed them ourselves. Between me, my brother and my father, we used to go through two cans of spray starch a week.

"I sometimes carried a twelve-gauge shotgun under my overcoat. It was like the Wild West, man. You'd have homeboys on the roof, homeboys behind the trees, guns everywhere. For a while, when the National Guard had the streets barricaded, you could only get in by police escort. If a house got burned, the fire department wouldn't go in until sunrise. It was up to you to put it out. We was down, homeboy, wasn't nobody meaner."

In 1979, the media discovered the gang problem by the sea. The *Los Angeles Times* published its special report—an entire section. There were stories of stray bullets, innocent victims, grieving mothers, shattered lives, midnight death.

"THE TROUBLE IN OAKWOOD," read a subhead on the front page. "Swept by smog-free ocean breezes, bordered on the south by the affluent playground called Marina del Ray," the text read, "Oakwood is a strangely incongruous center of poverty and tragedy. While crime and gang violence tear at the community from within, mounting coastal real-estate values threaten to crush it from without."

At that time, the drugs of choice in the neighborhood were *chiva* and PCP. *Chiva* is Mexican slang for "goat." In this case, it's also slang for black tar heroin imported from Mexico. When *chiva* was the thing, the Chicanos ruled the L.A. drug trade. They had the cars and the money and the guns. They sold the heroin to the *miatas* and reaped the profits.

Since crack came to the 'hood, the *miatas* have been in control. The struggle to stay high is a difficult job. The homeboys beg their mothers or their wives or girlfriends for five or ten dollars. They say they have to get a new driver's license, or they find some other official-sounding excuse. They say they need a new asthma inhaler or another small, expensive thing that they can rip off from a drug store and produce later to back up their story. Scam done, they buy a couple hits and smoke. Then they start all over again, scamming to get more. Many have sold their tools and their father's tools. There are amazing deals floating around Venice at three in the morning— whole automotive tune-up kits for under fifty dollars, VCRs for twenty-five.

Many in Venice have also sold their guns, which is probably another reason the Venice homeboys have been unable to muster the manpower to pay back Culver City. Lil' Sleeper, for one, sold his shotgun about a month ago. One night, someone offered me a .22-caliber semiautomatic Ruger rifle for the price of a twenty-dollar rock. Absent something of value to sell, the homeboys will do a robbery or burglary, though when you're sprung, that sort of business takes way too long. And then there's the business of fencing the goods—gratification too long delayed.

"The worst thing," says Joe Alarcon, a former Lennox gang member who now works for Youth Gang Services, "is that at this point we don't have much to offer Venice. The problems are even bigger in South Central. Down there we're getting, like, five homicides a week. The black areas are really bad. On a daily basis, something like 85 to 90 percent of all crimes in Los Angeles are being committed by Bloods and Crips. Those guys are crazy; they just don't care. Because our resources are limited, we've had to concentrate on the areas that are the worst. We've kind of let Venice fall through the cracks, I'm afraid."

***

Another day in Yogi's room. Yogi, Lil' Sleeper, and Margarita are on the bed.

Lil' Sleeper: "How much *fedia* you got?"

Yogi: "Two dollars, homes."

"I got two, too," says Lil' Sleeper. Really, he has five. He turns to Margarita. "You got *fedia*?"

Margarita's eyes are large, brown, empty. She looks like a beautiful, underage zombie model. One at a time, she works three crumpled dollar bills out of the front pocket of her super-tight denim mini-skirt. Finished at last, she holds the bills aloft like a prize.

"That's six," Lil' Sleeper announces. He snatches the bills from her hand.

"Seven," Yogi contradicts.

"Wha'?"

"Two and two plus three equals *seven*."

And then: A series of hard knocks on the door—*bang bang bang*.

Everybody ramrods. Eyes like saucers. *What the fuck, ese?*

Yogi turns down the radio and the fan. He calls out, innocently, musically: "Who's theeeeere?"

"Me, motherfucker! Open up!"

Yogi and Margarita trade looks. Lil' Sleeper's eyes bulge. He looks like he's about to throw up.

Five years ago, when Lil' Sleeper was still known as David and was about to be jumped into the gang, he went to Sleeper and asked him could he have his name. It is a common tradition, like adoption in reverse. Sleeper was honored. And he was willing. But there was a problem—another homeboy was *already* calling himself Lil' Sleeper. The thing was, *that* Lil' Sleeper had turned out to be a cheese eater. Sleeper was sorry he'd ever said yes to that *vato*. So, he said, if David wanted the handle for himself, Sleeper told him, he could have it. All he had to do was beat up the other Lil' Sleeper and take the name away.

The fight was bloody but short. David became Lil' Sleeper. Thereafter, he owed his allegiance to Sleeper.

Now Lil' Sleeper chews on his thumb, trying to think. "Open the door," he says at last.

Sleeper is hype. And he's even more pissed for being made to wait outside Yogi's bedroom door like some, like some.... *What the fuck, ese?* His jaw is clenched. The veins in his neck are tight. He points a dirty calloused finger at his namesake.

"What have you done to pay back Culver City?" he demands.

Lil' Sleeper looks up at him defiantly. "We ain't gonna do *nothing*," he says.

"We ain't gonna do *nothing*," Yogi repeats. He's got his homey's back. Little Banditos 4-ever.

"You got shot at the other day in your own neighborhood, homeboy! You got shot at *three times* in one week!"

Lil' Sleeper shrugs. "Why's it up to *me* to do something? There's other people who live here, too."

Sleeper stares at him in disbelief. *Can you believe this punk?* Then his eyes drift down to the carpet. There are lots of little white pieces of paper and lint and cloth and cigarette ash down there. To him, each piece looks like a rock. Could be a rock. He wants to reach down and...

"Gimme a blast," Sleeper demands. His lips are pulled back in a tight grimace.

"We was just going to get a ten from Binky," Yogi says.

"A ten?" Sleeper chews his thumb, considering.

Yogi brightens. "Maybe we could get him to kick us down a little more."

"Hand me that pipe," Sleeper says. "Is there any residue in there?"

"What about Culver City?" asks Margarita.

"We'll get them later," Sleeper says.

Rolling Stone, 1988

DUNKIN' DONUTS WITH MANUTE BOL

Manute Bol measures seven feet seven inches tall and weighs 208 pounds. The first time he tried to dunk, on a makeshift basket in his village in Sudan, he broke a few teeth on the rim. Now he's the NBA's newest star. He ejected Kareem Abdul-Jabbar's dunk, Larry Bird's lay-up, Kevin McHale's fadeaway jumper. But he still forgets to duck into doorways now and then.

Two guys in an old gym, a basketball, a game of horse.

The tall, skinny one is named Manute Bol. In sneakers he measures seven feet seven inches tall. The first time he tried to dunk, on a makeshift basket in his village in Sudan, he broke a few teeth on the rim. Now he's the NBA's newest star.

The other guy is Chuck Douglas, five foot nine inches tall. A young PR man for the Washington Bullets franchise, he is wearing loafers on his feet, a few extra pounds of pizza and beer around his waist. Bol calls him "Chief." It's his job, basically, to do whatever Bol needs.

Right now, it's a game of horse: The Chief versus the Dinka Dunker.

"Okay now, Chief. Watch this one," Bol says. "I'm gonna shoot between my legs, one hand."

"Well quit talkin' about it and shoot already," Chief says. "Let's see it!"

"Here I go. I'm gonna kill you, Chief."

Bol bounces the ball once, twice, then starts for the basket from twenty-five feet out, a graceful, lumbering giraffe, a man on stilts, eyes deep and bright in the blackness of his face, cheeks streaked with sweat, forehead scarred, three scars, a Dinka puberty rite.

Four, five steps cover the distance. Not so much a move to the basket as a series of moves: deliberate, jerky, animated, like a pupil at Arthur Murray, one-two and three-four.

He's been playing basketball for only six years. He's been in America for almost four years. There was a year learning English at Case Western Reserve in Cleveland, a year at the University of Bridgeport in Connecticut, a summer in Rhode Island with the United States Basketball League, a rookie season with the Washington Bullets in the NBA. The newness of his game still shows, stiff like a pair of new jeans.

Bol stops, plants, center key. Bends his knees like hinges. Cradles the ball down around and under one leg. Lets go. *Swish.*

"Allllright!" he cheers.

"Damn!" says Chief.

Chief and Bol are about the same age, 24, or they think they are. Bol doesn't really know how old he is. In 1983, when he came to this country from Sudan, his passport said he was 21. It also said he was five foot two. But anyway, Chief and Bol are nearly the same age, and even if there is two feet of difference in their height, they've been pretty close since their first meeting, on a summer morning at the Bob's Big Boy, near the Capital Centre.

And now he's in trouble. He's got to make that impossible shot.

He frowns, sets.

Bounce, bounce, run.

Down around and ... *boink*, off his knee.

"Ah ha-ha, you got H-O-R. Two more, you out, Chief. I kill you. Okay? *Okay?*"

Bol takes back the ball, explains his next move. "Now I'm gonna dribble this way, go to baseline and ah, reverse. Watch *this!*"

Douglas doesn't watch. He knows the shot. He *taught* Bol the baseline reverse. And so many other things, too. The behind-the-back pass Bol first used against the New York Knicks. The between-the-legs move he debuted against Boston. The names of things:

It's not a "train for the rug," it's a "vacuum cleaner."

They're not "little animals." They're "flies."

It's not a "fly spear." It's a "swatter."

No, your "left nose" isn't "broken," you just have a cold.

Douglas was hired in the summer of 1985, while still a senior at the University of Maryland. The Bullets wanted him to be, well, more than just an escort to Bol, and he is indeed. He's Bol's constant companion. His man Friday. His best friend, speaking of the day to day. Chuck drives Bol around, calls the power company and arranges to have his electricity turned on, shows him where the video arcades are, where McDonald's is, where he could buy a music component system with a "mote control."

"I don't know why, but he likes me," Douglas says of Bol. "At first, I kind of felt sorry for him. I thought he was just this tall guy who couldn't speak English. But he's funny. Like the other day at practice, he looks over and yells, "Dudley Bradley, you are the next contestant on *The Price Is Right*. Come on *doooooooown!*' I take him to get a shower curtain, or take care of moving, stuff like that. I showed him how to use the microwave and the washer-dryer. And he wanted me to pick out his furniture. I don't know why, but I guess he thought I knew what to get. I helped him choose. He spent six thousand dollars in one day.

"We like to have fun. We just wing it. He gives me tips on handling girls. He says, 'Chief, you have to be nice guy.' We go play pool or something. He loves pool. He's gonna get a table in his house. He says, 'I'm the man.' I say, '*Pleasssee*, Bol.' We go back and forth. He says, 'I'm like the Boston Celtics of the pool table and you're like the Knicks, Chief.' We just give it to each other back and forth."

Chief's nickname is part of the back and forth. He earned it after teaching Bol how *not* to react when you get into a car accident. Soon after the duo were paired, Chief's 1962 Falcon was hit by another car on the way to a press engagement in Baltimore. Douglas got out fuming and spitting at the other driver, an old man. But the old man didn't seem to be hearing him. He kept saying, over and over, "What's the matter, Chief?"

Since then, the Falcon has been replaced by a big Ford LTD, and Douglas has been called by the name Chief. Bol has recruited a Bullet teammate, Charles Jones, to teach him how to drive. He's already ordered a Ford Bronco with a specially designed front seat. After assigning Jones to the task of being his teacher, Bol told Chief, "I think you are too busy to teach me how to drive."

Not that Douglas has no influence on Bol. The other day, when he dropped off his charge at his townhouse, Bol said, by way of parting, "Nice seeing you, Chief."

Chief replied, with good humor, "It was nice to be seen."

Bol cracked up. Like it was the most hysterical thing he'd ever heard.

The next morning, before practice, when the pair made their ritual stop at McDonald's for Bol's usual "Big Breakfast"—scrambled eggs, sausage, hash browns and an English muffin—the woman at the drive-in window told them, "Have a nice day."

To which the Dinka Dunker replied: "Nice to be seen."

Bol laughed as they pulled out of the drive-thru, totally proud of himself. "I got her that time, didn't I, Chief?"

Bounce, bounce.

Bol is ready for his next shot.

Chief has H-O-R. "I'm gonna kill you, Chief."

Bol lumbers for the basket, for the baseline, the reverse. It is after practice at Bowie State College in Maryland. The rest of the Bullets have showered and are outside flirting with groupies, sitting in one another's Mercedes, listening to rap music, while steam from sewer grates billows across the quad like clouds.

In games, Bol plays more defense than offense. He has a few shots he's working on. A right-handed, flat-footed hook. A left-hand shuttle lay-up. A right-hand set shot that travels down at the basket. A soft but commanding dunk.

He doesn't, however, have the reverse layup.

Boink.

"Oh, shit. Oh, *shit*," cries Bol, an echo of Eddie Murphy in Bol's favorite movie, *Beverly Hills Cop*.

In games, displeased with a call, Bol will sometimes tell a referee, "*Get outta here!*" mimicking Bill Murray doing his lounge-lizard routine on reruns of *Saturday Night Live*. When the Bullets' trainer jokes with Bol, tells him there's a rumor going around that he's a Homosapien, Bol will say, "I don't get no respect," doing his impression of Rodney Dangerfield—he calls him "Rodney Danger."

"Rodney Danger kill me," Bol says.

Now it's Chief's turn to come up with a shot. "I'm gonna dribble this way, behind my back, and lay it in like this . . ."

Boink.

"No good, no good!" Bol rejoices, a good-natured taunting.

Bol's turn again: "Three-pointer, Chief. I'm gonna *kill* you."

Bol moves out to thirty feet. Standing there, poised to shoot on the battered floor-boards of the Theodore R. McKeldin Gymnasium, Bol looks otherworldly.

Legs that start at the junction of his feet, then zoom a thin two-lane to the speed-bump of his chest. Legs so long that when he sits, he appears to be the height of an average tall person—only his knees rise to the level of his chin.

Seven foot seven, 208 pounds.

Neck: fifteen and a half inches. Outseam: fifty-six inches.

Sleeve: forty-three and a half inches.

When he's reclining in the backseat of the LTD, and Chief is dallying outside the car, Bol will sometimes reach up, across the front bench seat, and tap on the horn. His arm covers the distance easily.

An ordinary door in a house is only as high as his shoulders; he has to stoop like an old man to pass through. His own townhouse has cathedral ceilings (but regular sized doors). His gray sofa has four sections instead of the usual three. He paid cash for all of it, including the matching black-and-chrome-and-glass accessories and the coffee table with the "see-yourself shine."

Of credit cards, Bol says: "American people don't want to pay for what they buy. Bol can pay."

Bol's fingertips are longer than a man's thumb, and way too large to handle the clasps of his three gold neck chains. The clasps are another of Chief's jobs. Bol's hands are the size of two extra-large slices of pizza, his favorite meal (with everything except bacon, ham, olives, and "fishy things"). His other favorites are lasagna, barbecued chicken, and ribs, all prepared for him and frozen by a cook at the restaurant part-owned by the Bullets' trainer, John Lally. Whenever Bol is hungry, he can just take something out of the freezer and pop it into the microwave. Despite the convenience of the microwave, Bol actually lost weight during his first season. This past summer, after a four-week vacation at home in Sudan—where he lost ten more pounds—Bol was sent to New Orleans for fattening.

Under the supervision of a nutritionist, Bol went through extensive medical testing and a fitness program involving flexibility exercises, sprints, weights, and "explosion sit-ups" (when he sat up, he threw a ten-pound medicine ball; when he sat back, one was thrown at him). Bol was also put on a 5,500-calorie-a-day diet. He trained on equipment specially designed by Universal to accommodate his size. By summer's end, had put on 30 pounds. He now tips the scales at nearly 230.

Still, people will no doubt continue to stare. Everywhere he goes, people stop and smile and shake their heads. They try to sell him Herbalife nutrients. They ask him about the weather up there. ("What do I look like?" he says back, smiling. "A weatherman?") They do this not because he blocked more shots last season than any other player in the league, not because he blocked more shots than *ten* teams in the league combined. They do this because he's the tallest person they've ever seen, and they all have to tell him so. Even when he's sitting, they walk over and ask him to stand.

"Can't stand. Leg broke." he tells them.

Bol's size 16 shoes are about the length of Tiny BB, the dachshund dog that chases rubber balls across the court during time-outs at Bullets games at the Cap Centre. Bol's feet, inside the shoes, are reminiscent of the long, gnarled roots of desert shrubs or, perhaps more closely, the roots of swamp trees after the annual flooding of the Bahr al-Ghazal River in southern Sudan, where the men of his Dinka village used to fish while he was tending cattle.

Right now, while he's earning, between salary and endorsements, about 333 times the annual income of the average Sudanese citizen, his sister, Abouk, 21, and six foot eight, is tending the family herd of cattle, warming herself by dung fires, using the ashes for mouthwash.

Bol has not talked to Abouk for some time. There is fighting in Sudan, and the few telephone lines in his village have been cut. Once, he told this to someone. Next thing he knew, the press was headlining the disappearance of his sister. People were coming up to him in the streets, asking, "After the season is over, are you going to go find your sister, Bol?"

After a while, Bol got tired of this question. He got tired of "silly Americans." He began answering with a long, straight face, "No, I think she been eaten by another tribe."

The press made almost as much of his disappearing sister as it did about the lion he killed with a spear. Stories said he'd tracked down the predator that has eaten some of his cows.

"Track him down? Shiiiit," Bol says with a laugh. "I find lion. He sleeping. I throw spear and hide behind tree. I not crazy."

Along the same lines, when a woman telephoned a cable-TV call-in show and asked him about the length of his "spear," he replied, "It long enough." Long enough, in fact, to make a young woman drive all the way to the Sheraton Hopkins Airport Hotel in Cleveland at two-thirty in the morning to visit him.

And to come back, the next night, with her mother.

Of his newfound celebrity, Bol says "Mostly, everywhere I go, kindness. Some cruelty, but nothing hurts my feelings, because I feel comfortable. Except in Cleveland, where I catch cold. Ah ha ha! Because God made me this way, I'm not mad. I have fun all the time. Oh, man, I just want to be a good basketball player."

He's getting there. After his first dunk, after the broken teeth, Bol decided, "This a stupid game." It was a hot day in the village of Gogrial, and his cousin Ding had just returned from prep school in Egypt. Ding had learned about basketball at school and thought

Bol would be a natural. And even while the blood was still wet on the rim—and Bol was saying he was quitting—Ding persisted. When Ding mentioned the possibility of a million dollars from the pros, Bol decided he would give it a go.

And so the odyssey from cattle herd to roundball began. The young grandson of a seven-foot-ten Dinka chieftain took the train six days overland to Khartoum, the capital of Sudan, and earned a spot on the 1982 national team, which lost to a pre-Dream Team U.S. squad by only four points. The Sudanese team was coached by Don Feeley, formerly of New Jersey's Fairleigh Dickinson University. It was Feeley's idea to bring Bol to America and to the NCAA. According to some reports, Feeley hoped to use Bol to gain a spot as assistant coach at Cleveland State. A Boston restaurateur was to help finance the move. In return, he would become Bol's agent.

Ding made the trip with Bol, but Bol didn't play for Cleveland State, and Feeley never got his job. Bol couldn't read or write English, so he couldn't go to college. Instead, he took beginner's English and worked out with Cleveland's pro team.

The next year, he won a scholarship to Bridgeport, and led the team to a 26 and 6 record before sellout crowds. Bol averaged 22.5 points, 13.5 rebounds, and seven blocked shots a game. He was named a Division II All-American.

After the season, Bol turned pro, signing a $25,000 summer contract with the Rhode Island Gulls just minutes before their USBL opener. When he blocked sixteen shots in that first game, the NBA took notice.

The Bullets surprisingly chose him thirty-first overall in the draft, calling their 190-pound prize "a long-term project." They took him out to meet the press. They said he'd play in two years.

Then, all of a sudden, Bullet center Jeff Ruland was injured. Bol was called into action.

He didn't disappoint. He swatted Kareem Abdul-Jabbar's dunk, Larry Bird's lay-up, Kevin McHale's fadeaway jumper. World B. Free had to alter his shot to get one over Bol's outstretched hand. Moses Malone stuttered, pumped, and stuttered again, finishing 8 for 26 in one game against the Bullets. When Knick's leaper Gerald Wilkins met Bol in New York's Madison Square Garden, well, let Bol tell it for himself:

"He tell me he gonna dunk on me. And I tell him, 'Not this year. I don't think you're gonna dunk on me this year.' And he say to me, 'I have to,' and I say, 'Okay, go ahead. But don't tell me. Just do it. Why you talk that bullshit?'

"So Wilkins, he stole the ball from somebody, and he went up. He jump high, man. Nobody believe I'm gonna block it. I caught the ball in one hand like this, man, and I came down with the ball in my hand. People went crazy! Next time we play them in Washington, I do it again."

Nobody plays well against Bol. There's never been anyone like him in the league.

Says Boston coach K.C. Jones, "I tell you, they can win a championship with this guy."

Says Abdul-Jabbar, "Now I know how people feel when they play me."

Every day, his talent seems to grow. A behind-the-back pass one game. A double-pump fake the next. A seventeen-foot sky hook the next. A soft bank from fifteen feet the next. Here is a center who can stand flat-footed and dunk easily. Other NBA centers, usually the best percentage shooters in the league, shot 41 percent against Bol last season, against the man that Dallas coach Dick Motta predicted would "break like a grasshopper does. An arm here, a leg over there."

In fact, Bol did not miss a game last season because of injury, and he was voted to the league's all-defensive team. With the Bullets trading for Moses Malone in the off-season, Bol will come off the bench this year, easing some of the pressure from his bulked-up shoulders.

"This a good country, basketball a good game. Better to play basketball than to work for a living. This a much easier life than in my country. How could I not like it?" he says.

Now, back to the game of horse, it is Bol's shot again. "Three-pointer," he calls out. "Here goes, Chief . . ."

From thirty feet. *Swish.*

Now it's Chief's shot.

Boink!

"Now you have H-O-R-S," Bol says. "One more, you dead. I kill you, Chief. Same shot. Three-pointer."

"No way you're gonna make that shot, Bol."

"No way? No way? Watch . . ."

By now, some of the Bullets have returned to the gym. They're watching the game between Bol and Chief for amusement. The other guys have picked up on their friendship, and now they refer to Douglas as Chief, too.

About Chief, Bol will later say: "He a nice guy. He make my life very easy. Sometimes he late to pick me up, but that okay, because he a very nice guy."

About Bol, Chief will later say: "I guess I like him so much because he's innocent. He's like a little baby, everything's so new to him. Because I'm always with him, and he's been interviewed a lot, I'm always interviewed. But it always comes off like I'm just his chauffeur or something. It doesn't matter. I know we're friends. We spend a hell of a lot of time together. So much time that sometimes I think I'm him."

Now Bol lets fly from thirty feet.

Swish!

The other players cheer.

Chief grimaces theatrically.

"You a horse, Chief," says Bol. "But don't feel bad. Come now, I buy you some lunch. You get the car now."

GQ, 1986

APPENDIX:

A few early stories from the *Washington Post*, 1980-1983

Author's note: Sometimes, when I'm working with younger writers, I show them some of the earliest of my professional writing. Here are some of my favorites.

Fond acknowledgement here to Walt Harrington, who introduced me to the New Journalists and to his own practice of "Intimate Journalism," the ideas of which are well presented in his iconic textbook of the same name.

THE FORGOTTEN AT FOREST HAVEN

Forest Haven was a live-in facility for children and adults with Intellectual Disability located in Laurel, Maryland, and operated by the District of Columbia. The site was opened in 1925 and closed on October 14, 1991, by order of a federal judge after years of alleged abuse, medical incompetence, and several deaths. *The commonly used vocabulary of the era is retained.*

D uring his first 34 years at Forest Haven, Benjamin, 38, spent most of his time alone on the cold concrete floor of his ward, tied to a pole near the nursing station with a bedsheet.

When he cried, as he often did in the early days, his face was sprinkled with water. An early memo also advised the staff to give him "love, affection and hugs."

Sometimes, the staff would untie him, but as he grew older he got wilder, raging through the ward, ripping sinks off walls and drinking from toilets. So the staff would tie him down again. Years later, they realized Benjamin's treatment was causing his outbursts. He would rage because he was restless, drink uncontrollably because the heavy doses of drugs used to calm him down were making him thirsty.

It was just last spring that his drug dosage was reduced, his bonds untied, and this toothless, stubble-haired man has come a long way since. He was labeled an "imbecile" by a D. C. court and sent to Forest Haven in 1945, after his frustrated father tried to drown him.

Today, he has learned to eat with a spoon. He helps the staff dress and take to the toilet the 38 others in the dank, cinderblock barracks where he lives. He still can't talk, but he is on a program that rewards his good behavior with candy and fruit, and he works with an eight-man group that picks up trash on the grounds several times a week. He seems to like that, the staff says. He doesn't run away much anymore.

And though Benjamin sometimes smokes three cigarettes at a time, he no longer eats them. Progress.

Change your perspective a little if you go to Forest Haven, tucked as it is in the forests of Laurel, MD, far from the heartbeat and high life, of a proper federal city where many would rather not know about grown men and women who wear diapers and bang their heads against walls for attention.

Spend 48 hours there, sleeping, eating and living with 780 of the most severely disabled citizens of Washington, and life becomes a series of pictures—sad, sickening, gut-pounding pictures. People living out their lives in the "Compound," 250 acres of brick and concrete sprawled across softly rolling hills: a warehouse in a time capsule, a playground for the forgotten.

During the last 55 years, federal investigators have often criticized the facility, finding urine on the floor and feces on the walls, documenting incidents in which staff members have beaten and abused the residents. Several times, the institution's eligibility for Medicaid funds has been in jeopardy.

Almost three years ago, U.S. District Court Judge John Pratt, appalled at the conditions and abuses documented at Forest Haven, issued an order to gradually close the institution and resettle the residents into community-based homes. There they could receive more specialized and practical training and live in a setting where they could have the opportunity to work and live like normal people.

Since Pratt's decree, 110 people have been transferred to foster homes, group houses, and private apartments, where they "change overnight because they are getting real role models instead of institution ones," according to Charles Inlander, who was appointed by the city to head the phase out of Forest Haven. Some have jobs on department store loading docks and in fast-food stores. They are making money and paying taxes, taxes that go to their own care.

But they are the prodigies, the less severely disabled staff and administrators quickly volunteer. For the others, it is more difficult. Today at Forest Haven, progress is getting a 50-year-old woman with the mental age of an infant to keep on her underwear or to learn to use the bathroom instead of a diaper. It is teaching a deformed child to use a spoon, training a 30-year-old to say his name.

The staff, says volunteer coordinator Loretta Clark, "tries to do the best with what we have. At least we care. Somebody has to."

***

Benjamin is found this morning, on a day like every other, in the playroom of the West 2 Ward in the Curley Building, home to the seriously disabled men at Forest Haven. His left hand and jaw tremble from his years on drugs as he shuffles the brown, concrete floor, breathing air thick with the smells of urine and soiled diapers and of the ammonia that never quite covers, stopping here and there to slap a palm against the wall. He is a short man, frail looking at times. Doctors say he is unable to control his adrenaline, giving him at times extraordinary strength.

Bathing and breakfast over, the rest of the guys are into their daily routines: sitting in the hallway, rocking and groaning, picking their eyes or their ears or their noses, staring at "Sesame Street" on the television or at a fixed point somewhere in their minds. Some have the crusty remnants of the morning's eggs, milk, and toast on their shirts.

Benjamin is edgy, a nursing assistant says. Illness and city hiring restraints have brought the staff at West 2 down from seven to four, and there is no one to take his group out for work. There is no one to do training of any kind.

The last time the staff was short and Benjamin didn't go out to work for three days, he pulled a sink off the wall.

Raymond P. Ragosta is Benjamin's psychologist, one of two at the institution. An energetic but frustrated man who carries more than six times the number of cases he says he can effectively handle —handwritten lists of his patients' names on legal-size paper cover a five-foot-long space on his tiny office wall—Ragosta says Benjamin is testament to the history of misunderstanding the mentally disabled.'

"We're looking at someone who came in before they really knew how to evaluate retardation," Ragosta says. "We want people to behave normally, yet we put them in an abnormal environment. A normal 3-year-old shares parental attention with maybe only a few others.

"Here, he has to share that attention and training with a whole ward of people and has parents who work eight-hour shifts. He has learned what he needed to learn. He reacts with instinct. He learned that when I bang my head, someone pays attention to me, that when I sit quietly, I get no attention.

"But the institutional response was that we need to control the head banging, not to discover what causes it or to educate the person in some way. Back in the 1940s and 1950s, they used to drug people to control them. And that was a breakthrough. Prior to that, there was this "One Flew Over the Cuckoo's Nest" mentality that you cut out parts of someone's brain to help them.

"Now, we have learned that mentally disabled people don't learn differently, they learn slower. They need patience and a simplified technique. Think about it. Going to the bathroom is a 12-step-process. We learn at age 2, but for these people, it has to be broken down and taught step by step.

"We know the technique but we don't have the manpower to implement it. These people are getting older much faster than they are learning. If we have to worry about getting the money for milk on the table, sheets and towels, having enough staff, how can we give the residents the time and attention they need?"

"It will take nothing short of a miracle to get these people trained enough to be able to place them in community-based group homes," Ragosta says.

***

Night falls on Forest Haven and from all over the compound, less severely disabled residents who can feed themselves move towards the service center, the main cafeteria. A tiny woman walks the line slowly, collecting whitefish, carrots, salad bread, fruit, cookies, and milk. Her T-shirt reads, "I Am Confused."

As the residents eat, shoveling spoonfuls of mashed potatoes and chattering among themselves in tongues only they seem to understand, a screaming youth bursts through the door and runs toward a visitor who is seated at one of the tables. He grabs her arm and groans: "Take me home with you, take me home with you." His other arm goes around her and several staff members hurry over to pull him away. Chairs and shoes scatter, his screams bounce off the gray-tiled walls. After 15 minutes, four men carry him out. The residents continue eating.

"Don't mind Danny," a resident named Joe says, absently fingering a thick black birthmark that runs down his forehead and across his nose. "He just goes off sometimes."

Joe is sitting with Rita, who he says is his girlfriend. He is tall, carved and muscular with darting, dark brown eyes. She, pear-shaped and soft. Neither are sure of their ages. "I'm 20," Joe says and then looks at the ceiling. "No, I'm older than that. I don't know. I could be 20 and I could be 50."

Both Joe and Rita are residents of Jones Cottage, a high-rise "apartment complex" for the mildly disabled, where each resident has a private room. Joe says the two of them get together "for a little fun." Rita giggles, turning her head away. "It's something to do," Joe says.

Life at Forest Haven is what you make it.

Down the hill from the cafeteria is Spruce Cottage, the home for 44 mildly disabled men from the ages of 30 to 80. Smiling residents pour out the door. Billy, a small, jagged-toothed baldish man, takes a visitor's hand and leads him down a corridor decorated with snapshots of the recent Spruce fashion show featuring the men at their houndstooth and hatted best, and stick-figure crayon renderings of the cottage and staff.

Jabbering a kind of "baby talk," as the staff calls it, Billy points to the little red wagon piled with toy trucks and cars he keeps by his bed. His possessions.

Sam, nearly 80, walks shakily down the hall carrying a tin of fish to feed the three cats the staff lets him keep out back. He is the oldest at Spruce, the cats his privilege of age. He's proud of those cats, and though he can't tell you that, you can see it in his eyes as he squats on the ground in the cold, feeding them each piece by piece.

Louis shuffles up and points to a visitor's cigarette, making a smoking motion with his fingers to his mouth. When he is given one, he strikes his palm with a finger, asking for a light. His request fulfilled, he smiles and shuffles away. Later he will repeat similar requests for coffee and spare change for the soda machine. A staff member advises: "You can give him what he wants, but make him ask."

Mr. Smith has a single room he calls "the best in the house." The blue cinderblock walls are decorated with pictures of Jesus Christ. Red and blue plastic flowers and color-coordinated candles still in their wrappers sit on doilies on bureaus and tables around the room. He has six radio-alarm clocks.

"I just like being on time," Mr. Smith says. But in truth, he rarely leaves his room. In the mornings he rises at five o'clock, the groaning and coughing of other stirring residents muffled behind his closed door, to tidy up and brew coffee from his private stock.

In another room, a visiting reporter approaches a white-haired man who will be his roommate, but only for the next two nights, the visitor explains. "You'll only be here two days?" says Mr. Bryce, shaking his head. "That's what they all say."

***

The next day brings a chill autumn rain, and streams of muddy water wash orange and yellow leaves through gullies in the patches of exposed dirt pitting the compound.

It is lunchtime at The Martha M. Eliot Infirmary, four wings of adults and children who cannot walk. In the narrow hall, a bony young boy with a fine-haired goatee turns silently round and round in his wheelchair, bumping now and then into doors and walls, a sheet tied around his middle to keep him from falling out.

A 40-year-old woman who looks about 10 stares at the ceiling from her crib, her eyes unmoving and cocked to opposite sides of her head. A thin layer of translucent skin covers her veiny limbs, angled stiffly, entangled. A soap opera plays on a television above her, the red-haired young protagonist weeps softly for the cameras.

Across the aisle is Susan. She is 20, her chart says, and barely two feet long, her body misshapen under her blue and red dress. A rare disease, osteogenesis imperfecta, has shortened and deformed her limbs and made her bones so brittle she can only be moved by two specially trained staff members. One of them walks up and places a bowl of chopped spaghetti and pureed peas by her right ear and a spoon in her right hand. Though she can only move her wrist, Susan feeds herself, flipping the spoon from bowl to mouth. She gurgles contentedly when a visitor strokes her hair.

An elderly woman who has volunteered for 10 years as a foster grandparent sits in a chair nearby, spooning food first to one stiff child sprawled across her lap, and then to another seated in a wheelchair. "These are my babies," she explains, softly wiping one's mouth.

Janet, a 15-year-old, weighed one pound, 18 ounces when she was born at home to a 19-year-old Washington woman. When Janet was three, her mother brought her to D.C. General Hospital, where doctors found her suffering from pneumonia, dehydration, and measles, and noticed she couldn't walk or talk and wasn't responding like a normal child. She was soon ordered to Forest Haven by the court. Her mother hasn't been heard from since.

Janet's big breakthrough came last month, when she finally learned to feed herself, clutching the spoon like a handlebar on a bicycle, waving it hesitantly toward her mouth and finally in. "I just thought she could do it, so I kept trying," says the medical health technician who has worked with her. It took eight years.

Across the street, several hours later in Curley's women's ward, hazy light filters through one of the few windows while a woman and two men, kept there because they were abused by the more violent residents in the men's ward, sit in wheelchairs before a stereo. One of the men has a tom-tom, the other a tambourine. The girl is on maracas and they rock back and forth to the heavy soul sounds of a disco station, beating in time with the music. Tanya crawls slowly around them, lost in her own space and time, wiping her hand on the floor like she's looking for something.

The unit supervisor here on East 2 is Gertrude Green, a licensed practical nurse who has worked the ward for 15 years. She calls her charges "babies", though the oldest is 70. "When I first started," she says, "I didn't think I could do it. I cried for two days. But you get used to it. They are such sweet things."

On the other side of the building, the program "Flo" is on television in Benjamin's ward and the men line a narrow corridor, staring. Charlie walks to the set and touches Flo's image with his thumb. Turning slowly, his eyes glazed, he weaves around the others and gazes at a female visitor, hesitantly reaching out and touching her arm. He walks back toward the television and repeats the process.

Meanwhile, the younger boys in West I are having milk and cookies. They grab for their rations and go back to perch on chairs, stuffing their mouths. When they finish, they scrape the floor for crumbs. One well-muscled youth does an impromptu ballet, swirling gracefully on powerful legs like Rudolf Nureyev in the center of the room.

Another walks toward a visitor, looks him up and down, grabs his cigarette from an ashtray and pops it in his mouth. Padding back to his chair, he gulps it down with a nod, smiles broadly and goes back to rocking and patting his cheek.

With bedtime near, the visitors leave the building, stopping first to talk with a staff member who has been sitting quietly in a dimly lit room, reading a romance magazine and watching a boy in a wheelchair and a green checkered straight jacket. Drool drips from his lips, blood oozes from one of several knots on his forehead the size of ping-pong balls.

"You must come back for the holidays," she advises. "We make it real cheerful around here."

November 6, 1980

© **"The Forgotten at Forest Haven," 1980, The Washington Post**

THE HAUSSLINGS: ALL IN THE FAMILY

Ruthann and Henry Haussling of Northern Virginia have seven adopted sons, all under 13 years old. To the social service agencies of Virginia and the District of Columbia, they were burdensome special-needs children whose natural parents could not raise them. But up the gravel road past the cornfield, in a big brick house on a hill, the boys are just Hausslings.

When the Hausslings went to the counter of a fast-food restaurant the other day and ordered $21.43 worth of hamburgers, fries, and shakes, the mob scene of raised hands and shouted orders prompted a stranger to ask: "What is this, a boys' club?"

"No," said Damien Haussling softy. "It's a family."

And what a remarkable family.

The seven adopted sons of Ruthann and Henry Haussling of Northern Virginia are of all sizes and backgrounds. James is the oldest at 13; Luke is the youngest at 3. Ruthann and Henry are white, the kids are black.

To the world in general, the kids were problems. To the social service agencies of Virginia and the District of Columbia, they were special-needs children whose natural parents could not keep them, whose lives carried too high a price.

But up the gravel road past the cornfield, in a big brick house on a hill, the boys are just Hausslings, and Ruthann and Henry are just Mom and Dad.

They all belong there, along with Ollie the one-eyed tomcat and Bun-Bun the rabbit.

Thirteen years ago, when they married, the Hausslings thought they would have no children of their own and perhaps adopt one or two. But they went the adoption route first and decided to keep adopting. "Seeing how many kids needed homes," explains Ruthann, "we didn't see a need for producing more."

As the Hausslings quickly discovered, most of the children who needed homes were kids with mental or physical problems. Birth control, abortion, and society's willingness to accept unwed mothers were factors in the steady decline of healthy infants put up for adoption. In Virginia, for instance, the number of healthy infants up for adoption declined threefold in the last decade, from about 1,400 to 400.

But the Hausslings do not want to be considered part of a modern-day adoption trend. Nor do they want to be considered extraordinary. With the $37,000 Henry earns as a computer specialist, the $9,000 the family receives each year in state and federal subsidies, and a priceless amount of togetherness, this family tries to live as normal a life as possible. "The thing I find irritating is when someone says, 'Oh, you're so wonderful' and puts you up on a pedestal," says Ruthann. "These are my boys. We didn't plan to have this many. It just happened."

***

It is Saturday—Doughnut Day—at the Hausslings. While Mom gets ready upstairs for her quilting class in town, Dad is downstairs in the playroom with the kids.

Earl, Nick, and Damien swivel in chairs by the bar, mouths caked with powdered sugar. The babies Luke and Jesse sit at a doll-sized table nearby, cinnamon doughnuts dwarfing their tiny hands. Andy darts around, shrieking and smiling. Jimmy is upstairs eating grapefruit; Mom thinks he's getting pudgy.

Twenty-one doughnuts disappear very quickly. Three are left. Four kids want more.

Nick begins to whine. "There aren't enough, Dad."

"Sure there are. What's 3 divided by 4?"

Damien answers first. Often, the frail 9-year-old sits alone and writes out multiplication tables while the sturdier boys roughhouse. "Three remainder 1," he offers.

"No," says Dad. Others shout answers.

Then Nick to Earl: "You can't figure it out."

"Neither can you, sucker," snorts Earl, with a street-wise inflection he learned from Jimmy.

Dad glares at Earl, and the 10-year-old's smile buckles into remorse. He leans toward Nick, hugs him from behind, kisses his neck.

"I'm sorry, Nick."

Eight years ago, the Hausslings sought to adopt a baby girl. Instead they got 1-year-old Earl, the first of their sons. He was crying when the caseworkers brought him to the house that day in late September. They put him down on the floor in the living room, near the window overlooking the red and yellow leaves of the old crab apple tree. He moaned and banged his head. Ruthann was ready to cry. She recalls: "They assured me I could still change my mind."

She didn't, but things with Earl got worse. He hit himself in the mouth, picked at his skin. Meals ended with food on the dining room wall. At Georgetown University, Earl was diagnosed as hyperactive, bordering on autism. "There [are] places for such children," the family doctor told the Hausslings.

That was eight years ago. One recent day, Ruthann showed a visitor a paper Earl wrote for school: *When I was at the beach I was having lots of fun swimming. One day I saw something coming up on the shore. It was a brown bottle and it had a small message.*

The message said, "This message is for you. You are the best person here."

***

On a fine spring day, the Subaru Pirates are meeting the Thomas Co. Giants.

Henry deposits Andy, 7, on the Pirates' bench and nods distractedly as the coach explains in great detail his whiffle ball, string, and clothesline technique for teaching toddlers to bat. He takes Luke, 3, and Jesse, 4, to a spot up the first-base line. There, he sits down with the morning papers, avoiding the other fathers, who swagger in twos and threes around the infield waiting for the game to start.

After sitting out the first two innings, Andy comes to bat in the top of the third. Pulling the batting helmet gingerly over his dual hearing aids, he strides to the plate. Quickly, he strikes out.

He walks off the field and leans dejectedly against the backstop. Andy cries a lot, and that warning look is descending slowly over his face, a curtain of despair. Henry walks toward Andy.

"Good cuts," the coach calls to Henry. "He took some good cuts, real good cuts." Henry points to the coach, signs his message to Andy, who bounds off to where the other kids are and gets into a dirt-throwing battle with another boy.

Meanwhile, on the sidelines, Luke takes a toy car from his older brother Jesse. Jesse begins crying. He has been outside for an hour, and the heat makes him weak, aggravates his sickle-cell anemia. His last sickle crisis left him in the hospital for six weeks, a $10,000 expense covered by Henry's government health insurance. All Jesse remembers at the hospital are the cartoons. The Hausslings don't have a television.

Watching a visitor trying to stop Jesse's tears, a blond-haired little boy standing nearby runs to his father and takes one of three toy trucks from his lap. "I'm going to let that black kid play with this," he says.

The Pirates lose by one run. One of the mothers distributes watermelon. Dad urges Andy to eat quickly; Earl, Nick, and Damien are on another team and their game starts in a few minutes. Another Pirate approaches Henry. "Andy loves watermelon. He came to our class picnic and ate four pieces, and two brownies, and a cookie."

"Everybody in town knows Andy," Henry says later. "He makes so much fuss and so much noise they can't help it."

But the neighbors treat Andy like a VIP. At his brothers' game, one little boy gives him two "Star Wars" bubblegum cards. And while the other kids stand at a distance and watch each motion jealously as a mother unwraps a candy bar, breaks it in half and hands it to her two daughters, Andy comes forward and hits his chest, shouting, "Me! Me!"

The mother takes the pieces back from her daughters and breaks off a share for Andy.

At home, Ruthann allows no such liberties. "I never wanted a situation where any of the kids are put on a pedestal because of their differences," she says. Andy is learning that if he goes and slugs people, he's going to get decked himself.

"A large family is like a minisociety," Ruthann continues. "There's a pecking order among the kids, and they'll fight with Andy like nobody's business." But that's at home. One time the kids came home from school and told Jimmy another kid was picking on Andy on the school bus. Jimmy was ready to go down there the next morning and take care of the bully.

Recalls Ruthann: "I said to Jimmy, 'But you're always hitting Andy yourself.'"

"That's different," Jimmy said. "He's mine."

***

Five pounds of hamburger, three pounds of coleslaw, two liters of soda.

With dinner time nearing, Ruthann flicks on the trash-masher and turns to the mail. One letter brings a smile. It contains Jimmy's birth records, information the doctors at John Hopkins University will need when Jimmy goes there for testing later this summer. At the top of the sheets is a whited-out name. "I'll bet this will tell us Jimmy's real name," Ruthann says.

Savoring her discovery, she holds a page up to the light, then shakes her head. "No," she says, "he doesn't look like a —— (saying another name); to me he looks more like a Jimmy."

***

The stars are bright in the big, dark sky that meets the valley below the Haussling house. Whippoorwills sing in the woods, crickets chirp. Inside the house with the yellow porch light, Jimmy pokes his face through the iron railing on the stairs.

Long after his parents have gone to bed, he walks the floor upstairs, stopping here and there to caress one of Mom's antique boxes or homemade wall hangings. He peers intently at the shelf of antique doll-house furniture, then sits down in a rocking chair and looks into the distance.

"What're you thinking about, Jimmy?" a visitor asks.

"Nothing," he says. He places his chin on a fist and rocks.

Jimmy doesn't like the dark. When the 13-year-old first came to the Hausslings at Christmas, he never slept in his bed in the alcove between the two rooms downstairs where Andy and Earl and Damien and Nick sleep in bunk beds. First, he carved out a nest of clothes and towels in a closet. Then he slept under the desk in Andy's and Earl's room. Once, Ruthann found him crammed between the shelves under the bar. These days he mostly uses the bed, but still demands a night light.

Jimmy was given up for adoption when he was 4 months old. Before he was adopted the first time, he lived in four different foster homes—the second and third moves, the report says, resulted from community pressure about his mixed racial background. His mother, white and 24, told the hospital staff at first that Jimmy's father was black, then changed her story and listed the father as Italian.

The first adoption ended after three years when, records say, "Jimmy's adoptive parents blamed Jimmy for the trouble their neighbor was having at the time." The "trouble" was that the neighbor was being prosecuted in court for beating Jimmy when she baby-sat for him.

Three years later, he came to the Hausslings. Aside from his fear of the dark, there was the matter of his jacket. Red and shiny, boys' size 18, he wore it to meals and to bed, indoors and out. When it was being washed, he waited patiently outside the laundry room. "It was a kind of security blanket for him," Ruthann said.

But in school, Jimmy's special education teacher saw the jacket as a behavioral problem. On the chalkboard each day, she wrote: "Jimmy should not wear his jacket in the classroom." One day, Jimmy shoved his teacher. The woman called Ruthann and told her, "Next time, I'm going to hit him back." Ruthann took Jimmy out of school the following day.

Jimmy no longer wears his jacket; he ran it over with the family lawn mower this spring. And he gets his education at home—two hours a day with a county tutor, the rest of the day with Ruthann—in one of the three upstairs bedrooms that has come to be known as "Jimmy's School Room."

In Jimmy's special education class at school, "They had him on a survival-skill program only," Ruthann says. "I can't see a 13-year-old boy whose only reading experience is, 'The gnats sat on the hat.'"

Next year she'll teach him the classics, she says. She's already made puppets of the characters and plans to put on little plays. And together, Ruthann and Jimmy will study Spanish.

This summer, Ruthann also has plans to form a family Caveman Club. Using the barn as a cave, Ruthann and the kids will wear furs, grunt instead of talk, and draw pictures of animals.

Ruthann says some of her boys, like Jimmy, "can't set limits for themselves. When a situation is unstructured, and they have to set down their own parameters, it makes them anxious. For Jimmy, he's been hurt so much; his ego is so fragile." To counter this, Ruthann and Henry have given Jimmy an important role in the family. As the oldest, he helps out with the others and takes them each day to the bus, letting each take his turn as line leader.

Nick has really taken to Jimmy. Although Nick has freckles, green eyes, and straight red-brown hair, he recently wrote a paper in school in which he described himself as having "shiny black eyes and hair." Nick also likes the urban dialect Jimmy brought with him to the Haussling home. "He liked the way Jimmy talked and the way he walked, all his scowls and stuff," Ruthann says.

One day the two came to Ruthann and said they'd be happy if they were the only children in the family. "The other kids have too many problems," they told Ruthann.

"Okay," Ruthann said. "Who should we get rid of?"

They went down the list, but kept saying, "No, we can't get rid of Earl. No, not Jesse . . ."

They ended up keeping everybody.

June 7, 1981

© **"The Hausslings: All in the Family," 1981, The Washington Post**

FARMERS HARVEST FRUIT OF BOUNTIFUL SUMMER

Ninety miles west of Washington, D.C., at the foot of the Blue Ridge Mountains, fall has come to Greg Smith's farm in Culpeper, VA. The sun is round and low; the verdant countryside is fading, and the smell of mature Yellow Delicious apples hangs sweet in the crystal air. Winter is coming; there is much to do. There are signs the coming cold will be long and deep.

*With special thanks to Walt Harrington, who helped conceive and edit this early piece of ours and may have added a flourish or two. I learned from his every keystroke.

CULPEPER, Va. – The dawn is chill inside the barn, and Greg Smith's breath hangs in the air like puffs from a hand-rolled smoke. A Holstein stands motionless before him, and he strokes the cow's black and white face with a rough, stained hand. A few steps away, the sun outlines the open barn door on the earth, and there summer lingers, warm to the skin.

It is autumn, harvest time at Ashland Farm. And while Smith still rises, with the certainly of the chime, at 5:30 sharp, the sun dawdles 60 seconds more each morning and moves imperceptibly to the south. Smith pulls a handful of brown corn silage from the trough, stirring the kernels and the chopped pieces of cob, stalk, and shuck with a finger. He closes his hand tightly. When it opens again, the coarse, fluffy matter springs back to size. Perfect. The right amount of moisture to last through winter.

It has been a good year at Smith's 1,112-acre dairy farm, so bountiful the feed crops he grew in his fields—the corn, barley, alfalfa, and soybeans—have filled, all five of his 60-foot silos. This year, he has had to buy two enormous white plastic bags to hold the extra bounty. They rest, bloated, in front of his clapboard farmhouse like two 50-yard caterpillars, gorged and sleeping off their feast.

A year ago, Smith was not so pleased. Drought had withered the crops, and food for his 750 head of cattle barely lasted the winter. Fewer cows and steers could be bred, less milk produced. Through that summer, he had matched his Heinzman travelling irrigation gun against that heat, sending it rolling through the fields, the fine spray leaving rainbows over the manicured rows. Still, the crop was poor.

But that is history as time on the farm goes. It has been a good season and nature's new fidelity can be measured in bushels. By noon, Smith, 41, his brother Ken, 38, and their five hired hands have reached the middle of their 15-hour day. They have fed and milked the cows, picked and shelled and dried corn, raked and baled alfalfa, planted rye and replaced a fuel pump and a tractor belt.

Ninety miles west of Washington, at the foot of the Blue Ridge Mountains, fall is a time to prepare for winter, when the ground and the ponds will freeze and life itself will seem to be suspended. The verdant countryside is fading, and the smell of mature Grimes Golden and Yellow Delicious apples hangs sweet in the crystal air. The sun is round and low, and light splashes now across the fields more like a spreading coat of varnish than summer's sheer garment of translucent silk. Soon, the cows will linger in the barn, favoring the warmth of their extra winter issue of straw and sawdust over the cool grass by the pond, shadowed in the afternoon by Mount Pony.

Greg Smith is a quiet man, one who usually wears his sentiment, like his work shirt, tucked tightly under his belts. But, this day, in his rush, he still has time to see. "You see such a beautiful world," Smith says, "and you think, 'How can people not believe there's a God?' To see a calf born, to plant a seed in the spring and see corn and alfalfa grow up tall by fall…"

He doesn't finish. Instead, he climbs into his red pickup truck and drives the several hundred yards to the house, which once was a hospital for Confederate soldiers.

Inside, Greg's wife, Doris, is giving a covered-dish lunch. "Just a bunch of us girls getting together to eat and sit around gabbing," she says

Doris is a hearty woman with a straight-faced wit that makes a person shake his head seriously until he realizes she is making fun. "I suppose you think we're going to feed you lunch," she says, her vowels as country-round as her shape, her smile signaling the fest. She hands a plate, and then one to her husband, who first takes off his blue Ashland's Farms cap and tosses it toward a dowel on the wall. The cap falls and he eyes it a moment, choosing to leave it there. He turns and accepts the plate. Already it has been a long day.

In the dining room, he helps himself to food from casseroles in straw baskets, cheese and broccoli, hamburger and beans, sausage and cheese. He turns to the kitchen to eat.

With the coming of fall, the eight women spooning homemade peach cobbler and vanilla ice cream onto their plates no longer gather at Linda Stapleton's pool or go wading in the Rapidan River near Irma Peters' place. Except for rare occasions like this one, they are too busy. In the basement are hundreds of cans and jars of peas, lima beans, corn, tomatoes, freezer jellies, and pickles that Doris has recently preserved. Hill onions in her quarter-acre garden, a few tomatoes and green peppers and two bushels of pears still await her attention.

These days, Doris must cook for three sittings of breakfast, one for Greg and herself, one for her two children, and one for Greg's grandmother. She cooks two lunches, two dinners.

Besides these duties, a variation of which all the women perform, Dorothy Walker, a slight woman with a white sweater draped around her shoulders and buttoned at the neck, says she always is hurrying the 12 miles to town or the 30 miles to Fredericksburg for parts when a tractor or a combine breaks down. "It never fails that when I get there, I can't describe it and have to call home," she says.

Mostly, the women have been busy winterizing, securing the trapdoors of basement stairways, airing electric blankets, caulking windows, cleaning flues. Apples for cider, sauce, and pie filling must be picked and, at night, after their husbands have set the propane corn dryers for one more load, there are tired arms and sore backs to be massaged.

With the exception of Rita Wells, whose favorite color is orange, none of the women at Doris' table much likes fall. The season brings more chores, more responsibilities for them and their husbands. Beside the harvest, pipes must be wrapped against the freeze, behemoth John Deere tractors filled with antifreeze. The coats of the cows grow thick and their udders must be shaved to ensure that the milk is sanitary.

And fall precedes winter, which is a slow, gray, desolate time. "It's so quiet in winter," says Gay Duckett, another of Doris' friends. "The crickets are gone and you look out and all you see is bare trees and death."

At Ashland Farms, there are whispers that the coming cold will be long and deep. The caterpillars are furry and black. The walnuts, coated in their spongy green skins, and the hickory nuts, acorns and persimmons are unusually abundant; the foliage on the trees is thick.

The next time Doris Smith will go wading in the Rapidan River near Irma Peter's place, or her husband, Greg, will plant a seed and watch the corn grow tall, or the dawn will have no chill or the sun will lay a garment of silk across the fields is another world away.

October 5, 1981

THE HUNT: SPECIAL BOND FOR FATHER, SON

A hunt is a ritual: the guns and the gear, the primitive milestone of the first kill, the lore of manhood passed from generation to generation. For father and son Jim and Troy Norine, the hunt is not about killing. It's about holding yourself real still, the smell of damp earth and distant woodsmoke. It's about love and kinship and being together in the great outdoors.

The sun glows orange as it dips behind the ridge, back-lighting a silken spider web, laying long hardwood shadows across the valley. The father sits on a mound of damp earth, back against a stump. Leaves chatter in the breeze, his stomach gurgles the moose sausage he had for lunch. He is perfectly still, cold as the blue-steel barrel of the Ruger 7mm magnum he cradles in his lap.

He hears a rustle deep in the thicket, the sound a child makes kicking leaves in a gutter. He sees no movement, yet he can feel the motion in his chest and fingertips, hear its progress toward him. An artery pumps in his neck. Buzzards circle the cloud-swept sky, a squirrel stands on the limb of a hickory tree.

"Deer," he whispers.

Up the hill and out of sight, 200 yards away, the son sits on a platform high in a tree. Behind him is a golden meadow of wild wheat, before him a red-clay road and dozens of fresh deer tracks. He, too, hears a rustle and turns his head to the meadow. His is the face of the father: rounder, softer, yet unmistakable; green eyes so clearly the same. He blows a Leon's Turkey Call, and his gobble, that of a young tom, crosses the woods.

"He's spotted one, too," the father whispers. He gobbles back. It is a low, rasping gobble, the call of the lead tom.

It has been this way for years: the father, Jim Norine, and the son, Troy James Norine, together in the woods. Troy was 4 when Jim started him fishing. Jim would put on his rubber waders, pack Troy inside with him and walk, the two stepping as one, into cold, fast-running Minnesota streams in search of trout.

Troy bagged his first Canada goose at 10, his first buck two years ago at 15. The trophies, a glass-eyed bird and two eight-inch horns, sit now at home in the laundry room, unobtrusive symbols of a bond between father and son, a link fashioned of time and love, blood and beauty.

The Norines live today in the tract-house suburbs of Springfield, and Jim works in downtown Washington, a world away from the tiny, midwestern farming town where he was raised, where people smiled and waved on the street, called each other by name.

Hunting is Jim's chance to get away from the darting eyes—"the lack of common decency"—he encounters every day in Washington, to be independent and self-reliant, to see that his boy learns the lessons of the farmhouse as well as those of McDonald's. In the woods, what's important to the father becomes important to the son.

The hunt is ritual: the guns and the gear, the primitive milestone of the first kill, the lore of manhood passed from generation to generation. For Jim and Troy Norine, the hunt is not about killing. It's about love and kinship.

***

Today, they hunt for deer in a forest southeast of Charlottesville, near Palmyra. It has been a long day: up at 2 a.m., gone at 4, in the woods by 6:30. It is not the time but the wait that is wearing. For the hunt is not really a hunt at all.

Troy and Jim pick spots and lie in ambush. They hold statue-still, fighting sleep and cold and the itch that starts on the instep and, left unscratched, spreads across the body like a rash. Deer, though color-blind, can pick up a movement at 500 yards; their hearing is so acute they can be spooked by an eddy of the wind.

Jim is wearing a hot orange golf cap so he will not be mistaken for a deer by other hunters. The cap is pierced with a National Rifle Association moose lapel pin he got for taking a 1,000-pound bull moose in Alberta, Canada. His pants—supported by red galluses—and coat are red wool. He is a strong, healthy man of 42 who tempers his coffee with cocoa.

The man Jim Norine admires most is former UCLA basketball coach John Wooden. Jim used Wooden's running offense and his zone presses when he coached at Blaine High School in Anoka, Minn. Today, as director of the Hunter Services Division for the NRA, he still adheres to Wooden's "Pyramid of Success." A copy of it hangs on a wall in his dark-paneled den, next to a coyote hide and a certificate for being the WCCO radio and Fairway/Super Fair Stores coach of the week.

A handsome man, Jim wears glasses, as do his wife, Barb, Troy, and daughter, Tanya, 12. But in the two family portraits in their living room, Jim is the only one who removed his glasses.

Jim searches the brush, waiting for a sign—for a twig to snap or a tail to flash, for a deer's eye to glow, as it will in the slanting light of autumn, not much brighter than fox fire.

"I know that critter's out there," he thinks. Jim hopes the deer won't smell him and be spooked; he is sitting upwind from the brush, but just to be sure, he has set out Skunk Skreen. Designed to help the hunter against an animal that can smell him a third of a mile away, the pungent artificial scent comes in two bottles. Separate, the clear liquids are odorless. But mixed like epoxy on wood or rock, they send out the powerful rotten-egg stench of an angry skunk.

Jim hears the rustle again, this time only a few steps away through the heavy brush. Five minutes pass. Ten more. A gnawing sound, like a saw cutting wood, pierces the gentle symphony of the creek, the leaves, the chipmunks, the crows. A buck is rubbing his horns against a tree.

November is breeding, or rutting season. The rack a buck grows each fall emerges covered with felt. And as autumn proceeds, the buck polishes and hones his antlers, which will become his weapon for locked-horn matches with other bucks that would contend for his rights to a doe.

Jim's eyes dart and his hand grips the rich, walnut stock of his rifle, just behind the trigger. His is a high-powered, bolt-action hunting rifle, eight pounds. The sight is a Leupold Vari-X, a four-lens, barrel-mounted telescope with a cross-hair sight that will make a deer standing at 200 yards appear to be only 20 yards away. When the trigger is squeezed, Jim's 150-grain, steel-coated, hollow lead bullets rocket from the grooved barrel, like a well-thrown foot-ball pass, at 3,800 feet per second. Deadly accurate to 400 yards.

But Jim will not touch the trigger, even click off the safety, unless he can see the deer's horns clearly. Jim hopes that if he can't get a clear shot, the deer will wander toward his son, who will.

Troy's first deer was a spike buck, a young deer with only two spike-shaped horns. He and Jim were hunting in the Appalachian Mountains in Bath County, and Jim posted Troy in the bottom of a draw, and then circled behind a thicket to flush a buck Jim had seen earlier. Spooked, the buck ran toward Troy, stopped and looked over its shoulder. Troy killed him with one shot in the lungs.

"My dad knew just what he was going to do," Troy says. "Boy, it was great . . . Dad said 'Good shot, buddy.' I think he was more excited than I was."

Troy hasn't dropped a buck since, and Jim thinks it's time he got another, even though Jim didn't get his first buck until he was 18. It wasn't Jim's father, but his Uncle Mike who decided it was his time on a hunting trip in northern Minnesota.

Jim, the oldest of three boys by five years, hunted with Mike a lot in those days. His father owned a poultry business and worked

12 to 14 hours a day. "It took a lot out of him," Jim says. "We didn't hunt deer together until I was out of college."

It was just after dawn when Mike flushed the big white-tail down a trail about 150 yards from Jim. It had a 12-point rack—antlers with 12 limbs—and weighed 265 pounds. Jim shot it once through the heart.

***

Troy, still in the tree stand, looks across the meadow. He raises a pair of binoculars toward the spot where he heard the rustling. He is also wearing a hot orange golf cap—his says "NRA Freedom" on the crown—and a leather NRA belt and buckle from which hangs a six-inch razor-sharp Browning hunting knife. His 30.06 also is a Browning.

Hunting deer, he says, is like looking at a jigsaw puzzle: You have to see one of the parts and then put it together with others. "If I were deer where would I go?" Troy wonders. "There might be a whole herd out there I can't see."

Troy, a senior at Robert E. Lee High in Fairfax, has a lot of friends who hunt, but two of his closest, Froy Saldana and Kevin Riordan, don't. Troy and Kevin like to argue and give each other a hard time. They argue about whose mom makes the best pecan pie and about who is smarter in algebra. Kevin insists he is, Troy insists he is. They both got Ds last quarter. They agree, however, that if it weren't for Lisa LaChance, neither would have gotten through algebra last year.

When they're not doing schoolwork or putting in hours at the Franconia Amoco, where Troy is the night manager, they hang out at McDonald's or go to a midnight movie. Sometimes they drive into Washington and cruise along 14th Street, yelling at the hookers. Kevin says his parties are "known to get a little wild." Last summer he gave a "four kegger" and in September he had a "bring your owner."

"That one got real wild," Kevin says. "Three tables got busted, some kid threw up all over my room, and another kid threw up all over himself. My parents let me have the party, but that's the last one I'm having."

Troy says he drinks a bit himself. Once, he came home from a party after having had two beers. When Jim smelled them on his breath, Troy confessed and was grounded for two weeks. "I'm working with him on not being a member of the herd, to be an individual," Jim says. Nevertheless, Jim says Troy's mom believes Jim is a little easy on the boy. "Troy respects his mother a lot," Jim says, "but he loses some of his independence around her. She's always telling him to clean his room and pick up his socks."

Jim was as straight as a kid can be when he was young. No drinking, chasing girls, hot cars, or late nights. But that was in rural Cokato, Minn., population 2,056. "Times are different," he says, "and Springfield isn't Cokato."

Troy has a blue, 1967 Firebird with a black top, chrome wheels, and Mohawk Super Mac 60 wide tires on the back. It has no heater, but it does have a set of $60 Pioneer triaxial speakers that can blast AC/DC's new album, "For Those About to Rock," at 60 watts. "Everybody at school takes their music pretty seriously," Troy says.

Last summer, Troy and Froy took the Firebird to Rehoboth Beach. It was four days of cruising the boardwalk and the pinball arcades, buying surfer shirts. "We were typical guys at the beach, just looking for girls," Froy says.

Troy met one, too, a pretty brunette from Greencastle, Pa., named Angie. Froy says Troy believed she liked him because he wasn't wearing his glasses. For Christmas, he's asked Jim to buy him contacts.

Now Troy hears a rustle again and trains his binoculars. In the distance he can see a hunter walking out of the woods. A boy, perhaps 5 or 6 years old, walks at his side.

***

The sun has disappeared below the ridge and bright orange stripes alternate with clouds under a cold, blue sky. Sitting on the dirt, Jim is a conflicting mix of tension and calm. His hand still grips the rifle tightly, his eyes still dart, though he hasn't heard anything from the woods in 20 minutes. He leans back as if he is at home in his favorite floral-patterned chair in the rec room, eating peanuts and watching Kansas City play Detroit on Thanksgiving Day.

"These days," Jim says, "you see so little of that trust factor among people. You pass them on the street and they are too hurried to say hello, even nod their heads. By golly, I wasn't raised that way. I was raised to have a kind of common decency. The gap seems to be widening between people instead of getting closer.

"But then you come out and go hunting and you can get away. You can daydream or fall asleep, let random thoughts rampage through your mind. You get good memories out of it. Maybe I just remember the nice things, times I've frozen my tail off and got soaking wet.

"It doesn't sound like something positive, I know, but it's a matter of being out there and doing something because you want to. Just being out there is enough. You don't remember the bad things, either. I remember when my team lost in double overtime and didn't get into the state finals, but I really don't care if I shoot a deer or not. That's not the whole reason for being here."

Neither Jim nor Troy has seen a deer all day, and darkness is now approaching. Jim stands, decides to circle around the thicket and see if the buck's still there.

Over at the stand, the man and the boy reach Troy.

"How you doing today?" Troy says.

"Just fine," the man says.

"Doing any good?"

"No." The man scrapes the dirt with his boot. "I'm afraid I'm gonna have to ask you to leave. This is private property."

Troy climbs down and the boy scoots up.

"I'll bet you shot a lot of deer off that stand," Troy says.

"Yep, sure have. Sorry you can't have one of them."

***

Troy walks through the woods a couple of hundred yards to the road, where he meets his father. Jim tells him about the buck, about the rustling of the leaves and the rubbing sound like a saw cutting wood. "Don't know where he got to," Jim says. Troy tells him about the hunter and the boy.

"You know, I put a whole puddle of Skunk Skreen up on that platform," Troy says. "I hope that little boy puts his fingers in it and rubs it on his nose."

"Come on, Troy," Jim says sternly.

"I'm just kidding, you knucklehead," Troy says, and the talk dies. Troy looks up at his dad, into the face and green eyes so clearly his own, and touches the shoulder of Jim's wool jacket.

"Let's go home, Dad."

"We'll get one next time, Son."

December 6, 1981

© "The Hunt: Special Bond for Father, Son," 1981 the Washington Post

EAGLE AT SEA: THE RIGOROUS LIFE BEFORE THE WIND

The USCGC Eagle is a 295-foot sailing barque used as a training ship for future officers of the United States Coast Guard. Each summer, Eagle deploys with more than 300 Coast Guard Academy cadets on various missions around the globe. A story of a reporter's three weeks at sea, with nary a sight of land, on a ship that looks a lot like a pirate's.

Three hundred miles off the coast of Bermuda, the sea is sapphire and sparkle, a saucer meeting sky. Waves swell and break in muted roar, and flying fish skim across the whitecaps.

Eagle heads east-northeast through the Atlantic, her sails curved against the clear blue day—22 Dacron triangles and squares that layer her three masts like clouds. She makes seven knots, rising and dipping through the eight-foot swells, leaving a trail of foam, looking like a ship that Blackbeard sailed.

On board is a city of people, all wearing dark blue baseball caps. They climb rope spiderwebs or stand around and talk, leaning at an angle as if drunk. Some mop while others hose, their portable water pumps revving like lawn mowers. The deck vibrates, a bit wet with the ocean spray.

Eagle had left Washington seven days before, motoring down the Potomac and then setting sail for the ocean, her course the direction of the wind. Her crew numbers 200, most of them Coast Guard Academy cadets, and their cruise is a lesson on the sea. In two weeks, they will cover 2,000 miles of mid-Atlantic, going east almost to Bermuda, south as far as Charleston, S.C., and then heading back to the mainland and liberty in Norfolk.

For all that time there will be no sight of land, no television reception, no afternoon beers. After a while, the miles of ocean will look the same, and their minds will numb and the beauty of the ocean will blanch. After a while, they will feel like the world is only Eagle, a sailing ship the length of a football field.

She has masts 15 stories high, four galleys and four levels of deck, two teak helms. On board are electric, metal and woodworking shops, lounges with leatherette couches, a suite with mahogany walls, labyrinthine passageways that smell of detergent. The crew sleeps stacked in triple-decker bunks, 20 men or 20 women to 10-by-15-foot compartments. In the hold are stores for four months: steaks, peanut butter, popcorn, fruit, olives, taco shells, and toothpicks with cellophane feathers on the ends.

There are no mail calls on Eagle, and news comes late, if at all. Time is measured by the smell of sizzling bacon, the clang of a brass bell, the silver blast of a boatswain's pipe. Without compass, chart and sextant, the rise and fall of the sun and the moon, Eagle could be anywhere, anytime. "Just over the horizon could be Africa or Europe or Connecticut," says Capt. Martin Moynihan.

Eagle is an island under sail. She makes her own water, turning salt to fresh at a rate of 7,500 gallons a day, makes electricity with a turbocharged generator. She carries an M16 rifle and a couple of .45-caliber pistols, a doctor on loan from a Navy submarine base, and a barber who doubles as chief cook.

Her sails capture 21,500 square feet of wind and are controlled by 170 lines tied to brass pins on teak rails. When the brass is polished, a cadet can see the reflection of a speck of dirt in his eye. Her decks are steel, painted with a gray mixture of epoxy and sand that is good for footing but bad for shoes. She can make 18 knots under sail, and if the wind gives out, she can fire up the 1,000-horsepower diesel that the snipes in the smoke hole call Max, and make 11 knots.

Sailing is really physics: The setting of a dynamic airfoil, a sail, in opposition to a static hydrofoil, a boat, in such a way that a desired vector, or course, results. But on Eagle, sailing is an enlisted man named Tramp who carries a picture of Eagle in his wallet, an executive officer who sits high in the ship's rig and reads law books, the captain named Moynihan who wept when the citizens of Cork, Ireland, turned out in hundreds to welcome Eagle to their port, and the chief warrant officer who wants to die on Eagle.

It is the third-class cadet who leans over the rail and stares, breaking silence to say only that the ancient mariners believed that sea foam is made when a mermaid dies, the first-class cadet who once dreamed of "big gigantic spiders" hanging from the masts and gobbling up Eagle's deck crew. It is a cadet who chose the Coast Guard over West Point because she liked blue uniforms better than green, an enlisted man who joined because it was "the least military of all the services," and officers who make pizza on morale night while two dozen of the crew dance a dance called the James Brown to a song called "Drop the Bomb" that blares from a boogie box.

Sailing on Eagle is getting a truck driver's tan, brown from the bicep down, tasting salt water above the lip, climbing the foremast rigging at night to kiss the Coast Guard pennant, and then lingering at 147 feet 6 inches to watch a full moon burn a path across the midnight sea.

Sailing on Eagle also is being military, following orders, rules and procedures: the book. In this case the book is "Eagle Seamanship," copyright 1979 by the Naval Institute Press in Annapolis.

Eagle is working 20-hour days but learning, as a weightlifter or runner learns, that progress often is measured in pain. Sailing on Eagle is a poem and a metaphor, an insight into nature and an insight into self.

"You know," says First Class Cadet Pete Chittenden, "the weird thing about Eagle is coming home after a cruise. You walk on the street and know that all these people have no idea you were out at sea on Eagle. You can show them pictures, but somehow the pictures never show the feelings I had when I took them. And when you try to explain .... Well, to talk about it is to kind of put it down, if you know what I mean, to make it trivial.

"It's like trying to explain how you feel about life."

***

Sail stations sound on Eagle and suddenly 150 people are hustling across her deck.

First-Class Cadet Paul Ferguson, U.S. Coast Guard Academy, is on the bridge. He is lanky, and when he shouts commands, his Adam's apple bobs. His eyes are darting, but no one can see them behind the dark glasses on this sunny day. Behind him is the mizzenmast. In front of him, down a 10-foot ladder (there are no stairs on a ship) is the waist, Eagle's main open deck from which the mainmast rises. Farther forward, up another ladder to the forecastle, is the foremast.

Mr. Ferguson has "the conn." He is the controlling officer. He wears the binoculars on this shift. Having the conn is an honor, having the conn is heady; having the conn is fun, yet it isn't fun. There is exhilaration, and also a sweat tide of responsibility.

Mr. Ferguson, age 21, is in command of the ship—almost. An officer has the deck, and the deck governs the conn. Mr. Ferguson's job is to call out the orders he gets from the officer of the deck, who gets them, in quieter tones, from the captain, or from the executive officer, who also gets his orders from the captain.

The captain is governed by rules, procedures, the book. That is how the military is run and that is how Eagle is sailed on this Mid-Atlantic training cruise, the only way. Even though Eagle looks like a pirate ship, it is a military vessel. Every member of her crew has signed away some portion of his or her life in exchange for the benefits of a steady job or a free education. They have agreed to do what other people tell them, and if they don't want to, or they think they know a better way, or even if they just don't like the guy, they still answer, "Yes, sir."

Eagle's book is "Eagle Seamanship." Everyone on board carries it. If it is lost, a new copy can be bought for $8.95 in the ship's exchange. The copies are kept on the rack with the Eagle mugs and the Eagle full-color photos.

The book allows Mr. Ferguson to give a few orders of his own. He can ask the helmsman, a younger, third-class cadet, to mark the ship's bearing by the gyrocompass. He can tell the helmsman to come left 15 degrees. He can order the phone talker, another third-classman, who wears a headset and communicates with other phone talkers around the ship, to ask the ship's information center about the range of, say, an oil tanker on the horizon.

Then the helmsman or the phone talker will call out the bearing or the range, and keep calling until Mr. Ferguson yells, "Very well" or "Aye." Among first-class cadets, yelling "Very well" or "Aye" is a practiced art. They swell their chests and throw it from the diaphragm, then clip it off at the lips.

Right now the wind is blowing 12 knots, swelling the ocean 300 miles off Cape Hatteras to eight feet, and Mr. Ferguson is not asking the helmsman or the phone talker any of these things. Right now 150 people are at sail stations, manned and ready on lines all over the ship, waiting for him to shout his commands.

Mr. Ferguson surveys the masts: fore, main, and mizzen. He checks for other ships in the area and sees none. He swallows and his Adam's apple bobs, and then the grips his binoculars with his left hand and cups his right to his mouth: "On the main and on the fore, hold instructions and set and douse one of the main staysails and douse and furl the main t'gallant sail!"

Nothing happens.

On the main and on the fore, two other first-class cadets look puzzled. They are mast captains, and each, advised by enlisted men and officers, commands a force of third-class cadets. After a few seconds, one of the mast captains yells back: "Repeat, Mr. Ferguson."

Now the executive officer, Lt. Cmdr. William Hain, supersedes the deck. He steps forward: "What did you say, Mr. Ferguson?"

"I said, 'On the main and on the fore, hold instructions and set and douse one of the main staysails and douse and furl the main t'gallant sail,' sir."

"Say it again, Mr. Ferguson."

He says it again, louder.

"No, no, no, Mr. Ferguson. No! You're saying, 'Set and douse one of the main staysails.' Right now, all of the main staysails are set, so you have to douse them before you can set them again, don't you think, Mr. Ferguson? All we're going to do is take one down and put the same one back up again. We're going to douse and set, Mr. Ferguson, Douse and Set. Now, try again, Mr. Ferguson."

He does, and mast captains begin shouting and lines clutter the deck and cadets scurry around the ship in groups of three, four, eight, and they heave, hand over hand at first, then with their backs: "Heave, two, three, heave, two, three," and though the rope digs into their palms and makes them raw, each cadet can feel the power generated by the group, feel as if it is his or hers alone.

And with this, the main topgallant staysail runs down and up again. The second highest of four staysails that run between the mainmast and the foremast, it is attached with rings called hanks to a braided steel line called a stay. It looks like a giant shower curtain, and screeches the same way when it moves.

The main topgallant sail is doused with a great squealing of wood and metal pulleys. The second highest of five square sails on the mainmast, it hangs limp from the yardarm. Six cadets climb up rope and steel shrouds to furl it. They ran out across the yard, standing on two-inch-thick manropes that sway as the cadets shift their weight.

They clip themselves with safety belts and lean their stomachs over the tube-shaped yards. They pause a moment and look below. The people on deck look Lilliputian. Then, working in unison like soldiers folding a flag, they haul in an arm's length of Dacron sail at a time, folding and tucking as they go, until the sail lies flat. When certain there are no deadmen—no parts of the sail drooping —they lash the sail to the yard with gaskets, ties made of cloth and rope.

Within an hour they are back on deck and the mast captains are yelling, "That's well." It is done. In celebration, the foremost gang gives a cheer: "We're the fore, it's our mast: main and mizzen, up your—They stop here: taste and regulations.

Back on the bridge, Quartermaster Jessica Robinson, third-class cadet and keeper of the ship's log on this watch, approaches Mr. Ferguson.

"Mr. Ferguson?"

"Aye."

"Sir, which sail did we just put up?"

Mr. Ferguson says nothing. He stares at her for 30 seconds.

"What sail did we what, Miss Robinson?"

"What sail did we just put up, sir?"

"Miss Robinson, on Eagle we don't put up sails. We set sails."

"Yes, sir," Miss Robinson says and retreats, her question unanswered.

"You could say," Mr. Ferguson says as an aside, "the s— flows downhill here."

That it does. "You do lose a certain amount of freedom," says First Class Cadet Sharon Kiel. "But the Coast Guard is good because it puts you in your own little isolated bubble. You're responsible for yourself and your own actions, and sometimes for the actions of others, but they tell you when to get up, what to wear, when to eat, when to go to classes. They tell you almost everything. It's comfortable I suppose."

First-Class Cadet Barney Moreland, a star on the sailing and windsailing teams at the academy, knows the book by heart. He likes to demonstrate his knowledge, ask tricky technical questions that the officers cannot answer, but he also knows how to take orders.

"You'd be surprised how little problem you have learning to take orders... That's part of the attitude adjustment or whatever you want to call it, part of the way you become adjusted to the military," he explains. "You realize that a guy doesn't have to be smarter, better, more qualified. He's telling you to do things because he's been there longer, and you learn to respect him for it. After a while you realize that maybe I'm not as smart as I thought.

"Everything is laid out in a pattern so that as little as possible is left to judgment. Judgment in a crisis situation can be really poor. You get used to thinking along prescribed patterns and it becomes a damned nice crutch, a damned nice crutch.

"It's true that you could tack this boat differently. You could do a lot of things differently around here. But then again, if you really had a pressing urge to do so, you probably wouldn't belong on Eagle anyway."

***

The wind whips up and the world rolls over on its side. Sunny-side becomes scrambled, sausages hit the deck. The cabin boy is pinned against the bulkhead. He catches a bottle of ketchup, sidesteps a bowl of fruit.

Suds from the washing machine drain into an officer's sink. The officer had been putting on his pants; now he is on the floor.

Topside, Eagle's crew dances with gravity. When she lurches to starboard, they lurch to port. They walk like Groucho Marx. The sails strain, the deck vibrates. It feels as if a whale has caught hold of the anchor and is swimming away furiously. On the bridge, veins bulge on the arms of the helmsmen as he tries to hold the rudder against rushing water. On the fantail, cadets are jumping in the air. If they time it right, and go up just as Eagle comes down from a wave, it feels like floating.

This is sailing Eagle, heeling 25 degrees. The sun is high and the wind is 20 knots south-southwest. The temperature is 77 degrees, four degrees warmer than the surface of the 6,000-foot-deep waters below. Four hundred miles off Charleston, S.C., course 287 by the gyro, the ship cuts a wake of aquamarine and foam, and the air is crystal, with a smell more like sugar than salt. The whole crew loves it—except the cook, the cabin boy, the officer on the floor, and a cadet who is sick on the rail.

It's an adrenaline day, a day to step lively or fall, a day when every muscle in the stomach flexes to hold the rest of the body upright. It's also a day of learning, for heeling has a way of making green cadets remember that nature does what she wants. She'll offer fine winds on occasion, but the price of exhilaration is a certain amount of sausage on the deck, and the realization that the same wind that tousles hair can capsize a ship.

So they learn to cope with life on an angle, filling glasses half full, lying salt shakes on their sides, putting the dishes back into spring-loaded wells. The camera goes under the pillow, the half-empty soda in the sink, and the ashtray in the top drawer of the desk. They discover that they'd better hold on when they sleep, especially on the top of a triple-decker rack.

On Eagle, the greater message is this: Men are tiny against a 14-story mast and a mast is tiny against an ocean. "It's frightening at times when you think about it." says First-Class Cadet Paul Ferguson. "There's so much water out there, you have to respect it; know how powerful it is. If somebody goes overboard in heavy seas, the chances are slim and none that we'd ever find them. It would be like being lost in space ... I'm not obsessed with the fear of the sea. We all just know what we're dealing with."

Seaman James Ahl is straddling the main royal yardarm, the highest on the mast. He loves to climb in the rigging, never hooks his safety belt, either. He especially loves it on a day like today, when Eagle is heeled and the mast is arching from side to side as she bobs through the waves. Ahl compares it to the weightlessness of pole vaulting.

"If you fall, you're either going to splat on the deck or break your back on the water," he says. "But if you're going to die you're going to die." Ahl may enjoy danger, but whenever he climbs the mast he pauses a moment to kiss two crossed anchors painted there. They mark the spot where a man was killed two years ago when the main royal yardarm gave way.

Fourteen stories below, Captain Martin Moynihan smokes his pipe. Moynihan has thick brows over eyes a shade lighter than the sea, and the finely etched wrinkles of a man who has spent 22 years on Coast Guard cutters looking into the wind. While his crew lurches and stumbles, he is planted like a punching bag with sand in its bottom for ballast. He's been sailing since he won a week at a summer camp on Long Island, a prize for being a Newsday honor paperboy. He still respects the sea.

Once, when Moynihan was commanding a cutter out of New England, his crew rescued a man off a fishing trawler near Cape Cod. The man's hand had been mangled and a finger would need amputation. After the man was taken to sickbay, Moynihan went below to see him. "It was the first time I really got a look at him. He must have been 60 or 70 years old and I told him how sorry I was about his finger. He said I shouldn't worry about it; that it was the third one he'd lost.

"That's when I realized about the sea, that's when it all came home. I used to like to have swim call now and then, but when you jump off the ship, it's like jumping into a bottomless pit. Look around you. You see nothing but sea. You can get burned to a crisp by the sun, drenched by the rain, beaten by waves. But darn it, you get a good wind like you have today and it's darn exhilarating."

Too much exhilaration can get tiring as Eagle's crew learned last year. Eagle was six hours out of her home port of New London, Conn., headed for Cork, Ireland, when she hit a gale. To reach Ireland on schedule the crew had no choice but to take the straightest line, a position that put them just before the storm's 40-knot winds. Heeled at 40 degrees, Eagle rode the winds like a surfboard for 18 days. The crew almost could stand on the walls.

After a few days, though, the angle got old. Few in the crew could keep from falling out of their racks, so there were arguments over who would claim the few lounge couches that ran abeam of the ship. The waves washed over the rails, onto which scores of cadets were hooked by safety lines in a nonstop, sea-sick vigil. Twenty cases of stomach-settling saltine crackers were gone in a week.

The washing machines were useless. Someone rigged a net, out in the clothes and threw it overboard. It took two hours to wrestle the net back in, but the rushing water had balled the clothes to tightly they had hardly gotten wet.

Formal meals were suspended. "It was a hand-to-mouth kind of thing," remembers Lt. Cmdr. William Hain, Eagle's executive officer. "Most of the people couldn't eat. The rest of us ate baloney and cheese sandwiches for 18 days. They would put the baloney and cheese on a platter and replenish the supply each day, until the stuff on the bottom of the pile was really rank."

But on this day and on this cruise, there is no gale and no particular course Eagle must sail. It is getting late now, and the orange sun silhouettes the rigging, puts a glow on the sails as it drops toward the horizon. The order is given to fall off the wind. After nine hours on her side, Eagle rolls upright.

At this, some of the older hands in the enlisted ranks are briefly puzzled. They see that the Coast Guard pennant atop the foremast is still whipping but Eagle's sails are empty, and they blow forward and then snap back, making a sound like thunder. Lines clang against the masts. Heads shake side to side in disgust.

"This isn't sailing. This is bull," says one enlisted man. "The only reason they changed course is because it's time for the evening meal. The officers don't want their food in their laps."

***

Tramp, Woody, Winding, and Doc are standing with a handful of other enlisted men on Eagle's deck. The rain hits their yellow hoods and echoes in their ears. Sky and sea are thick and gray, like wool, and blasts from the fog horn come in groups of three.

It could be just before dawn or just after dusk, but it is 4:30 in the afternoon, about the hour the crews on many pleasure craft would be mixing their first martinis. But there is no liquor aboard Coast Guard sailing ship Eagle, so this is simply the hour before dinner, when the pace slows and the smell of fried chicken hovers over the deck, and Tramp and Woody and Wingding and Doc can only talk about having martinis.

Three hundred miles at sea, nine days since the last drink and five days to the next, Wingding and Tramp agree they'd prefer their martinis with olives, while Doc says he'd like his with an onion. Woody, from Willaford, Ark., says he'd rather have beer.

The cadets around the enlisted crewmen are untempted by such fantasies, preferring instead to wind down from their 16- or 20-hour work days with push-ups and sit-ups and jump rope. They wear stretchy athletic shorts that sag with the weight of rain.

Petty Officer Sam Meyer, 25, is walking across the deck when he's smacked in the head by a plastic-coated jump rope. He rubs his hand on the spot, checks for blood. Seeing none, he says nothing and joins his friends. He has a thick beard that starts just below his eyes and ends at his chest, and his accent pegs him to Savannah, Ga. He went to sea rather than work in Ben Portman's Music Center, which his grandfather built from a pawnshop into a chain of music stores.

Meyer looks back toward the cadet who ambushed him and shakes his head. Her name is Cathy Kurzy, a third class cadet with pierced ears but no earrings, long eyelashes and dirty fingernails. She is 19 and can do 135 push-ups. She chose the Coast Guard Academy over West Point because West Point "looked like a dungeon" while the Coast Guard Academy "looked like a real college campus," and because the Coast Guard has blue uniforms while the Army has green. She had worn a green uniform at Lumen Christi Catholic School in Jackson, Mich., and was sick of the color.

"Jesus," says Petty Officer Second Class Meyer, rain dripping from the end of his nose. "They're getting dangerous. We gotta find them more work so they'll get tired."

The other man laughed with him. They are close to the cadets in age, but they are a spicier lot, onion rolls compared to white bread. On board, they are called by their nicknames. The cadets are addressed by last names, always preceded by Mr. or Miss, like the officers.

The enlisted crew stays with Eagle all year. They take her to dry dock in Baltimore's Curtis Bay Shipyard and spend the winter tearing her apart and putting her back together, mending the sails and repairing the rigging and sanding the decks when the work allows, they sleep on her as well in their berthing compartment heated by steam.

They do all these things all winter so that each spring they can sail Eagle to the academy in New London and turn her over to the cadets and their officers for the summer. The officers are academy instructors, men who went to the academy and were once cadets themselves.

When Eagle sails into port, to hundreds or thousands of landlubbers screaming and waving and clapping, it is the cadets who go up in the rigging and wave back. The enlisted men must stay on deck. There is little glory for the enlisted. The Coast Guard calls what they do advising. The enlisted men call it babysitting.

Now there is yet another new crop of jumping, pumping cadets to contend with. The enlisted men know all the faces; the names don't matter much. They know the types sure as bass know minnows. There are third class cadets like Erin Dorrian, 19, from York, Maine, whose father commands a Coast Guard cutter, and 19-year-old Joe Re of Fairfax, whose father is retired Navy, and Jeanne Schiller, 18, a lawyer's daughter raised on a 25-acre farm in Sunbury, Ohio, who "wanted the structure and discipline of the military," and Cameron Lewis, 19, who comes from six generations of Rhode Island fishermen and yachtsmen.

First Class Cadet Sharon Kiel, 20, came to the academy from Middletown, N.J., for the free education, and because "I was afraid if I went to a regular college I would party too much." Her classmate, 21-year-old Barney Moreland of Pensacola, Fla., accepted his appointment because, "I was feeling pretty high on myself, thinking I could join this organization and be the hottest hot shot." He based his view on his "well roundness," something he picked up in high school when he worked summer days as a longshoreman and summer nights as a flutist in a band.

On the other hand, Seaman James Ahl enlisted because he used to hang out on street corners in Oakland, Calif., dressing in a style he calls "tennis-shoe pimp" and heading on "a slow shuffle to nowhere." Tramp's first name is Chris. He is 20 years old and wanted to join the Coast Guard since he was 12 and saw a TV ad that showed a 44-foot Coast Guard rescue boat that could swamp and then right itself like a kayak. The catalyst, however, was six months of trying to find a job after high school. "What it came down to was the unemployment rate in Michigan," says Tramp, a native of Jackson, Mich.

Wingding is 22 and his real name is Jeff Weigand. He had finished three years in chemical engineering at his hometown University of Akron in Ohio, when his scholarship ended. He chose the Coast

Guard over the Navy because he was getting married. "I wanted to be out on the water, but I didn't want to be out there for eternity at a time."

Cadets and enlisted men have a special bond, a mixture of the affection of a master for his apprentice and the resentment of an agent for his star. At sea, an enlisted man frequently will ask an inexperienced cadet to get him a length of shore line, a mooring rope that is always left behind on the dock when the ship sails. He might ask a cadet to get him a quart of prop wash, the wake the propeller makes behind the boat, or to get him the key to the main engine. There is no key.

Yet, when a cadet asks an enlisted man to get him an Eagle Crew T-shirt, something the cadets aren't allowed to buy, the man almost certainly does so, maybe taking a Coast Guard Academy T-shirt in trade. Petty Officer Meyer will spend an hour teaching a cadet how to blow his silver boatswain's pipe, just because the cadet would like to know. And when Ahl goes up in the rigging with the cadets to furl a sail, he keeps up a constant chatter: "Everyone all right? . . . Watch your step here, it's slippery . . . You're doing a fine job, that's it."

On the last port of liberty in Washington, Seaman Pete Marcucci took it upon himself to introduce some cadets to the 14th Street strip. Cuch, as he's known, is only 25, but he's the elder cool guy on the deck force, like Fonzie with a Newport, R.I., accent and a pair of mirror shades and so much knowledge about sailing that people say he could sail Eagle by himself. He joined the Coast Guard because he didn't know what else to do after backpacking for six months in Alaska.

He has a square knot tattooed on his forearm, a sailor's symbol of having sailed to the four corners of the world, and standing around with his arms folded, he looks like salt personified. He says he took the cadets to a strip joint, then to a "model and escort service."

"I told them they could go in and look, but that they shouldn't buy anything or touch anything," Marcucci says. "I mean, these kids have to learn about things, you know; they'll be going to a lot of ports later on. I just didn't want them to get hurt or anything. They're only cadets, you know."

***

The night is clear, a poem of stars and cool sea air and porpoises playing in the wake, but Third Class Cadet Joe Re is thinking about Shalimar, the perfume his girlfriend wears.

It has been more than a month since he's seen her, and as soon as the Coast Guard sailing ship Eagle docks in Norfolk, he plans to catch the first bus to Fairfax, and he doesn't care how late it leaves. He'll have three days of liberty, and on Saturday night he's going to take her to Annapolis and buy her an expensive dinner at the Maryland Inn. There will be matches on the table with his name inscribed in gold letters.

Tonight, however, Re is standing watch in the pilot house, watching the scanner arm play around and around the radar screen. On each pass it echoes little blips that are nothing more than white-caps and throws yellow light across his face, deepening his eyes, shadowing his nose. He is here, but his mind is there, until a fly buzzes by his ear.

It bounces against the radar screen, and into a wall, and then out of the door. "Haven't seen one of them in almost two weeks," Re says and then he smiles. "I think we're supposed to see land by tomorrow."

He becomes silent and his smile fades. He pushes a finger toward the stars Polaris and Kochab and the constellation Drago, and calls them by name, savoring the words as they roll off his tongue. He swells a little as he does this, as if he is pointing out someone important in a restaurant, someone important he has come to know.

"I'm going to hate getting off Eagle," he says.

On a night like this, the end of a 2,000-mile ocean voyage, if you don't know what you feel, you know you feel something. You stand and watch the night and you know you're looking at something beautiful, but you can't be still to appreciate. You're not really seeing anymore. You're numb and you're sorry you are. You feel like you need to leave this ship, yet you are unwilling to let go.

Two weeks earlier, every sight and sound and every touch had been a needle in your brain. You saw water bluer than you'd ever seen and you couldn't stop staring. Here was a world of new definitions.

You began to notice that swells always came in groups, and that a rain storm would first appear as a gray blur on the distant horizon— you could just about tell how much time you had to go down below and get your slickers. You learned you could make that blind step down the shrouds without plunging 14 stories to the deck. The rock and roll of the ship came to have a pattern, and soon you could anticipate and shift your weight, almost walk a straight line.

You learned that if you set the sails a certain way, aimed the bow a certain direction, you could get a 100-foot ship to go where you wanted. Two hundred people had made that happen, but somehow you felt it was a triumph of your own. You thought maybe you were nature's peer.

But after a while you began to drown in your senses, realized how tiny you were. You felt the wind whip up suddenly and you found yourself falling. You were wet for days at a time, even when below deck. When the life-sized dummy was thrown overboard in a drill, you watched it get smaller and smaller while it took forever to turn the ship about and lower the lifeboat.

And finally, you just needed to be alone, needed something finite. You needed home and dry land. You felt lost and trapped in all of this magnificence, and it seemed like nothing at all.

Then came a common housefly and you wanted to stay forever, though you didn't know why until Eagle was finally moored and you stepped on solid ground after two weeks, and the buildings rocked and swayed as if you were still at sea.

You remembered those six days on board when sunspots blocked all news from the world and how you didn't miss it, and how when it did come—word of war, a flood, an international summit—you went back to watching the second reel of "Bronco Billy." You thought again about the sapphire ocean and the pale blue sky, the flying fish and the porpoises, the smell of bacon and the sound of breaking waves and the echo of rain in your ears.

You remembered the taste of salt on your lips and the way you felt weightless when you sat on the mast during a heel, the way you jumped up when Eagle came down from a wave and how you felt like you were floating.

And then you remembered that you were on land again, and no matter how late it was, you caught the first bus home.

June 27-31, 1982

© **"Eagle at Sea," 1982, The Washington Post**

POTTER'S FIELD: FAIRFAX COUNTY'S DREARY GRAVEYARD FOR THE DESTITUTE, ADRIFT OR ANONYMOUS

The first to be buried here, in 1946, was John Doe. Two John Does and two Jane Does followed, followed by a Christine Marie Doe, Infant Unknown. Though the others there have names duly recorded on small granite headstones, the histories of nearly all have been lost in the shuffle of paperwork and time. But not all were forgotten. An investigation back in time.

P otter's Field in Fairfax Country is 10 rows of flat gray stones, a ceramic lamb without a nose, a vase of plastic flowers, and six azaleas, all within a chain-link fence within five acres of gravel.

The grass is matted and where the graves have sunk, muddy water collects in pools. On a warm day the moisture rises, mingling in the air with the odor of exhaust and the din of engines from the buses and trucks in the country maintenance yard to the north.

Gathered in these paupers' graves are people from a different Fairfax Country, a place of violence and misfortune amid comfort and affluence, a place where people die and have no one to bury them or insurance to pay the cost.

In Potter's Field are the fallen like Charles B. Degges, *Washington Evening Star* reporter and school board member, and the criminal like Thomas Lalayette White, tough and knife-scarred from the streets of Baileys Crossroads. They are immigrants like Ibolya Jenes, who served up daily specials at a cafeteria in Tysons Corner; the destitute like Wallace Gill and his two daughters, who lived in Chantilly in a shack without plumbing, and local characters like Andy Smith, who waved to commuters each morning from the edge of Pickett Road.

"They're the kind of people you hear about but rarely see in Fairfax," says the Rev. Wallace Hale, a retired infantry chaplain who has buried many in Potter's Field. "People who are adrift, people with no home, people who lost touch with a certain stability that seems so important in the suburbs. They are the ones who are buried in Potter's Field."

Today, 149 persons are in Potter's Field, also called Fairfax Country Cemetery, the most recent buried on Feb. 4. Dedicated in 1946 to the drifters found dead along the highways and train tracks of a county just blossoming after the war, the graveyard was isolated then, forest and meadow off Jermantown Road near the old county Poor House, across from the old county dog pound.

The first to be buried there was John Doe. Two John Does and two Jane Does followed, as did Christine Marie Doe, Infant Unknown. Though the others there have names duly recorded on small granite headstones, the histories of nearly all have been lost in the shuffle of paperwork and time.

Until 1969, there were neither head stones nor fence, and school buses and abandoned cars were parked atop the graves. The vehicles were moved and the headstones, azaleas, and fence were placed only after the public learned that the field was such a mess that the county had rejected a boy's request to visit his mother's grave.

The azaleas were planted by two women who saved the bushes from tractors clearing land for the county office building. A man now buried in the field helped build the fence. Since then, five to 10 people have been buried there each year.

When people die in Fairfax without money or survivors or friends, they are handed over to the county, becoming the "Indigent. Unknown, or Unclaimed Human Bodies" of Procedural Memorandum No. 67. Seven agencies are responsible for each burial, paid for through prearranged blanket purchase agreements. Costs total $925, up from $825 in 1981.

Death without money in Fairfax includes transport in a black Chevy station wagon to Everly Funeral Home in Fairfax City, which is managed by a man who wears a tie tack in the shape of a shovel. There is standard embalming and cosmetic work if needed, and burial garments from Louis Drygoods in New York City. A man's suit without belt loops or pockets costs $75. A woman's dress with a false slip is $45.

If the decreased has family or friends, a one-hour viewing can be held. If not, the pine or pressed wood coffin is closed and driven in a hearse to the grave, dug four feet deep. Hale delivers a 10-minute service, usually in the presence of only two maintenance men and the tractor they will use to push the pile of uncovered dirt back into the grave.

Thirteen years after Katherine Gill saw her husband and two daughters buried in this way, she cannot recall the color of her daughters' hair or the place of her husband's birth.

"After a while, though you don't want it to be that way, you kinda lose the picture of someone in your mind," says Gill, who has no photos of her family. "You change your ways and you stop going to see them. But I guess they don't never change. They'll always remain what they were."

The Hard Man

Thirteen people saw Ronnie Hall shoot Thomas Lafayette White. White had a grudge, and he came looking for Hall at the Lacy

Boulevard crap game, already heated at midday in September 1976, in a junkyard down a pitted road in Bailey's Crossroads.

Hall had losing dice on the plywood table and a .45 stuck in his belt when he saw White coming and he was in no mood to hassle. He said nothing, just reached for his gun. The three shots that echoed across a field of weeds set two mangy shepherd dogs to howling, and the game scattered. When the police arrived, the only one left was White, dead at 24.

It took the county two years to bring Hall to trial. No one would testify. Finally, the commonwealth's attorney persuaded an eyewitness to talk. He was so scared the judge had to clear the courtroom. After the trial, the witness moved to another state.

Even today, with Ronnie Hall doing time in Camp 26 near Haymarket for second-degree murder, mention of White and Hall inspires one man who saw the shooting to swear he isn't who the mailman says he is. But that's how it is around Lacey Boulevard, and around Munson Road and Moncure Street, blighted back lanes of the suburbs where the code is inner city.

This is where Thomas Lafayette White grew up, where he got a five-inch knife scar on his right biceps, where he got shot in the gut and refused to go to the hospital, preferring instead to raise his T-shirt and show the infected wound to the dudes.

White came to the Crossroads an infant, left by his mother with the county. He was raised in a yellow clapboard house on Munson by a foster mother named Minnie Peyton, who'd already raised other foster kids and worked 36 years and two weeks as a teacher's aide in the D.C. schools.

"Tommy was a good boy until he found out I wasn't his real mother," says Peyton, now 94. "After that, Tommy got into that dope and running around the neighborhood. He was a real smart-mouth. Thought he was the man of the Crossroads."

The day before the shooting, Peyton remembers, White and Hall came to the house. White has been drinking. "He came in spittin' and cussin' and I told him to shut up and get out," Peyton says. She closed the door on him and he put his hand through the screen, then reeled around and broke a window.

Hall had known Minnie Peyton a long time and, like many others in the neighborhood, called her Mom. He yelled, "I told you not to be messin' with Mom!" and the two went at it on the lawn.

The next day, White came to Peyton's house looking for Hall. White had a gun and he waited in the woods across the street. "He fired it once to let us know he had it," Peyton says. A few hours later, he was dead.

"All I know is I had done my part by him, and he didn't respect me or himself or nobody." Peyton says. "I said, 'Let the Lord take him in His hands and do what He will with him.'"

The Reporter

Charles B. Degges was a well-spoken, dapper man with a pencil-thin mustache and a resume as impeccable as his demeanor.

He had studied at the Corcoran School of Art and the Philadelphia Academy of Fine Arts, worked as a reporter for *The Washington Evening Star*, *United Press*, and *The Oakland Tribune*. He was secretary of the D.C. school board and the first director of the Alexandria Tourister Council.

"Charlie was a superior-talking kind of guy," recalls his sister-in-law, Albyne Leckert. "He was very flattering, very opinionated. Smooth."

In 1977, at the age of 74, Charles Degges died in the care of the Fairfax Department of Social Services. He was blind, alcoholic, and alone.

"Charlie had alienated everyone by the end," says a neighbor who lived near Degges in Belle Haven, south of Alexandria. "He resented going blind. He talked about how life had been against him."

It didn't seem so when, after seven years of covering the District school board for *The Star*, Degges was appointed board secretary in 1934. During his tenure, Degges caused a minor scandal when, in 1936, he breached board policy and gave the home addresses of city school teachers to Rep. Thomas L. Blanton. The Texas Democrat mailed the teachers a speech in which he claimed "incontrovertible proof" of a scheme to "communize the public schools." Degges was denounced by the board and resigned soon afterward.

He returned to newspapers, covering Washington for UP and then for *The Oakland Tribune*. In 1948, while covering Harry S. Truman's whistle-stop campaign for the *Trib*, he proposed to Marion Olivet in the dining car. One week later they were married.

Degges became head of the first Alexandria Tourist Council in 1962, but six years later, after unsuccessful surgery for cataracts, he was asked to resign. "He developed an absenteeism problem because of his health, and members of the board saw signs of a drinking problem," says council spokeswoman Diane Bechtol.

For the next nine years, Degges and his wife lived as recluses, supported mostly by Marion's sister, Leckert. By the late 1970s, a neighbor recalls, Degges was asking him to pick up liquor about once a week. "The in-laws didn't like that we got them liquor," he says. "But we finally came to the conclusion that, what the hell, they didn't have anything else."

By then, the spacious Degges house was dirty and unkempt, the heat was set at 90 degrees, and the television in the living room played constantly. Marion Degges, dying of cancer, would lie on a daybed, a bottle of Cabin Still bourbon and a bucket of ice by her side. Charlie would recline on a couch across the room. He, too, had a bottle and a bucket. When Marion was near death in 1976, she called the ambulance herself, Leckert says.

"Charlie, I won't be back," Marion told her husband. Charlie was too drunk to respond.

The 'Lover'

In the mornings, come time for commuting, Andy Smith would rouse himself and his yellow dog Russ and walk the short way from his trailer at the old Fairfax City sewage treatment plant to his chair on Pickett Road.

The traffic would already be thick when he arrived, and he'd spend an hour waving to the drivers on their way to work. When one honked back, it made his day.

On weekends, he'd go to the Little League fields across the street. Wearing a yellow hat and vest given him by some parents and children, he'd direct traffic before the game, occasionally giving a short-breathed toot on the whistle a city policeman had donated.

Andy Smith was an ageless man. Some said 50, others said 70. He said he didn't know himself. He was just always there. A remnant of the old days of Fairfax County, he grew up on a farm near Popes Head Road and went to school in a segregated, one-room schoolhouse.

For many years he worked on a farm. Later he lived in a ramshackle trailer on a patch of land his former employer left him when he died.

So, when they took his lot for George Mason University, Smith got a new trailer and a rent-free site on the grounds of the sewage plant, with water and sewer and electricity included.

Women and Sunday school children bought him food and a television, a radio and boxes of cigars, and even another trailer when Hurricane Agnes destroyed the one the city had given him. But Andy Smith was no charity case: Need was his gift, appreciation his payment.

"The world needs a lover and Andy Smith loves everybody," former Fairfax City Mayor Nathanial Young once said.

Though Smith was shabbily dressed and spent his days collecting deposit bottles from the roadsides, he was still, in the opinion of one 13-year-old Little Leaguer, "A pretty cool guy." The kind of guy who talked to anyone.

"And the funny thing," says city Public Works Director James R. Shull, "is that everybody would talk to him. You'd see these people all dressed up in suits talking to ol' Andy. It was a real contrast for Fairfax City."

When Andy Smith died in 1978, old and infirm in a chair in front of the television set in his trailer, his funeral was held at Mount Calvary Baptist Church, and hundreds of people were there.

A young girl sang a solo in his memory, and a Sunday school teacher eulogized him for 10 typed pages. "Here you had all these people praying for an old colored man who done nothing in his life but be a good human being," recalls city Street Superintendent C. Wayne Marteny, who went to the funeral. "It was kind of inspiring."

The Family

Wallace Gill and two of his three daughters drowned late in the afternoon, when the sun was low and the lazy ripples on Goose Creek shimmered like candles. It was August 1970 when they went to the creek near Chantilly and stopped for a picnic at a bend in a road cut between a hill and a field of summer corn.

Looking back, those who knew the Gills thought it strange that Wallace would go to the creek at all. He couldn't swim, and even at 44 was terrified of the water. His neighbor, Fred Mosser, could never even get him to go sit on the bank of Carter's Pond to do some fishing.

But it had been a beautiful day in waning summer, and when two of Wallace Gill's friends suggested the outing, he went along for the sake of his girls.

This is what Katherine Gill believes. After 20 years of marriage, she knew her husband well enough to know, even if he never said so out loud, that he wished desperately he could have given his daughters more.

"It hurt him when he couldn't get the girls new clothes or shoes for school when he knew all the others kids had new things," says Katherine Gill, 51. "He wanted them to come up better than he did."

Wallace and Katherine had grown up dirt poor in West Virginia: she in Glace, he in a town she can't recall. When they married in 1950, they migrated to Fairfax to find work.

They rented a three-room shack without plumbing for $50 a month near the Chantilly Post Office, and Gill found occasional construction jobs. Working for a Merrifield fencing company in 1969, Gill helped erect a chain-link fence around Potter's Field. At home he raised chickens, rabbits, bees, and vegetables in the back yard, and Katherine worked three jobs as a maid, but still they stayed poor.

"I guess a lot of people around here looked at them as kind of out of place," says Georgia Mosser, a neighbor who frequently brought them food when their credit at the grocery ran thin. "They were a little ragged around the edges, but they were good-hearted country folks."

Then, for some reason, Wallace Gill put aside his fears and took his daughters on a picnic. Leonard Layman, a family friend also on the outing, remembers that at about 6 p.m. Betty Ann Gill, 16, and Sharon Gill, 12, were wading in Goose Creek within sight of their father. Layman was on his way to the truck with Denise Gill, 8, to get sandwiches and hot dogs.

"Suddenly, I heard all this screeching and splashing..." he says. "When I got there all I could see was Wallace's hand above the water. I guess the two girls were already gone, I jumped in, but I can't swim either."

Several hours later, divers untangled the Gills' bodies from a sunken tree under seven feet of water. Police suspect that the girls slipped into a deep section of the creek and that Wallace Gill jumped in to save them.

"You know," says Katherine Gill today, "I don't think they'd mind being buried in that cemetery. Wallace would have been proud. He helped build that fence around the graveyard. It looks real nice, doesn't it?"

The Immigrant

Ibolya Jenes and Ilona Szabo were inseparable, even told everyone they were sisters. They had fled Hungary together and landed in America together, worked and lived and banked together, pooling their money in one account.

Then, on the night of Oct. 8, 1978, Szabo shot Jenes in the chest with a high-powered rifle they had bought to protect themselves in their Oakton apartment. Even today, with Szabo free after pleading guilty to first-degree murder and serving one year of a 20-year sentence (with 15 years suspended), the shooting remains a mystery to prosecutors.

Jenes and Szabo had made a remarkable pair, each the other's closest friend. Jenes, 14, was 5-foot-5, 190 pounds, with jet black hair and leveling black eyes. Szabo, two years younger, was a wisp in comparison, small and delicate and reserved.

"Ibolya was so domineering, and very protective at the same time," recalls Gerlinde Kuchmanich, herself an immigrant from Germany, a confidante of the pair, and the manager of the Marriott Cafeteria in Tysons Corner, where the two worked for a year in 1977, the longest they had worked anywhere since coming to this country in 1971.

"They were a little like Laurel and Hardy. Ilona was dependent on Ibolya on the outside, in public. But Ilona took care of all the money, did the driving, cooked all the meals. She spoke much better English, too."

Jenes and Szabo relied on each other, developing their own ways of adjusting to life in a frightening new world where custom and nuance often escaped them. "They were always afraid that somebody would come and make them pay for leaving their own country," says Kuchmanich.

"They loved having the freedom to work and move as they pleased. Once they just picked up and moved when they heard about some factory jobs in Minnesota." Yet, Kuchmanich says, after having lived in America for six years before the shooting, they didn't know how to go about becoming naturalized citizens. "They were afraid to call someone and ask."

At home they read Shakespeare and listened to Bach and Beethoven, though the walls of their one-bedroom apartment were decorated with posters from Niagara Falls and rabbit hides from Luray Caverns.

At work they got along well enough, though they would sometimes fight, Jenes screaming, Szabo crying, Kuchmanich says. But just as suddenly as they started, they would stop and hug.

So it is hard to say why Ilona Szabo shot Ibolya Jenes. Szabo told police she had pulled the rifle from under her bed because she saw intruders on the balcony, that the gun had gone off accidentally.

While awaiting trial, Szabo wrote to her lawyer: "I like to ask of you to tell judge I'm like to die by electric chair ... I all the times feel her blood in my hand ... It is not life I feel ... I like to die very soon, please." Today, Szabo is married. She could not be reached for comment.

Says Kuchmanich, "It was the two of them against the world and the two of them against each other. They had no one else to love and no one else to hate."

March 25, 1983

© "Potter's Field," 1983, The Washington Post

Acknowledgments

Dora Simons, Henry Schuster, John May, Albert Murray, Steve Jones, Walt Harrington, Don Graham, Ben Bradlee, Bob Woodward, Herb Denton, Stan Hinden, Gene Bachinski, Phil Smith, Jay Lovinger, Bill Hamilton, Tom Sherwood, Ken Ringle, Tom Morgan, Pete Earley, Jim Canfield, Rudy Maxa, Andrew Mayer, Bill Greider, Paul Hendrickson, Art Harris, Bill & Renee Regardie, Jack Limpert, Carolyn White, David Rosenthal, Jann Wenner, Bob Love, Bob Wallace, Robert Vare, Terry McDonell, David Hirshey, Bill Tonelli, Art Cooper, David Granger, Peter Griffin, Lisa Henricksson, Bob Scheffler, Kevin McDonnell, Andrew Chaikivsky, John Hendrickson.

The *Esquire* staff, 1997-present.

John Radziewicz, Lissa Warren, Will Balliett, Morgan Entrekin, Jamison Stoltz, Kathy Robbins, Flip Brophy, Lynn Nesbit, David Vigliano, Phil Raskind, Jeff Frankel. Jerry Bruckheimer, Mat Whittington, Malik Rasheed, William P. Smith, Matt Wallerstein, Alex Hedlund, Nick Antosca, Alex Hedlund, Nick Antosca, John Schoenfelder, Russell Ackerman.

Bob Greene, Sam Freedman, Hunter S. Thompson, Richard Ben Cramer, Peter Mehlman, Kurt Andersen, George Pelecanos, Barry Siegel, Patricia Pierson, William Pereira, John H. Richardson, Scott Raab, John Fennell, Patsy Sims, Kia Bowman, Kinsee Morlan, David Rolland, Angela Carone, Adam Elder, Michael Tisserand, Lisa Taddeo, Carter Harris, Bruce Kluger, Bill Zehme, Peter Mehlman, Gay Talese, Tom Wolfe.

Gerald Scheinker, Josh Scheinker, Harlan Levy.

Lee Cohen, Al Baverman, Hesh Beker, Scott Goldstein, Nate Braverman, Joe Chazen, Steven Sulcov, David Kelley, Geoff and

Maureen Diner, Marshall Keys, Eva Hamback, Federico Gonzalez Peña, Terrell Lamb, Chris Janney.

Andrew Greenstein, Darius Zagrean, Ovidiu Vlad, Laura Apetroaei, SF Appworks.

Siori Kitajima, Stravinski Pierre, Pamela Nettleton, Jean McDonald, Christopher Mele, Merv Keizer, Leorah Gavidor, Mary Beth Tweardy, Sohrob Nikzad, Jamie Ballard, Tanya Huang, Galya Lasker, William Fritz, Anna Fiorino.

Josh Schollmeyer, Michael Dubin, Donald Davidson, M.D.

Miles Sager, Beverly and Marvin Sager, Wendy Sager, Elizabeth and William H. Sager, Anne and Harry H. Sager, Sara and Lee Rosenberg, Frances and Richard Rosenberg, Debi and Steve Rosenberg, Betsy Compton Burke and Mitch Rosenberg, Karen and Rick Myers, Bonita and Robert Hauge, Danielle Rosenberg.

Permissions

A portion of "The King of the Cowboys" was excerpted as "The First Family of Rodeo" on Smithsonian.com on June 13, 2018.

The following stories were first published in different forms in *Rolling Stone*, and then again in 2008 in *Wounded Warriors*, published by Da Capo Press, all rights to which have reverted to the author: "Thailand's Home for Wayward Vets," May 10, 1984; "A Boy and His Dog in Hell," July 2, 1987; "Death in Venice," September 22, 1988; "The Ice Age," February 8, 1990.

The following stories were first published in different forms in *GQ*, and then again in 2008 in *Wounded Warriors*, published by Da Capo Press, all rights of which have reverted to the author: "Big," June 1995; "Generation H," September 1995.

The following stories were first published in different forms in *GQ*: "Dunkin' Donuts with Manute Bol," November 1986; "The Gospel According to Bill Hicks," September 1994; and "A Journey to the Heart of Whiteness," March 1996.

The following stories were first published in different forms in *Esquire*, and then again in 2008 in *Wounded Warriors*, published by Da Capo Press, all rights to which have reverted to the author: "The Sharpton Strategy," January 1991; "The Smartest Man in America," November 1999; "Kobe Bryant Doesn't Want Your Love," November 2007; "Wounded Warriors" (published as "Wounded Battalion"), December 2007.

The following stories were first published in the *Washington Post*. Published with the paid permission of the *Washington Post*. "The Forgotten at Forest Haven," November 6, 1980; "The Hausslings: All in the Family," June 7, 1981; "Farmers Harvest Fruit of Bountiful

Summer," October 5, 1981; "The Hunt: Special Bond for Father, Son," December 6, 1981; "Eagle at Sea," June 27-31, 1982; "Potter's Field," March 25, 1983.

Also by Mike Sager

NONFICTION

Scary Monsters and Super Freaks:
Stories of Sex, Drugs, Rock 'n' Roll, and Murder

Revenge of the Donut Boys:
True Stories of Lust, Fame, Survival, and Multiple Personality

The Someone You're Not: True Stories of Sports, Celebrity, Politics &
Pornography

Stoned Again: The High Times and Strange Life of a Drugs Correspondent

Vetville: True Stories of the U.S. Marines at War and at Home

The Devil and John Holmes - 25th Anniversary Author's Edition:
And Other True Stories of Drugs, Porn and Murder

Janet's World:
The Inside Story of Washington Post Pulitzer Fabulist Janet Cooke

Travels with Bassem:
A Palestinian and a Jew Find Friendship in a War-Torn Land

The Lonely Hedonist:
True Stories of Sex, Drugs, Dinosaurs and Peter Dinklage

Tattoos & Tequila: To Hell and Back with One of Rock's Most Notorious
Frontmen

FICTION

Deviant Behavior, A Novel

High Tolerance, A Novel

About the Author

Mike Sager is a best-selling author and award-winning reporter. A former *Washington Post* staff writer and contributing editor to *Rolling Stone*, he has written for *Esquire* for more than thirty years. Sager is the author or editor of more than a dozen books, including anthologies, novels, a biography, and textbooks. In 2010 he won the National Magazine Award for profile writing. Several of his stories have inspired films and documentaries; he is editor and publisher of The Sager Group LLC. For more information, please see www. MikeSager.com

About the Publisher

The Sager Group was founded in 1984. In 2012 it was chartered as a multimedia content brand, with the intent of empowering those who create art—an umbrella beneath which makers can pursue, and profit from, their craft directly, without gatekeepers. TSG publishes books; ministers to artists and provides modest grants; and produces documentary, feature, and commercial films. By harnessing the means of production, The Sager Group helps artists help themselves. For more information, please see www.TheSagerGroup.net.

THE SAGER GROUP

Artifex Te Adiuva

www.ingramcontent.com/pod-product-compliance
Lightning Source LLC
Chambersburg PA
CBHW022043020426
42335CB00012B/524